The Jour~~~~~~~~ I~~~~~~~~~

The journalistic
imagination

Today the media exert enormous political, ideological and cultural power, yet journalism retains a precarious position within literary culture and academia. By focusing on the journalism of ten celebrated writers from Britain, the United States and France, this text identifies some of the elements that make up the journalistic imagination and explores the reasons why it has so long been devalued and misunderstood.

The Journalistic Imagination draws together a group of top English and journalism academics in a unique collaboration – examining the neglected work of famous writers and celebrating the specific literary qualities of journalism as a genre. In the process, it highlights:

- the ways in which the writers blur the boundaries between journalism and literature in a variety of areas (eyewitness reporting, political campaigning, arts reviewing, column writing, war reporting, crime reporting, cultural commentary, sketch writing);
- the evolution of a specific journalistic sensibility and creative, literary style;
- the functions of journalism both within the public sphere and for the individual writers.

Writers include: Daniel Defoe, William Hazlitt, George Sand, Charles Dickens, Willa Cather, Graham Greene, George Orwell, Martha Gellhorn, Truman Capote and Angela Carter.

This text will be of interest to students of journalism, English, media studies, creative writing and cultural studies in general.

Contributors: Charlotte Beyer, Jane Chapman, Kirsten Daly, David Finkelstein, Richard Keeble, Jenny McKay, Nick Nuttall, Linden Peach, John Tulloch and Deborah Wilson

Richard Keeble is Professor of Journalism at the University of Lincoln. His publications include *The Newspapers Handbook* (fourth edition, 2005), *Ethics for Journalists* (2001) and *Secret State, Silent Press* (1997). He is also joint editor of the academic quarterly *Ethical Space*.

Sharon Wheeler is Field Chair in Print Journalism, PR and Publishing at the University of Gloucestershire. She is completing *Feature Writing for Journalists* (2007) and has contributed to *Print Journalism* (2005). Sharon is editor of http://www.reviewingtheevidence.com and is part of the blogging team at http://heydeadguy.typepad.com/heydeadguy/

The Journalistic Imagination

Literary journalists from Defoe
to Capote and Carter

Edited by
Richard Keeble and
Sharon Wheeler

Routledge
Taylor & Francis Group

LONDON AND NEW YORK

First published 2007
by Routledge
2 Park Square, Milton Park, Abingdon, Oxon OX14 4RN

Simultaneously published in the USA and Canada
by Routledge
270 Madison Ave, New York, NY 10016

Routledge is an imprint of the Taylor & Francis Group, an informa business

Editorial selection and material © 2007 Richard Keeble and Sharon
Wheeler; individual chapters © 2007 the contributors

Typeset in Baskerville by
Bookcraft Ltd, Stroud, Gloucestershire
Printed and bound in Great Britain by
Antony Rowe Ltd, Chippenham, Wiltshire

British Library Cataloguing in Publication Data
A catalogue record for this book is available from the British Library

Library of Congress Cataloging in Publication Data
The journalistic imagination : literary journalists from Defoe to Capote
and Carter / edited by Richard Keeble and Sharon Wheeler.
    p. cm.
    1. English prose literature. 2. American prose literature. 3. Journalism.
    I. Keeble, Richard, 1948– II. Wheeler, Sharon.
PR1285.J66 2007
823–dc22   2007008735

ISBN10: 0-415-41723-6 (hbk)
ISBN10: 0-415-41724-4 (pbk)
ISBN10: 0-203-93976-X (ebk)

ISBN13: 978-0-415-41723-5 (hbk)
ISBN13: 978-0-415-41724-2 (pbk)
ISBN13: 978-0-203-93976-5 (ebk)

Contents

Contributors

Charlotte Beyer is Field Chair for English Literature at the University of Gloucestershire. She teaches North American women's writing, and American literature from the nineteenth century and the contemporary period. She has previously published on Margaret Atwood. Her research interests are in the areas of Willa Cather's journalism, and contemporary fiction from North America and Australia.

Jane Chapman is Principal Lecturer in Journalism at the School of Journalism, University of Lincoln, where she is in charge of post-graduate programmes. She is the single author of three recent textbooks, all published by Polity Press: *Comparative Media History* (2005), which was a nominee for AEJMC/AJHA best book award; *Documentary in Practice* (2006); and *Issues in Contemporary Documentary* (2007). Jane is currently co-editing an anthology for Routledge entitled *Broadcast Journalism: a Critical Introduction*. She is a former television producer and news reporter with more than 200 factual programmes and documentaries to her credit.

Kirsten Daly is a lecturer in English Literature at the University of Gloucestershire. Her research interests include the Romantic period. She has published in the area of Romantic poetry and her current interests involve Romantic drama.

David Finkelstein is Research Professor of Media and Print Culture at Queen Margaret University, Edinburgh. His publications include *The House of Blackwood: Author–Publisher Relations in the Victorian Era* (2002), *An Index to Blackwood's Magazine 1901–1980* (1995) and the co-authored *An Introduction to Book History* (2005). He has also edited *Print Culture and the Blackwood Tradition* (2006) and co-edited *The Book History Reader* (second edition, 2006), *Nineteenth-Century Media and the Construction of Identities* (2000) and *Negotiating India in the Nineteenth-Century Media* (2000).

Richard Keeble is Professor of Journalism at the University of Lincoln. His publications include *The Newspapers Handbook* (Routledge, fourth edition, 2005), *Ethics for Journalists* (2001) and *Secret State, Silent Press: New Militarism, the Gulf and the Modern Image of Warfare* (1997). He is also the joint editor of *Ethical Space: The International Journal of Communication Ethics*.

Jenny McKay worked in newspapers, magazines and television before she began to teach and write about journalism. She has taught in several UK universities and is currently Director of the Journalism Programme at the University of Stirling, Scotland. The second edition of her book *The Magazines Handbook* was published by Routledge in 2006. As well as magazine journalism, Jenny's research interests include literary journalism and reportage. She has an MA in Old and Medieval English language and literature from Oxford University and a Diploma in Music from the Open University.

Nick Nuttall is a senior lecturer at the University of Lincoln School of Journalism. His current research interests include the journalism of the *fin de siècle*, Jack Kerouac and the 'beat' writers, New Journalism and 'gonzo' journalism of the 1950s and 1960s. Other publications include contributions to *The Encyclopedia of Interior Design* (1997) and a chapter on investigative journalism for the latest edition of *The Newspapers Handbook* (2005).

Linden Peach is the author of the first published monograph on the novels of Angela Carter. He has published widely on modern and contemporary writing, including books on the contemporary Irish novel, Virginia Woolf and Toni Morrison, for which he has been twice honoured by the Toni Morrison Society, University of Georgia. His most recently published book is *Masquerade, Crime and Fiction: Criminal Deceptions* (2006) and his *Contemporary Irish and Welsh Women's Fiction: Gender, Desire and Power* is forthcoming from the University of Wales Press. He is also part of the team working on the definitive edition of Virginia Woolf's work for the Cambridge University Press. In 2006 he was awarded an Honorary Research Fellowship at the University of Wales, Swansea. He is Professor and Head of the Department of English and History at Edge Hill University, Lancashire.

John Tulloch is Professor of Journalism and Head of the School of Journalism, University of Lincoln. Recent work includes jointly editing, with Colin Sparks, *Tabloid Tales* (Maryland: Rowman and Littlefield, 2000); and articles in scholarly journals such as *Journalism Studies; Journalism: Theory, Practice and Criticism; Ethical Space; Media Education Journal*; and chapters in a number of forthcoming books. His principal focus is press conduct and coverage, on a range of subjects including news management, human rights, extraordinary rendition, the Iraq invasion, grief, and the military. He has taught and undertaken consultancy in the Middle East, Central Asia, and India.

Sharon Wheeler is Field Chair in Print Journalism, PR and Publishing at the University of Gloucestershire. She is completing *Feature Writing for Journalists* (2007) and contributed to *Print Journalism* (2005). Her research interests include sport in the media, crime fiction, fandom and cult TV. Sharon is editor of http://www.reviewingtheevidence.com and is part of the blogging team at http://heydeadguy.typepad.com/heydeadguy/

Deborah Wilson is the Programme Leader for the BA courses at the University of Lincoln School of Journalism. Formerly a full-time broadcast journalist, she now combines the practice of journalism with teaching and research. The latter concentrates on early female foreign correspondents, the history of broadcast news and the development of community radio with particular reference to aspects of social gain. Deborah has given research papers on broadcasting and journalism at national and international conferences, including a series of presentations on current and historical trans-Atlantic influences on UK radio for the Broadcast Education Association in the US.

Introduction

On journalism, creativity and the imagination

Richard Keeble

Robert Fisk, veteran war correspondent of the London-based *Independent*, is back from Baghdad in February 2005 at his flat in Beirut. A bomb goes off down the road, and he writes:

> I ran down the street towards the bombing. There were no cops, no ambulances yet, no soldiers, just a sea of flames in front of the St George's Hotel. There were men and women round me, covered in blood, crying and shaking with fear. Twenty-two cars were burning, and in one of them I saw three men cowled in fire. A woman's hand, a hand with painted fingernails, lay on the road. Why? Not bin Laden, I said to myself. Not here in Beirut. I was staggered by the heat, the flames that crept across the road, the petrol tanks of vehicles that would explode and spray fire around me every few seconds. On the ground was a very large man, lying on his back, his socks on fire, unrecognizable … Then through the smoke, I found the crater. It was hot and I climbed gingerly into it. Two plain-clothes cops were already there, picking up small shards of metal. Fast work for detectives, I thought. And it was several days before I realized that – far from collecting evidence – they were hiding it, taking it from the scene of the crime. I came across an AP reporter, an old Lebanese friend. 'I think it's Hariri's convoy,' he said.
>
> (2005: 1,278–9)

Notice the narrative urgency, the meticulous attention to detail in this eyewitness account ('a hand with painted fingernails', 'socks on fire'), the emphasis on the personal drama, the sense of the news value in rooting out corruption (the cops taking away evidence from the scene of the crime). There is horror here but it is not over-sensationalized. This is journalism at its best: based on facts and authentic experience – and displaying great sensitivity to language, tone and rhythm (see Tulloch 2006a).

According to the American media historian and theorist Michael Schudson (1996: 96; cited in Tulloch 2006b): 'Reporters make stories. Making is not faking, not lying, but neither is it a passive mechanical recording. It cannot be done without play and imagination.' Similarly, G. Stuart Adam (2002: 7–40), in providing a 'preliminary' definition of journalism, argues that journalism is a 'form of expression that is an invention. It is a creation – a product of the imagination'. Such views lie at the heart of this text – and they can transform our perceptions of the epistemology, functions, form and content of journalism. For, by stressing the creativity of journalism (for instance, of the sort we see in Fisk's eyewitness account), we can identify it as a specific literary field, yet one closely linked to fiction – and the other arts.

The implications for journalism education are also substantial. As Adam comments (ibid.: 9): 'I believe that much of journalism teaching – whether it is concerned with professional practices or with social and political effects – is too functional.' Neither the practitioners nor the social scientists 'are sufficiently inclined to lift journalism out of the bureaucratic settings in which journalists are likely to operate'. Adam is talking about the situation in the United States but his view could equally apply to Britain – and elsewhere. Journalism education, in short, needs to encourage the creative spirit just as practitioners need to acknowledge and further explore its creative possibilities. Indeed, by focusing on the journalism of a few celebrated writers, this text is aiming to identify some of the elements that make up the journalistic imagination and explore the reasons why it has so long been devalued and misunderstood.

Certainly today the media exert enormous political, ideological and cultural power. Yet journalism retains a precarious position within literary culture and academe. One result is that the journalism of authors, poets and playwrights is usually either forgotten or marginalized. Thus, commenting on Dickens's journalism, John M. L. Drew (2003: 1) says that 'relative to the letterpress inspired by his novels and short fiction, it is not well known and it is very widely scattered'. So this text is seeking to retrieve from the dustbins of literary and cultural history the journalism of these writers and to celebrate it. In the process, it presents journalistic texts (the 'flights of journalistic imagination', as Jane Chapman comments in her essay here on George Sand) as worthy of close analysis.

Journalism and literature are too often seen as two separate spheres (one 'low', the other 'high'). As Richard Ingrams comments: 'Journalism is a dirty word to some and the journalist is considered an inferior species compared, say, to the writer of novels or history' (1995: 249). The essays collected here show how these two spheres, in fact, constantly overlap. Journalistic genres constantly avoid neat categorizations and theorizing, thriving on their dynamism, contradictions, paradoxes and complexities. And journalism's functions are diverse and ambiguous – being variously associated with democratic debate, education and entertainment as well as myth, fabrication, disinformation, polemic and propaganda (see McNair 2005: 28).

Within the intellectual economy of modern societies, authors, editors, publishers, campaigners and academics are found regularly changing roles. Indeed, for so many men (and women) of letters since the eighteenth century the continuous flow of writing has incorporated journalism, books, reviews, polemics, sociological research or poetry even. And as the essays here demonstrate, a range of textual and thematic continuities and contrasts can be identified between authors' journalism and their novel or play writing. Journalism will be seen not as a marginal literary pursuit, but as a central cultural field which writers exploit for a variety of reasons and where, crucially, they self-consciously construct their public identities (Hartley 1996).

Journalism's low status

Complex factors (historical, cultural, ideological, political) lie behind journalism's low literary and academic status – and the marginalization of the journalistic imagination. Since their emergence in the early seventeenth century in Europe's cities, particularly London, the 'news media' (variously known as corantos, diurnals, gazettes, proceedings and mercuries) have been associated with scandal, gossip and 'low' culture. As Craven comments (1992: 3), these publications 'brought sex and scandal, fantasy, sensationalism, bawdiness, violence and prophecy to their readers: monstrous births, dragons, mermaids and most horrible murders'.

By the early eighteenth century the derogatory term 'Grub Street' had come to be associated with all forms of struggling, low-level publishing. Originally applied to Milton Street, a warren of garrets and tenements in Moorfields where poor writers lived, by the 1720s 'Grub Street' had spread through the impoverished wards on the edges of the city, close to Clerkenwell and St John's Gate – home of the *Gentleman's Magazine* in the 1730s. Around the same time the word 'hack' (and 'hackney') came to be associated with writers and prostitutes – basically anything overused, hired out or common (Uglow 1998: 1). Even after hundreds of years of cultural change, the words 'hack' and 'Grub Street' are still associated with journalism.

In the United States, too, early forms of journalism were often linked with 'vulgarity' and 'corruption' (Schudson 1978: 13). As the novelist James Fenimore Cooper commented in *The American Democrat* (1838):

> The press tyrannizes over publick men, letters, the arts, the stage, and even over private life. Under the pretence of protecting publick morals, it is corrupting them to the core, and under the semblance of maintaining liberty, it is gradually establishing a despotism as ruthless, as grasping, and one that is quite as vulgar as that of any christian state known.
>
> (Cited in ibid.: 13)

A 'higher', 'extraordinarily rich' form of journalism evolved in Britain during the eighteenth century (Adam 2002: 17): 'It included the literary essays of Addison and Steele; the polemical writing of Lord Bolingbroke, Cato and Junius; the legislative reports of Dr Johnson in the *Gentleman's Magazine*; and, later, of Woodfall, one of the first Gallery reporters, in the *Public Advertiser*' (see also Italia 2005). By the mid-nineteenth century, as Gross comments (1969: 63), an 'unprecedented number of serious journals of opinion' were prospering, including the *Saturday*

Review, a reinvigorated *Spectator*, *Fortnightly*, *National Review*, *Macmillan's* and *Cornhill*, the latter under the command of the novelist William Thackeray (1811–63).

Yet overall the low status of journalism has persisted. While the term journalist was imported from France in the 1830s to refer to writers on periodicals (distinguishing them from writers of literature), the identification of journalism largely with newspapers and mass culture has had a profound impact on the sensibilities of writers. For instance, in her chapter here on William Hazlitt (1778–1830), Kirsten Daly suggests that he was a literary journalist in two senses: he was both a literary writer and a writer who discussed literature. In other words, he practised the 'higher' journalism. Yet his journalism was deeply inflected by his belief in the marginal position of journalism in relation to the 'aristocratic' writers of 'literature'. As a result, his literariness became (like Keats's) intrinsically combative. According to Daly, Hazlitt's essays amount to a defence of the craft of literary journalism as a valid form of creative writing. Hazlitt, she suggests, puts forward an alternative model of creativity which values quotation: the effective articulation of someone else's words.

In his chapter on Charles Dickens (1812–70), John Tulloch argues that journalism in Britain is marked by a particular 'uncertain social esteem' since it lacks the secure role given to it in America by the First Amendment to the Constitution and because it is more distant than its European neighbours from the world of literature.

Tulloch suggests that another reason for the low status of journalism in Britain has been its perceived lack of creative control by the author compared to the control allegedly associated with the 'artist'. He argues: 'Arguably one of the malign effects of Romanticism in British culture was to define the "true" artist's status as not having a patron but a soulful relationship to the audience that precluded writing for anything as vulgar as the market.' Certainly the issues of creative control and his relationship to the mass audience fascinated Dickens as he strove (in the end with remarkable success) to become a major editor and proprietor with his magazines *Household Words* and *All the Year Round*. Dickens published about 350 articles – over a million words – in magazines and newspapers. But only in recent years has the scale of his achievement as a journalist been acknowledged.

By the middle of the nineteenth century the philosopher John Stuart Mill was attacking journalism with these words:

> In France, the best thinkers and writers of the nation write in the journals and direct public opinion; but our daily and weekly writers are the lowest hacks of literature which, when it is a trade, is the vilest and most degrading of all trades because more of affectation and hypocrisy and more subservience to the baser feelings of others are necessary for carrying it on, than for any other trade, from that of the brothel-keeper up.
>
> (Cited in Allan 2004: 19)

Indeed, in France, journalism's eighteenth-century roots lay in a more literary and 'explanatory' form. As Rodney Benson comments (2005: 96): 'The full title of a prominent early, and enduring, journal testifies to this twofold allegiance: *Le Journal des débats politiques et littéraires.*' And the persistence of this political/literary tradition, reinforced by George Sand in her many press campaigns, as Jane Chapman illustrates in her chapter here, has tended to modify cultural critiques of journalism in France.

Journalism and the literary marketplace

On a basic level, journalism has provided writers with an income. Yet this very fact has reinforced journalism's position as a sub-literary genre. For while literature is often seen as the fruit of 'scholarship' – hence pure and disinterested and above market considerations, including those of being readable and accessible – journalistic writing is viewed as distorted by the constraints of the market, tight deadlines or word limits. Moreover, journalism tends to be identified in Anglo-American mainstream debates with a mass audience (uncultivated) as opposed to an elite (cultivated). Accordingly, mass audiences are characterized as being easy to manipulate, emotional and irrational; elite audiences are more likely to be linked with notions of rationalism (Meyer and Lund 2006: 53).

The poet Samuel Taylor Coleridge (1772–1834), for instance, wrote throughout his life for a variety of journals (such as the *Morning Post* and the *Watchman*, which he ran for just ten issues in 1796) in a range of genres – non-political essays, profiles, leading articles, parliamentary reports. But these are largely ignored by the academy. While Marilyn Butler (1981) has argued that Coleridge may well be considered one of Britain's first 'modern journalists' or 'professional intellectuals', his journalism was never a source of pride for him. He much preferred to think of himself as 'a very humble poet' (ibid.: 25). As Leader (1998: 24) comments: 'If the attitudes Coleridge expressed towards journalism live on, they do so in the academy, not just today because it is the academy which shelters many poets and virtually all philosophers but because academic writing in general – "scholarship" – is meant to be pure and disinterested, above mere market considerations, including those of readability or accessibility, as also above such contingencies as tight deadlines or word limits.'

By the 1930s, the critic Cyril Connolly was bewailing the 'victory' of journalism over literature. Its plain style, he claimed, had thrust aside the 'Mandarin style' 'characterized by long sentences with many dependent clauses, by the use of the subjunctive and conditional, by exclamations and interjections, quotations, allusions, metaphors, long images, Latin terminology, subtlety and conceits' (1930/1961: 29–30).

He continued: 'There can be no delayed impact in journalism, no subtlety, no embellishment ... Prose, with the exception of Conrad who tried to pep up the grand style, began to imitate journalism and the result was the "modern movement"; a reformist but not a revolutionary attack on the Mandarin style which was to supply us with the idiom of our age.' Literature was merely responding to market demands and the democratization of culture epitomized in the growth of the mass-selling media: 'books grew cheaper and reading them ceased to be a luxury, the reading public multiplied and demanded less exacting entertainment'. And these trends horrified Connolly.

Another victim of this common devaluing of journalism as a creative field was the American writer Willa Cather (1873–1947) whose vast journalistic output has received scant attention from critics. Yet, as Charlotte Beyer demonstrates in her chapter, Cather carried these negative attitudes into her own writing, making a clear distinction between her 'serious writing' and the 'journalistic stint': the hundreds of thousands of words she wrote simply to keep afloat. Similarly, Martha Gellhorn (1908–98) constantly stressed she needed the money from journalism to fund her 'writing' – implying, as Deborah Wilson points out in her chapter here, that journalism was not even a form of 'writing'.

Journalism as a distinct category worthy of special attention

Another effect of the 'low' status of journalism has been the tendency amongst critics to see it as a genre which writers exploit to experiment with styles, voices and ideas later expressed more fully in their 'higher' writing. The journalistic imagination is rarely considered worthy of special attention. Thus while Cather was influenced by the notion of hierarchical categories in the production of literary works, judging her journalism of 'lesser' value, Beyer is concerned here to consider it as a separate body of work equally worthy of analysis.

Virginia Woolf, though a literary journalist for much of her career, was very critical of the politics of the journalistic economy – seeing it as male-dominated. For instance, her original version of *Orlando* has a great deal to say on literary politics – censorship, men's opinions of women, the corruption of the literary marketplace, the idiocy of the Burdett-Coutts literary prize and the embargoes on women writers (Lee 1998: 123). In her poem, *Fantasy*, the journalist is depicted as a bug, repellent, crawling and blood-sucking (Brosnan 2000: 194). However, the failure of critics to acknowledge the significance of her extensive career as a journalist (1904–41) has produced a seriously distorted image of Woolf's literary project and personality. As Brosnan argues convincingly, in dismissing her non-fiction altogether 'critics perpetuate the construction of a literary figure, and the movement she is often deemed to exemplify, as separate from a whole sphere of literary and cultural production' (ibid.: 193).

Similarly George Orwell (1903–50), considered by many as one of the greatest, if not the greatest, UK journalists of the last century, was dismissive of journalism. In his *Tribune* columns, as Richard Keeble argues in his essay here, he displays a remarkable range of tones, styles and themes. But, throughout his career, Orwell constantly looked down on his journalism as mere pamphleteering and a 'lesser' form of literature. He had a horror of hack reporting and despised the 'dreary subworld of the freelance journalist' (see Bromley 2003: 125). And while his As I Please columns have received almost unanimous praise from critics, there has been no major critical assessment of their literary elements.

Yet, Keeble suggests, Orwell used his columns from 1943 to 1947 effectively to define a new kind of radical politics. It involved reducing the power of the press barons, facing up to racial intolerance, defending civil liberties. It also incorporated an awareness of the power of language and propaganda, a celebration of the joys of nature and an acknowledgement of the cultural power of Christianity. Above all, in the face of the vast political, cultural, economic factors driving history, it recognized the extraordinary richness of the individual's experience.

Likewise, Graham Greene's stints as a film reviewer have attracted little critical attention. Yet David Finklestein argues in his chapter on Greene that the author of more than two dozen novels was also 'one of the finest film critics of his generation'. And in the chapter on Angela Carter (1940–92), Linden Peach suggests her journalism is rarely acknowledged as a significant part of her output, worthy of serious consideration in its own right. In fact, Carter's journalism was an intrinsic part of her broader intellectual project – to scrutinize and resist dominant ways of thinking that constrain or distort intellectual, emotional, sexual and aesthetic development. 'As cultural and political commentaries, her journalism is as original, tough-minded, intelligent and astute as her other writings.'

Journalism and the 'here and now'

While concepts of 'high' and 'low' serve to keep journalism subordinate to literature, they have, in fact, never been clearly distinct categories – as the career of Daniel Defoe (1660–1731), often credited with being the first journalist, only too clearly highlights. An undercover agent for the government in 1707 and master of disguise, Defoe presented all his writing – even his now famous fiction such as *Robinson Crusoe* (1719) and *Moll Flanders* (1722) – as fact, and almost all of it anonymously (Wilkes 2002: 20–8).

Shirlene Mason (1978: 1) highlights the epistemological complexities at the heart of Defoe's work in this way:

> He often talked on both sides of an issue and he loved to construct paradoxical situations which defied easy analysis or solution. In addition his use of different personae as mouthpieces helps him to consider a problem from several angles without committing himself to one viewpoint. His fictional characters or the correspondents to the journals and to the *Review* may or may not speak for Defoe. When Defoe is supposedly speaking for himself, his use of irony can lead a reader astray. When Defoe wrote *The Shortest Way With Dissenters* he was put into prison because his readers did not understand the satire. A modern reader can have the same problem in trying to perceive to what degree each situation is being treated ironically.

In her essay on Defoe here, Jenny McKay highlights the historical context in which his extraordinary oeuvre emerged. While the first specialist women's magazine, the *Ladies' Mercury*, was launched as a monthly in 1693, the lapsing of the Licensing Act in 1696 unleashed a torrent of new literary forms. Not only did Britain's first recognizable newspaper, the *Daily Courant*, appear on 11 March 1702 but the journalistic imagination also expanded about this time to incorporate 'war stories, parliamentary proceedings, travel accounts, political editorials, book adverts, bills of mortality, cargoes of ships, biographies, bibliographies, Hebrew anagrams, lottery numbers, assize reports, literary criticism and social comment' (Raymond 1999: 132; see also Conboy 2004: 58–9; Applegate 1996: 60–3). Sommerville (1996: 114) suggests that the novel could only have developed out of such a diversified literary culture attuned to periodical news:

> The pace of the novel was the pace of news, which had come to seem the pace of life itself. The ordinary lives of novelistic characters were anchored in a social and physical world that had been made literary by periodical publications. And novels often returned the compliment, by masquerading as journalism. Daniel Defoe is the most notable example of a newsman who could step over into fiction – or novelistic fact.

McKay identifies the way in which Defoe captured in his account of a terrible storm in November 1703 one of the basic elements of the journalistic imagination: its concern with 'events in the here and now' (Adam 2002: 19). Significantly, in his examination of the social role of newspapers in nineteenth-century America, Michael Schudson highlights the special attractiveness of their 'continuous communication' and involvement in the 'here and now' to men and women of letters. He writes (1996: 42): 'The nineteenth-century newspapers were key instruments of urbanization, providing not only the advertising forum that made new institutions like department stores possible but also providing a community identity that held a city together when it was no longer a face-to-face community or even a "walking city".' After the rise of the press, private communication, rumour, word of mouth, the pulpit, and other forms of printed and hand-written propaganda (posters, handbills, etc.) all continued to constitute vital means of political communication. But unlike other aspects of print culture, the press held out the possibility for men and women of letters of 'continuous communication, of amplification and correction'.

Jeffery Smith (1999: 5) also stresses the impact the periodicity of the press had on the creation of American nationhood:

> To a great extent, original writings in periodicals and pamphlets were responsible for advancing the ideological debates of a nation in the act of creating itself. Books and European philosophers seemed to have played less of a direct role in the process than is often assumed. The press allowed large numbers of Americans to contemplate issues simultaneously and to respond to each other rapidly.

Journalism and the rhetoric of factuality

According to Adam (2002: 22), journalists are concerned with facts and information 'and they follow, however crudely and randomly' an epistemological procedure. They 'construct a picture of fact and information'. The epistemological issues here may not be as clear-cut as Adam suggests. The notion of 'fact' – along with the professional ideology of objectivity which came to dominate mainstream discussions about the responsibilities of journalists in the US and Britain from the late nineteenth century onwards – is problematic. And the boundaries between fact and fiction can often blur. Yet journalism generally succeeds on the basis of its claims to accuracy and authenticity. Thus Defoe was at pains to stress in his account of the storm the accuracy of his observations and the authenticity of the documents he drew on. There may well be ironies here. Yet within the diversified literary culture of early eighteenth-century England, Defoe's rhetoric of factuality became all the more necessary, if only to win the trust of readers – and the support of advertisers. As he commented in 1705: 'The principal support of all the public papers now on foot depends on advertisements.'

Similarly, in the only issue of the first newspaper in the American colonies, *Publick Occurrences, Both Foreign and Domestick*, Benjamin Harris stressed in his reports on England's campaign against Canada that he wanted to provide 'accurate news in a time of confusion' and promised to correct any mistakes (Smith 1999: 5). This rhetoric of factuality is translated in Dickens's journalism, according to John Tulloch, into a 'confident grasp of the sheer *thisness* of the material urban world, the buzzing universe of things'. Indeed, 'facts' derived from eyewitnessing might be seen as the blocks on which the journalistic imagination can be constructed. Take this sentence from one of Dickens's *Sketches*, published in the *Morning Chronicle* on 15 December 1834:

> On a board, at the side of the door, are placed about twenty books, all odd volumes; and as many wine-glasses – all different patterns; several locks, an old earthenware pan, full of rusty keys; two or three gaudy chimney-orna-ments – cracked, of course; the remains of a lustre, without any drops; a round frame like a capital O, which has once held a mirror; a flute, complete with the exception of the middle joint; a pair of curling-irons; and a tinder-box.

The list, Tulloch argues, transfixes us with 'its seemingly random specificity, the eccentricity of the objects, the traces of their former owners not quite effaced, trying to convince us of the authenticity of the observation'.

Like Defoe and Dickens, Truman Capote was always determined to establish the authenticity of his voice. His *In Cold Blood* (1966) was hailed on publication by both fiction writers and journalists and was to give birth to a new school of writing – the New Journalism – which stressed narrative, a participatory approach and literary style (see Sims 1984; Sims and Kramer 1995; Applegate 1996; Chance and McKeen 2001). Yet, as Nick Nuttall points out in his chapter here, Capote, while drawing from a range of literary conventions (the biography, crime story, the nineteenth-century episodic novel) was still concerned to stress the 'factual' basis of his writing.

In an interview, Capote claimed to have adopted 'a narrative form that employed all the techniques of fictional art, but was nevertheless immaculately factual'. And in the Acknowledgements section at the start of the book Capote stressed: 'All the material in this book not derived from my own observation is either taken from official records or is the result of interviews with the persons directly concerned.' For Wolfe (1975: 47), New Journalism's obsession with eyewitness recording of 'facts' is one of its defining features:

> the recording of everyday gestures, habits, manners, customs, styles of furniture, clothing, decoration, styles of travelling, eating, keeping house, modes of behaviour toward children, servants, superiors, inferiors, peers, plus the various books, glances, poses, styles of walking and other symbolic details that might exist within a scene. Symbolic of what? Symbolic, generally, of people's status life, using that term in the broad sense of the entire pattern of behaviour and possessions through which people express their position in the world or what they think it is or what they hope it to be. The recording of such details is not mere embroidery in prose. It lies at the centre of the power of realism as any other device in literature.

Yet notions of 'factuality' and 'authenticity' remain persistently problematic, with the journalistic imagination thriving on the complexities and contradictions. Despite the rhetoric, Capote could not resist the temptation to resort to fabrication – most overtly at the end of the book. As Nuttall writes, the chance encounter between Alvin Dewey and Susan Kidwell, Nancy Clutter's best friend, in the Garden City cemetery is pure invention. 'It clearly suits the demands of a fictional narrative, providing a sense of life carrying on, bringing us full circle, back to the place where the story began, rather than the requirements of a piece of journalism that it sticks to the facts.'

The human interest story and faction

A fascination with 'human interest' also lies at the core of the journalistic imagination. Significantly, McKay argues that Defoe's *The Storm* was a pioneering example of the 'human interest' story, making it particularly compelling for modern readers. By the mid-nineteenth century Henry Mayhew was building his remarkable sketches of urban life (first published in the *Morning Chronicle* and collected in *London Labour and London Poor*, 1851–61) on extensive, lively interviews with a vast range of sources – beggars, labourers, sweatshop workers, prostitutes (see Sales 2000). Dickens also based some of his more memorable sketches, such as 'On Duty with Inspector Field', published in *Household Words* on 14 June 1851, partly on interviews.

In France at the same period, George Sand captured the human interest dimension at the heart of her local newspaper campaign to expose the cruelty of the Catholic Church and the nonchalance, hypocrisy and inefficiency of the civil authorities in a particularly imaginative way – by creating a fictional correspondence between a Berrichon peasant (Blaise Bonnin), who represented the finer points of rural common sense, and his godfather (Claude Germain). As Jane Chapman comments in her essay here, this was a remarkable flight of the journalistic imagination with Sand utilizing her fictional skills to capture the authentic voice of the rural working class.

George Orwell, intriguingly, distrusted the interview as a way of revealing character and attitudes. During his assignment as war correspondent on the Continent for the *Observer* in 1945, he rarely recorded interviews but instead cited conversations, discussions and overheard comments (Keeble 2001: 398–9). The journalistic interview, after all, is a formalized event in which the reporter assumes a dominant, controlling position over the person being interviewed. The presence of a notebook emphasizes its artificial and contrived elements. In contrast, the conversation, the chat over a meal are more authentic, with all the participants occupying equal status. In his As I Please column of 28 April 1944, Orwell reproduces a conversation with a *Peace News* seller. But he claims no authenticity for his report: he says the conversation 'went something like this' and the 'youth' remains anonymous throughout. How much of this is fact, how much is fiction – or is it faction (a mix of both)?

On journalism's 'plain style' and public voice

Journalism also has its own voice and style. As Adam comments (2002: 26): 'Whatever else may be said about the language of journalism, it is fair to say that it is disciplined by its public and empirical character. Its vocabulary is the vocabulary of public discourse. It may strive to represent scientific ideas or the abstract notions of philosophy, but it does not adopt the vocabularies of those disciplines. It uses a vocabulary that can be understood in the street or in the marketplace.' Like other forms of rhetoric, 'journalism is an artifice with its own palette pointing to the concrete and the experiential' (ibid.).

At best, journalism's strength lies in its clarity of language and structure – and conciseness. Even the seventeenth-century 'mercurists' reinforced the veracity claims of their reporting with a sober 'perfect style of language'. And in the following century Defoe defined journalism's 'plain style' as one 'in which a man speaking to five hundred people of all common and various capacities, idiots and lunatics excepted, should be understood by them all'.

Dickens's capacity to observe, mirror and recreate popular speech was another crucial element of his journalism, as John Tulloch argues in his chapter. And Jane Chapman highlights the way in which George Sand's strategy of writing in the language of ordinary people was intricately linked to her desire to promote republican socialism through her journalism.

But journalism's 'plain style' does not mean it is incapable of capturing complexity. In her chapter on William Hazlitt, Kirsten Daly suggests his 'familiar style' in fact helped him negotiate the complex tensions inherent in his position as a literary journalist and theatre critic: the need to adopt a persona, whilst speaking honestly about the works under review, and the need to present authors' words to readers through the medium of print in a way that did justice to the original performance context. Moreover, according to Linden Peach, Angela Carter not only covered a wide variety of literary and cultural topics in her journalism in the *Guardian*, *London Magazine* and *New Society*, but often displayed the linguistic and narrative experimentation that characterizes her fiction.

For Jeffrey Meyers (2000: 266), Orwell's 'plain style' was 'the basic weapon in his arsenal' appealing to readers' common sense and persuading them of his honesty and good faith. 'At the same time his arguments are sophisticated, provocative and entertaining.' Whether he was writing a novel, poem, essay, review, column or polemic, Orwell was always 'journalistic', using direct and pared-down language. In his essay 'Politics and the English Language' (first published in *Horizon* in April 1946: see Orwell and Angus 4: 156–69), Orwell linked clarity of expression with sincerity: 'The great enemy of clear language is insincerity. When there is a gap between one's real and one's declared aims, one turns as it were instinctively to long words and exhausted idioms, like a cuttlefish squirting out ink' (ibid.: 166–7).

On the qualities of journalism

Significantly, all our contributors are concerned to stress the value and quality of the writing under review. Much academic commentary on the media (for understandable reasons) is highly critical. Either journalists are too trite, sensational, perpetuating stereotypes of various kinds (racist, sexist, militarist and so on) or they are purveyors of myth, propaganda and lies. Here, in contrast, are journalistic models worth celebrating and from whom students of English and journalism can learn such a lot.

The selection – building on the important work of John Gross (1969), Jeremy Treglown and Bridget Bennett (1998), Kate Campbell (2000), Iona Italia (2005) and the substantial American canon of texts on literary journalism, explored by Nick Nuttall in his chapter on Capote – is by no means exhaustive. Yet like these texts, *The Journalistic Imagination* is aiming to challenge the 'low' status of journalism. In addition to its many consequences already identified, this has meant journalism has been slow to gain respectability as an academic subject – particularly in Britain.

As Kate Campbell (2000: 1) comments, speaking of journalism and literature, 'literary studies have mostly kept them apart, neglecting and disparaging journalism'. It is hoped this text, bringing together academics from both journalism and English studies, will help in the cross-fertilization of ideas. Such a process, celebrating the diversity of the journalistic imagination, can only enrich the two disciplines – and cultural life in general.

The editors would welcome comments and criticisms from readers. Please contact Richard Keeble at rkeeble@lincoln.ac.uk and Sharon Wheeler at Larton.Media@ zen.co.uk

References

Adam, G. Stuart (2002) 'Notes towards a definition of journalism', in Clark, Roy Peter, and Campbell, Cole C. (eds), *The Values and Craft of American Journalism: Essays from the Poynter Institute* (Gainesville: University Press of Florida), pp. 7–40.

Allan, Stuart (2004) *News Culture* (Buckingham: Open University Press), second edition.

Applegate, Edd (1996) *Literary Journalism: A Biographical Dictionary of Writers and Editors* (Westport, CT: Greenwood Press).

Benson, Rodney (2005) 'Mapping field variation: journalism in France and the United States', in Benson, Rodney, and Neveu, Erik (eds), *Bourdieu and the Journalistic Field* (Cambridge: Polity), pp. 85–112.

Bromley, Michael (2003) 'Objectivity and the other Orwell: the tabloidisation of the *Daily Mirror* and journalistic authenticity', *Media History*, 9/2: 123–35.

Brosnan, Leila (2000) 'Monarch of the drab world: Virginia Woolf's figuring of journalism as abject', in Campbell, Kate (ed.), *Journalism, Literature, Modernism* (Edinburgh: Edinburgh University Press), pp. 191–210.

Butler, Marilyn (1981) *Romantics, Rebels and Reactionaries: English Literature and Its Background, 1760–1830* (Oxford: Oxford University Press).

Campbell, Kate (2000) 'Introduction', Campbell, Kate (ed.) *Journalism, Literature, Modernism* (Edinburgh: Edinburgh University Press), pp. 1–14.

Chance, Jean, and McKeen, William (2001) *Literary Journalism: A Reader* (Belmont, CA: Wadsworth).

Conboy, Martin (2004) *Journalism: A Critical History* (London: Sage).

Connolly, Cyril (1930/61) *Enemies of Promise* (Harmondsworth, Middlesex: Penguin Books).

Craven, L. (1992) 'The early newspaper press in England', in Griffiths, Denis (ed.), *The Encyclopaedia of the British Press* (London: Macmillan).

Drew, John M. L. (2003) *Dickens the Journalist* (Houndmills, Basingstoke: Palgrave Macmillan).

Fisk, Robert (2005) *The Great War for Civilization: The Conquest of the Middle East* (London: Fourth Estate).

Gross, John (1969) *The Rise and Fall of the Man of Letters: English Literary Life Since 1800* (London: Weidenfeld & Nicolson).

Hartley, John (1996) *Popular Reality: Journalism, Modernity, Popular Culture* (London and New York: Arnold).

Hartsock, John C. (2000) *A History of American Literary Journalism: The Emergence of a Modern Narrative Form* (Amherst: University of Massachusetts Press).

Ingrams, Richard (2005) *Muggeridge: The Biography* (London: HarperCollins).

Italia, Iona (2005) *The Rise of Literary Journalism in the Eighteenth Century: Anxious Employment* (London: Routledge).

Keeble, Richard (2001) 'Orwell as war correspondent – a reassessment', *Journalism Studies*, 2/3, 393–406.

Leader, Zachary (1998) 'Coleridge and the uses of journalism', in Campbell, Kate (ed.), *Journalism, Literature, Modernism* (Edinburgh: Edinburgh University Press), pp. 22–40.

Lee, Hermione (1998) 'Crimes of criticism: Virginia Woolf and literary journalism', in Campbell, Kate (ed.), *Journalism, Literature, Modernism* (Edinburgh: Edinburgh University Press), pp. 112–34.

McNair, Brian (2005) 'What is journalism?', in de Burgh, Hugo (ed.), *Making Journalists* (London and New York: Routledge), pp. 25–43.

Mason, Shirlene (1978) *Daniel Defoe and the Status of Women* (St Alban's Vermont: Eden Press Women's Publications).

Meyer, Gitte, and Lund, Anker Brink (2006) 'Making room for pluralism by redefining journalism: an essay on practical reasoning', *Ethical Space: The International Journal of Communication Ethics*, 3/2,3, 51–9.

Meyers, Jeffrey (2000) *Orwell: Wintry Conscience of a Generation* (London and New York: W. W. Norton & Company).

Orwell, Sonia, and Angus, Ian (eds) (1968) *The Collected Essays, Journalism and Letters*, vol. 1: *An Age Like This 1920–1940*, vol. 2: *My Country Right or Left*; vol. 3: *As I Please*, vol. 4: *In Front of Your Name* (Harmondsworth, Middlesex: Penguin).

Raymond, Joad (1999) 'The newspaper, public opinion, and the public sphere in the seventeenth century', in Raymond, Joad (ed.), *News, Newspapers and Society in Early Modern Britain* (London: Frank Cass).

Sales, Roger (2000) 'Platform, performance and payment in Henry Mayhew's *London Labour and the London Poor*', in Campbell, Kate (ed.), *Journalism, Literature, Modernism* (Edinburgh: Edinburgh University Press), pp. 54–71.

Schudson, Michael (1978) *Discovering the News: A Social History of American Newspapers* (New York: Basic Books).

—— (1996) *The Power of News* (Cambridge, Massachusetts; London: Harvard University Press).

Sims, Norman (ed.) (1984) *The Literary Journalists* (New York: Ballantine Books).

—— and Kramer, Mark (eds) (1995) *Literary Journalism: A New Collection of the Best American Non-fiction* (New York: Ballantine).

Smith, Jeffery A. (1999) *War and Press Freedom: The Problem of Prerogative Power* (Oxford and New York: Oxford University Press).

Sommerville, C. John (1996) *The News Revolution* (Oxford: Oxford University Press).

Treglown, Jeremy, and Bennett, Bridget (eds) (1998) *Grub Street and the Ivory Tower: Literary Journalism and Literary Scholarship from Fielding to the Internet* (Oxford: Clarendon Press).

Tulloch, John (2006a) 'Book review: *The Great War for Civilisation: The Conquest of the Middle East*', *Ethical Space*, 3/2,3, 62–3.

—— (2006b) 'The privatisation of pain: Lincoln Newspapers and the end of public execution in England', *Journalism Studies*, 7/3, 437–51.

Uglow, Jenny (1998) 'Fielding, Grub Street and Canary Wharf', in Treglown, Jeremy, and Bennett, Bridget (eds) (1998) *Grub Street and the Ivory Tower: Literary Journalism and Literary Scholarship from Fielding to the Internet* (Oxford: Clarendon Press), pp. 1–21.

Wilkes, Roger (2002) *Scandal: A Scurrilous History of Gossip* (London: Atlantic Books).

Wolfe, Tom (1975) *The New Journalism* (London: Picador).

The authors would like to thank John Gilliver, Nol van der Loop, John Tulloch and John Simons for their comments on an early draft (though the authors remain entirely responsible for the final version).

Chapter 1

Defoe's *The Storm* as a model for contemporary reporting

Jenny McKay

Daniel Foe was born into the family of a successful tradesman in 1660. As a young man he went into business too, dealing at various times in meat, hosiery, wine, tobacco, perfume, horses and bricks, often with disastrous results such as bankruptcy and imprisonment in 1692 and 1703. Defoe married in 1684 and was the father of at least six children, one of whom became a journalist, although without notable success. Foe added the prefix De to his name in 1695, perhaps, as some have speculated, to enhance his social standing by the adoption of a title that sounded more aristocratic (Richetti 2005: 19). He was educated at the Nonconformist Morton's Academy, renowned for its forward-thinking approach to education which stressed science, economics and modern rather than classical languages. Defoe acquired a strong interest in politics and social affairs as well as religion, at a time when deep divisions separated Catholic from Protestant in all aspects of life, including the accession to the throne. Along with his business activities Defoe held public office, but by the 1690s he was establishing himself as an energetic and eloquent writer of political, religious and moral polemic and satire. As a result he was condemned by the authorities and for a punishment he was made to stand in the pillory. From the early years of the eighteenth century, Defoe depended on high-level patronage for his livelihood and was employed as a propagandist and a secret agent charged with setting up an intelligence network, most notably for Robert Harley, Earl of Oxford, MP, Speaker of the House of Commons, a Secretary of State 'and prime minister in all but name' (Downie 1979: 2). Defoe developed his extraordinary facility with words to become a writer of astounding productivity and invention. He is widely credited with a role in the foundation of at least two genres – journalism and the novel, although his most famous fiction, *Robinson Crusoe*, was not written until Defoe was nearly 60. He died in 1731, alone and impoverished. For someone who wrote so much there is surprisingly little known about his personal and domestic life.

Most people know Daniel Defoe as the writer of the novels *Robinson Crusoe* (1719) and *Moll Flanders* (1722). His renown as a novelist has long overshadowed his reputation as a journalist even though he was successful, prolific and innovative as a writer of factual as well as fictional narratives. When his journalism is considered by scholars it tends to be the polemical pieces about religion, morals, economics and politics that receive attention. Or the journalism is used as a source of information by historians, especially those interested in politics or social issues. Much less often is it studied in its own right as a subject for literary and textual analysis.

Why, then, is so little of Defoe's journalism read today, even though it forms such a large proportion of his huge output? The most obvious reason is that journalism is considered ephemeral: it is, by definition, about current affairs. When Defoe was writing about the political and religious controversies of his time he could assume his audience knew the background and cared about the debate. Today's readers need specialized knowledge of the period to be gripped by some of Defoe's arguments. A second reason is that the quality and popularity of Defoe's novels mean readers may not think of looking beyond them. Then there is the question of canon-formation, of who gets to decide what is worthy of being read, studied or published. The English literature establishment is reluctant to accord literary status to journalistic writing, while much of the journalism establishment is equally reluctant to celebrate journalism for its literary merit. A kind of snobbery is partly to blame for this, which means that those who write for a living are looked down on as mere hacks and compared unfavourably with those whose motivation is thought to be the higher calling of the creative arts. Lastly, and partly for the reasons I have listed, there is the problem of access: the journalism of Defoe, like that of many other great writers, is not easy to find for readers who are not members of academic libraries.

Yet this neglect of Defoe's journalism is all the more surprising given the establishment in the academy in the UK over the past 30 years – and in the United States over more than a century – of the field of journalism studies. Here you might expect to find at least some of his vast journalistic output being read by students and lecturers keen to examine early examples of their own practices. In fact this hardly happens. This is to miss a great deal.[1]

Defoe's vast journalistic range

In addition to politics, Defoe wrote on a vast range of topics. A 'veritable writing machine', one recent biographer, John Richetti, calls him (2005: ix). Defoe wrote, argued, reported, and he edited. He founded his own magazine, the *Review*, and wrote it more or less single-handedly from 1704 to 1713, publishing three editions a week – an undertaking that included separate editions for Scotland where he was based for some of that period. For the *Review* he was a reporter, a political commentator, an agony uncle, a leader writer, a critic, a gossip columnist (or scandalmonger as the term then was), and, under the pen name Mr Review, he was the precursor of the growing legions of writers of opinion columns. 'For sheer fluency and day-to-day pertinence and insight, there is nothing else in English political writing then or since quite like this extended and unflagging performance,' writes Richetti (ibid.: 97).

Defoe argued vigorously in favour of educating women. He wrote about the 1707 Act of Union with Scotland, about road maintenance, about insurance schemes and against the idea that there is any such thing as a pure-bred Englishman. The press, magic, family life, the servant problem, religion, usury, ghosts, language and diplomacy were other subjects he tackled. He offered practical advice to anyone who might be willing to listen: for example, when, in 1721, it seemed likely that the plague was again about to cross the Channel from Europe he sought to influence the thinking of officials about how such a crisis could best be prepared for and dealt with. In this case, typically, he produced articles as well as two books out of his material: the overtly didactic *Due Preparations for the Plague* in 1722 and a month later the work which would now be classed as a historical fiction, *A Journal of the Plague Year*.

This book has long been acclaimed for its sympathetic and dramatic reconstruction of the outbreak of plague in 1665 in London. Written with the cool objectivity of an observer, the narrative is convincing in its realism and it has, like *Robinson Crusoe* which was published three years earlier, acquired the significance of a literary archetype.[2] *A Journal of the Plague Year* is the moving study of an individual and a society going through a period of intense crisis both tangible, in the disease, and intangible, in the moral dilemmas the outbreak poses. (*La Peste*, of 1947, by the French novelist and journalist Albert Camus, is perhaps the best-known successor fiction.) However, the weight that this seriousness implies is not burdensome. The novel is richly textured, warm and humane, and shows a compassion for the suffering of the poor.

Unlike a significant proportion of Defoe's writing, *A Journal of the Plague Year* leaves no doubt as to whether he was the author.[3] This is not true of all the works which have been attributed to him but even if you count only those texts about which his authorship is not in question, the range of his curiosity, the breadth of his knowledge, and his unflagging need to communicate with as many people as possible using language they could understand are remarkable. He was a fluent, opinionated, well-informed and versatile writer. These attributes are also, of course, a suitable description of those who would be most employable in the newsrooms of today, and this may help to explain the strength of his appeal for journalists of our time such as his biographer, Richard West, and the BBC's former political editor, Andrew Marr. According to West, Defoe was 'a great and not just a good reporter' (1997: 87). And for Marr, he was a 'writer of genuine genius' who created 'a journalistic style that lasted'. He wrote 'excellent, clear, uncluttered, reporterly English full of relatively short sentences of plain description' (2004: 8).

The Storm: landmark text in the development of British journalism

Fortunately some of Defoe's journalism and other non-fiction writing is now in print, most notably one of his earliest works, *The Storm*. For modern readers this provides a welcoming route into the journalistic writing of 'one of the most significant figures in the history of print journalism' (Ellison 2006: 91). It does not depend on much background knowledge as it is about a severe weather event, which readers can relate to their own experience. As a nation the British are known for their obsession with the weather and with disastrous-weather stories in particular: they like to hear about the physical damage to cities and country-side, about destruction, miraculous escapes, tragic deaths, about acts of bravery contrasted with acts of calculating cruelty. They like to apportion blame for what has gone wrong.[4] All of these are tropes with which modern journalists and their readers are familiar. And Defoe's *The Storm* offers all of them in a book which, by virtue of its publication date, can be seen as a landmark text in the development of British journalism and the writing of popular narrative.

It was written at a time when what we would now call journalism (but for which there was then no single collective term) was flourishing. After a period of tight government control over what was published, in 1695 the Licensing Act was allowed to lapse in England and this unleashed a torrent of news publishing in new forms and by new writers (Smith 1979: 45–7, 56). The first women's magazine, the *Ladies' Mercury*, was launched as a monthly from 1693, the first recognizable news-paper, the *Daily Courant*, appeared in 1702, and many other titles were to follow in the first decades of the eighteenth century. By the 1690s Defoe was already gaining a reputation, notoriety even, as a pamphleteer, and as his business activities became more calamitous he found himself poised to play a full part in what Ellison describes as 'a proliferation of texts and the expansion of … communication systems' unique in the history of the media (2006: 2).

The Storm: or, a Collection of the most remarkable Casualties and Disasters which happen'd in the Late Dreadful Tempest, both by Sea and Land, to give its full title, is one example of his activities. The book was published in 1704 and 'printed for G. Sawbridge and sold by J. Nutt' (Hamblyn 2003:1). It commemorated what remains the worst tempest ever recorded in the British Isles. The wind had swept across southern England for a week in late November 1703, destroying thousands of buildings, felling millions of trees, as well as killing thousands of people, including a fifth of the sailors in the British Navy. Little wonder that the monarch, Queen Anne, described it as 'a Calamity so Dreadful and Astonishing, that the like hath not been Seen or Felt in the Memory of any Person Living in this our Kingdom' (ibid.: xxxix). It is also likely that Defoe, who had recently emerged from debtors' prison and who had a family to support, recognized in the event a way of earning some much-needed money by using his writing skills. For most of his adult life until this storm, Defoe had earned his living from commerce, although during the 1690s he was also forging a career as a writer of poetry, journalism and polemical pamphlets.

The Storm is not a novel. Its first-person authorial voice states that it is based on true accounts of what happened during and just after the hurricane, eyewit-ness accounts solicited from all over the country by means of advertisements in the *London Gazette*, which was founded in 1666 as an official government news-paper carrying mainly foreign news, and the *Daily Courant*. Here is part of the advertisement:

To preserve the Remembrance of the late Dreadful Tempest, an exact and faithful Collection is preparing of the most remarkable Disasters which happened on that Occasion, with the Places where, and Persons concern'd whether at Sea or on Shore. For the perfecting so good a Work, 'tis humbly recommended by the Author to all Gentlemen of the Clergy, or others, who have made any Observations of this Calamity, that they would transmit as distinct an Account as possible, of what they have observed.

(*London Gazette* 3975, 13–16 December 1703)

The advertisements can still be viewed in newspaper archives, as can other documents such as *Philosophical Transactions*, the journal of the Royal Society (the learned society of scientists founded in 1660), on which Defoe drew for some of his research and from which he quotes in *The Storm*.[5] He refers to other traceable documents, as well as to the letters his advertisement elicited from clergymen, gentlemen, 'honest countrymen', an apothecary, sailors and even one woman who were scattered throughout the large area of England devastated by the storm. By this means Defoe seeks to establish the authenticity of the events and scenes he describes.[6] He developed this technique in his later narrative writing even when he was not composing a factual account. *A Journal of the Plague Year* is one example where he makes extensive use of documents, such as the Bills of Mortality (lists of the names of those who died and the causes of death) from London churches, to help verify what he describes within a fictional account of an event which had, in fact, taken place.

Like *A Journal of the Plague Year*, *The Storm* describes a society in the grip of catastrophic events which will have lasting effects both physical and psychological on the people who witness them. The order of magnitude may be different (the 1703 storm left around 8,000 dead, the plague in 1665 around 97,000) but a reading of both suggests a connection between the way the narratives were conceived by Defoe: it is hard to believe that his fictional account of London's plague would have been written in the same way if *The Storm*, a largely factual account, had not appeared first. *The Storm* was Defoe's first full-length book and in it we see him experimenting with ways of writing about experience which are later developed in his fictional narratives. One example is the use of eyewitness accounts. For *The Storm* these are gathered from the author's correspondents and contacts, to use the journalists' jargon of today. In his novels such as *A Journal of the Plague Year* the viewpoints of imagined 'eyewitnesses' are regularly used to narrate events, although it is probable that he had heard accounts direct from people who lived through the plague in London in 1665.

The Storm, then, is worth reading both for its own sake and for its significance as a founding text for both journalism and the novel. The journalist and biographer of Defoe, Richard West, argues that as a piece of reporting *The Storm* is 'a masterpiece, which puts to shame all modern accounts of disaster whether in books, newspapers, radio or television' (1997: 86). During what turned out to be 'the golden age of journalism' in the early eighteenth century, Defoe was 'the first master, if not the inventor, of almost every feature of modern newspapers' (ibid.: xiii). One of Defoe's main strengths, in West's eyes, was that 'he excelled in the art of telling a story', just as Richard Hamblyn, editor of the modern edition of *The Storm*, praises Defoe for his 'narrative instinct' (2003: xxvii).

Early master of modern journalism

West's suggestion that Defoe was an early master of modern journalism is easy for us to test, as the daily round of hard news production in our increasingly frenetic media age supplies us with many examples of disaster reporting, some of them offering direct parallels with Defoe's approach. Here are two quotations from people who lived through severe storms separated in time by 300 years. The first is from *The Storm*; the second is an eyewitness quoted on the BBC news website after a more modest gale.

> Several hundred of Apple-Trees and other Trees blown down: Most Houses damnify'd in the Tiles and Thatch ... Our loss in the Apple-Trees is the greatest; because we shall want Liquor to make our Hearts merry.
>
> (Defoe 2003: 97)

> Last weekend I thought I must prune the apple tree this autumn. Well no need to do that now – the wind blew it over. I don't know what has upset me more the fact that the tree has blown over or the realization that my annual intake of apple-pie will be seriously reduced this year.
>
> (BBC news website[7])

This endearing preoccupation with apple trees and consequent dismay about apple deprivation is the kind of detail which, as any journalist knows, brings a story to life. Andrew Marr, another of Defoe's journalist admirers as we have seen, praises Defoe for his understanding of the importance of developing trust between journalists and their readers and also for being a reporter who believed in seeing and hearing things for himself (2004: 9). For Anthony Burgess, Defoe, in his absolute 'devotion to the craft of reportage' (1966: 12), was 'our first great novelist because he was our first great journalist' (ibid.: 7). Burgess is drawing attention here to Defoe's contribution to the development of realism as a literary convention and noting the links between this development and early attempts by journalists including Defoe to make a literary record of reality. *The Storm* represents, at around 75,000 words, the first recognizable piece of modern journalistic reporting and book-length features journalism of a sort that is still, and increasingly, practised in English as well as other languages. It was the eighteenth-century equivalent of an instant book and was published within seven months of the disaster.

The idea of writing about this storm was not Defoe's alone. There are other accounts of it, as well as of other momentous events stretching back through the seventeenth century. One example is *The Wonders of this windie winter*, which was published in 1613 (Hunter 1990: 178–9). Other periodicals carried brief accounts of the storm within a few days, and the January and February 1704 edition of the Royal Society's journal, *Philosophical Transactions*, was, as Hamblyn observes, almost a storm special: three out of that edition's eight contributed letters were about the hurricane and a further one was about the earthquake which may or may not have been related to it (2003: xxxi).

Defoe offers these letters as some of the several documentary sources of information he uses to compile his own narrative. Of those who died, more than 1,100 were stranded on Goodwin Sands in the English Channel. One ship was blown from there, in the south of England, all the way to Norway. Defoe revelled in detail whatever his subject. For *The Storm* he presents scientific explanations and shows evidence of his research into the records of barometric pressure on the days before and after the storm struck, as sent to the Royal Society by a Mr Derham. He also presents the documentation relating to the terrible loss of life among sailors. His irrepressible and admirable drive to improve and manage things is shown by his inclusion of a table illustrating how sailors refer to the various strengths of wind: he then proceeds to set up his own table of wind strengths to make the measurement clearer. His table anticipates the establishment of the Beaufort scale by around 100 years.

Pioneering example of human interest story

It is as an early example of the journalistic human interest story that *The Storm* is most compelling for today's readers. It is a record of narrow escapes and loss of life. The Bishop of Bath and Wells was killed along with his wife

> by the Fall of two Chimney Stacks, which fell on the Roof, and drove it in upon my Lord's Bed, forced it quite through the next Flower [floor] down into the Hall, and buried them both in the Rubbish; and 'tis suppos'd my Lord was getting up, for he was found some Distance from my Lady, who was found in her Bed.
>
> (2003: 71)

In addition:

- Defoe records massive damage to property. He says he saw 17,000 trees down in the county of Kent alone before he stopped counting. In St James's Park 'above a Hundred Elms' were blown over, some having been planted in the sixteenth century (ibid: 62). In Gloucestershire one gentleman 'had many Woods; among which was one Grove of very tall Trees, being each near Eighty Foot high; the which he greatly valued for the Tallness and Prospect of them, and therefore resolv'd never to cut them down: But it so happen'd that

Six Hundred of them within the Compass of Five Acres were wholly blown down' (ibid.: 71).

- It is a record of cowardice, selfishness and inhumanity as shown by the townspeople of Deal who could see sailors trapped on the Goodwin Sands but for whom they could neither find boats to rescue them nor any help once they were saved (ibid.: 134).
- Defoe is at pains to celebrate heroism, self-sacrifice and generosity as shown by the Mayor of Deal. Infuriated by his townspeople's selfishness, he took boats by force to rescue several hundred men and paid from his own pocket for food and shelter for the wretched survivors. In a passage which has a certain understandable testiness about it, Defoe describes how the government was at first unwilling to help with the travel costs home for these men who were, after all, employed by the British Navy when their ships went down (ibid.: 134–6).
- And it is a record of comical moments, such as the story of the itinerant woman, offered lodging in a barn for the duration of the storm who found in the morning that all her clothes, hung up to dry out, had been blown away during the night along with the roof of her shelter. She had to climb out almost naked through the rafters (ibid.: 77).

This kind of anecdote is familiar to modern consumers of news media but when Defoe was writing it was not the norm. Literary historian J. Paul Hunter notes that it was a relatively new phenomenon in the late seventeenth century for people to be so interested in the immediate and the contemporaneous, and he ascribes this to a growing interest in discovery, enlightenment and novelty (1990: chapter 7).

Verification and reliability of sources

Such immediacy raises questions about sources and the reliability of testimony, questions which were on Defoe's mind too. As narrator of *The Storm* he says he cannot personally verify every letter he presents. Where he cannot verify, he publishes anyway but with a warning that it is second-hand testimony. In his 'Preface' he is at pains to establish the credibility of what he writes, explaining that writers carry a responsibility to posterity for the accuracy of their work:

> If a Book Printed obtrudes a falshood, if a Man tells a Lye in Print, he abuses Mankind, and imposes upon the whole World, he causes our Children to tell Lyes after us, and their Children after them …
>
> (2003: 3).

He condemns earlier 'Pen-men' whose 'prodigious Looseness of the Pen has confounded History and Fable from the beginning of both' (ibid.: 5) and seeks to distance himself from such 'ridiculous Stuff' as the Greek myths, proclaiming his own desire to 'keep close to the Truth' (ibid.: 8). He is aware of the responsibility he carries: 'I have not undertaken this Work without the serious Consideration of what I owe to Truth, and to Posterity' (ibid.: 5).

This leads him to explain why there is such variety in the writing style of the accounts he presents in his book. He makes 'Apology for the Meanness of Stile' of some of his correspondents and for reproducing it without alteration. Of one, he says the style is

> Coarse, and Sailor like; yet I have inserted this Letter, because it seems to describe the Horror and Consternation the poor Sailors were in at that time. And because this is Written from one, who was as near an Eye Witness as any could possible be, and be safe.
>
> (Ibid.:131)

Defoe is arguing that 'The Plainness and Honesty' of his witnesses' stories is more important than any lack of literary sophistication (ibid.: 8). He came from a family of religious Dissenters and therefore was not educated at a university where emphasis was laid on traditions of rhetorical writing based on classical models. Defoe's own education, at the Dissenters' academy in Newington Green, London, was strongly influenced by the Baconian tradition of intellectual inquiry which had led to the formation of the Royal Society in the 1660s. In her book *Defoe and the New Sciences*, Ilse Vickers (1996) describes how seventeenth-century precepts about language are demonstrated in Defoe's work: everyday, simple language without decoration or flourish was to be preferred as the most effective means of communication and, therefore, as the best way to contribute to the advancement of knowledge.[8]

This tenet is relevant to journalistic writing today and a look at any current journalism textbook reveals links between late seventeenth-century Plain Style and the way journalists are now taught to write. Here is one example from countless: 'What is needed is plainness, decorum, economy, precision – above all clarity. What is not needed is rhetoric or embellishment' (Hicks 1999: 124). Defoe strove to write clearly and simply and encouraged others to do the same, notably in the introduction to *The Compleat English Tradesman* (1726–7), a book aimed at young men at the start of careers in business. For advice about writing style many British journalists nowadays are able to refer back to the influential essay by George Orwell, 'Politics and the English Language', of 1946, in which he encourages all writers to strive for brevity, clarity and freshness of expression while railing against pomposity, euphemism and cliché (see Orwell 1970: 156–69). But how many know about earlier attempts to manipulate language written and spoken, even though these have a significant place in the history of journalistic writing?

Echoes of Defoe's journalism in current practice

Vickers's book describes other ways in which Defoe's methods have echoes in our current journalism practice. For example, she draws attention to the emphasis placed by the 'new sciences' on observation and the collection and classification of information gathered at first hand, on empirical enquiry, on accuracy and on sceptical questioning as a habit of mind (1996: 65). And as Robert Mayer argues, *The Storm* exemplifies the way in which 'the "scientific" methodology of the new history' could be used to create a work that 'depends heavily upon narrative and is intended to have popular appeal' (1997: 162).

In keeping with these principles Defoe's descriptions are made vivid by his own colloquial writing style and by the evidence he offers that he was there, right in the middle of the terrible event which is the subject of his book:

> The Author of this Relation was in a well-built brick House in the skirts of the City; and a Stack of Chimneys falling in upon the next Houses, gave the House such a Shock, that they thought it was just coming down upon their Heads: but opening the Door to attempt an Escape into a Garden, the Danger was so apparent, that they all thought fit to surrender to the Disposal of Almighty Providence, and expect their Graves in the Ruins of the House, rather than to meet most certain Destruction in the open Garden ... the Author of this has seen Tiles blown from a House above thirty or forty Yards, and stuck from five to eight Inches into the solid Earth.
>
> (2003: 30–1)

The reporter as eyewitness

This desire to 'be there' is a strong motive for all the best writers of journalism, an idea that will be familiar to those who have trained as newspaper reporters. Andrew Marr argues for the importance of journalists getting out of their newsrooms to go and report. So does Tom Wolfe in his essay 'The New Journalism' in which he praises feature writer Jimmy Breslin for his insistence on being able to 'leave the building, go outside and do reporting on his own, genuine legwork'. And John Carey, not a journalist but a literary critic, academic and anthologist of journalism, explains that reportage is at its strongest when it is based on eyewitness accounts, when it 'derives ultimately from people who can say "I was there"' (Marr 2004: 384; Wolfe 1973: 25; Carey 1987: xxix).

In *The Storm* we encounter Defoe in an early demonstration of the role of the eyewitness reporter during and immediately after a disaster, out and about in the streets, dodging danger (in this case flying roof tiles) as he talked to people. He asked, he observed, he counted, he made projections from the statistics, and he apportioned blame. That is very much what journalists do today. So too is adding up the cost, translating the human and physical disaster into money terms as a way of conveying to readers the impact of what has happened.

Indeed the City was a strange Spectacle the Morning after the Storm, as soon as the People could put their heads out of Doors ... The Streets lay so covered with Tiles and Slates, from the Tops of the Houses, especially in the Out-parts, that the Quantity is incredible: and the Houses were so universally stript, that all the Tiles in Fifty Miles round would be able to repair but a small Part of it.

Something may be guest at on this Head, from the sudden Rise of the Price of Tiles; which rise from 21s. per Thousand to 6 l. for plain Tiles; and from 50s. per Thousand for Pantiles, to 10 l. and Bricklayers Labour to 5s. per Day.

(Ibid.: 57)[9]

Defoe gathered quotes to bring his story alive. In this case, as we have seen, he sought written quotations from correspondents throughout the country. (This is a good example of the Baconian method for gathering scientific data being applied to create a journalistic record.) Journalists still advertise for informants through the media. Modern reporters still construct their stories from quotations, especially from eyewitnesses in the case of big events, but also when comments are needed.

Defoe uses his carefully gathered range of points of view to engaging effect in *The Storm* and his assertion that nothing can be more useful to 'the publick services than plain, naked, and unbyasst accounts both of persons and things' is at once Baconian and a useful summing up of what the better journalists try to do today, even if there is now a certain scepticism about how far the stories they write can ever be free of bias. Journalism is sometimes mocked for its pretensions to being, and inadequacies as, a first draft of history, but to make a contribution to the historical record of his time was clearly one of Defoe's motivations in writing *The Storm* and there is no doubt that he succeeded in constructing, as Ellison describes, 'a collective memory of the event' by drawing together 'multiple narratives of personal suffering' (Ellison 2006: 107).

Defoe also provides background information based on his own reading to put events into context, to try to explain, in this case, how winds in general occur and what might have caused this one in particular. For this he offers religious as well as scientific explanations. To take religion first:

The main inference I shall pretend to make or at least venture the exposing to publick View, in this case, is, the strong Evidence God has been pleas'd to give in this terrible manner to his own Being, which Mankind began more than ever to affront and despise ... I cannot doubt but the Atheist's hard'ned Soul trembl'd a little as well as his House.

(Ibid.: 6–7)

Besides arguing that the storm was sent by God to show atheists that he did, in fact, exist, Defoe suggests it is a punishment for wickedness, describing it as 'the dreadfulest and most universal Judgment that ever Almighty Power thought fit to bring upon the Part of this World' (ibid.: 9).

Religious explanations do not, however, preclude scientific ones. Against any readers who might see a contradiction in looking to God as well as to the laws of physics for explanations, Defoe argues that 'a Philosopher [we would now say scientist] may be a Christian, and some of the best of the Latter have been the best of the Former' (2003: 13). Chapter 1 is called 'Of the Natural Causes and Original of Winds' and in it Defoe recounts late seventeenth-century scientific thinking about the physical causes of winds, while proposing that God may have had an overarching purpose in sending this particular one.

Defoe's modernity

The Storm is a fascinating narrative because of the way Defoe pieces together recent tragic events of great social and personal significance and then tells the story as fully as he can. Practices we now take for granted in journalistic research and narration were part of Defoe's method: how research is conducted; how testimony is gathered and used; which news values inform the selection of material; the role in the narrative of the eyewitness and the expert; how the writer tries to establish the authenticity of his account; how blame is apportioned; and, not least, what kind of language is used to write up the material.

It can be seen as a milestone in the development of both journalism and the novel. This is to emphasize the strength of the link between two different kinds of realism: between writing which claims to present verifiable reality (journalism) and writing which aims to present invention as if it were reality (realist fiction). For anyone interested in the history of journalistic writing *The Storm* contributes to an understanding of how such writing came to be as it is and what it can achieve. For anyone interested in the history of literature *The Storm* contributes to an understanding of how the conventions of realist fiction began to be developed. For these reasons, in addition to its intrinsic interest as an account of an unfolding tragedy, and for its significance as an early, experimental narrative by a writer revered as one of the English language's greatest writers, *The Storm* is a text well worth reading.

Notes

1 The situation in the United States is better and improving, partly because there is a longer tradition of studying journalism in universities. However, as Hartsock explains, there remains a bias against journalism among English studies specialists, while in journalism and mass communications departments the 'literary' aspect of journalism is still marginalized (Hartsock 2000: 6).

2 Robert Mayer calls *Robinson Crusoe*, 'a central text of Western civilisation' (1997: 1).

3 The most definitive list of Defoe's writings is by P. N. Furbank and W. R. Owens (1998). Their 44-volume edition of Defoe's works is under way (2000–8), published by Pickering and Chatto.

4 Tom Fort's book *Under the Weather* (2006) and Kate Fox's chapter 'Weather' in *Watching the English* (2005) discuss this phenomenon from the respective perspectives of a historian and a social anthropologist.

5 *London Gazette* 3972, 2–6 December 1703 and *Daily Courant* 409, 2 December 1703; *Philosophical Transactions* No. 289, vol. 24, 1704–5, pp. 1,530–4.
6 There are letters of doubtful origin, in particular the one purporting to be from a sailor still stranded on a ship in the English Channel (Hamblyn 2003: xxxi).
7 www.newsvote.bbc.co.uk/mpapps/pagetools/print/news.bbc.co.uk/1/hi/uk/38756 99.stm, accessed on 8 July, 2004.
8 Vickers further argues that *The Storm* is 'the work in which Defoe first explicitly declared his adherence to the principles of Baconian science' (1996: 117).
9 It is poignant to note that Defoe's main occupation before 1703 was as a man of commerce, albeit one whose businesses had a habit of going bankrupt. It had happened a few months before the storm – the business in question being the manufacture of roof tiles!

References

Brayne, M. (2002) *The Greatest Storm: Britain's Night of Destruction, November 1703* (Stroud: Sutton).

Burgess, A. (1966) 'Introduction', in Defoe, D. [1722] *A Journal of the Plague Year*, Burgess, A. and Bristow, C. (eds) (London: Penguin).

Carey, J. (1987) *The Faber Book of Reportage* (London: Faber & Faber).

Defoe, D. (2003) [1704] *The Storm*, Hamblyn, R. (ed.) (London: Allen Lane, and (2004) Penguin).

—— (1726–7) *The Compleat English Tradesman* (London: printed for Charles Rivington).

—— (1997) *The True-Born Englishman and Other Writings*, Furbank, P. N. and Owens, W. R. (eds) (London: Penguin).

Downie, J. A. (1979) *Robert Harley and the Press: Propaganda and Public Opinion in the Age of Swift and Defoe* (Cambridge: Cambridge University Press).

Ellison, K. (2006) *Fatal News. Reading and Information Overload in Early Eighteenth-Century Literature* (London: Routledge).

Fort, T. (2006) *Under the Weather. Us and the Elements* (London: Century).

Fox, K. (2005) *Watching the English: The Hidden Rules of English Behaviour* (London: Hodder & Stoughton).

Furbank, P. N. and Owens, W. R. (1998) *A Critical Bibliography of Daniel Defoe* (London: Pickering & Chatto).

—— (2006) *A Political Biography of Daniel Defoe* (London: Pickering & Chatto).

Hamblyn, R. (2003) 'Introduction', in Defoe, D. (2003) *The Storm* (London: Allen Lane and (2004) Penguin), pp. x–xl.

Hartsock, J.C. (2000) *A History of American Literary Journalism: The Emergence of a Modern Narrative Form* (Amherst: University of Massachusetts Press).

Hicks, W. (1999) *Writing for Journalists* (London: Routledge).

Hunter, J. P. (1990) *Before Novels: The Cultural Contexts of Eighteenth-Century English Fiction* (New York and London: W. W. Norton & Company).

Marr, A. (2004) *My Trade: A Short History of British Journalism* (London: Macmillan).

Mayer, R. (1997) *History and the Early English Novel: Matters of Fact from Bacon to Defoe* (Cambridge: Cambridge University Press).

Novak, M. E. (2001) *Daniel Defoe: Master of Fictions* (Oxford: Oxford University Press).

Orwell, G. (1970) 'Politics and the English language', in Orwell, S. and Angus, I. (eds), *The Collected Essays, Journalism and Letters of George Orwell*, vol. 4 (London: Penguin), pp. 156–69.

Payne, W. L. (1951) *The Best of Defoe's Review: An Anthology* (New York: Columbia University Press).

Richetti, J. (2005) *The Life of Daniel Defoe* (Oxford: Blackwell).

Smith, A. (1979) *The Newspaper: An International History* (London: Thames & Hudson).

Sutherland, J. (1986) *The Restoration Newspaper and its Development* (Cambridge: Cambridge University Press).

Vickers, I. (1996) *Defoe and the New Sciences* (Cambridge: Cambridge University Press).

Watt, I. (1957) *The Rise of the Novel: Studies in Defoe, Richardson and Fielding* (London: Chatto & Windus).

West, R. (1997) *The Life and Strange Surprising Adventures of Daniel Defoe* (London: Harper Collins).

Wolfe, T. (1973) 'The new journalism', in Johnson, E. W. and Wolfe, T. (eds), *The New Journalism* (London: Picador), pp. 15–68.

Chapter 2

William Hazlitt

Poetry, drama and literary journalism

Kirsten Daly

Born in 1778, the son of a Unitarian minister who had settled in the Shropshire village of Wem, William Hazlitt grew up in the culture of dissent. His early ambition was to be a painter, but he also began to publish on diverse subjects: *An Essay on the Principles of Human Action* (1805), *The Eloquence of the British Senate* (1807) and *A New and Improved Grammar of the English Tongue* (1809). Neither of these courses of action was commercially successful, nor was an early foray into lecturing. Upon marriage to Sarah Stoddart and the birth of his son William, Hazlitt moved his family to London. He began his journalistic career as a parliamentary reporter on the *Morning Chronicle* in 1813. The following year he was made drama critic, and would spend much of his career writing on the theatre for various publications, including the *Champion*, the *Examiner* and the *Edinburgh Review*. In 1817/18, he started to become well known. This proved to be a mixed blessing. On the one hand, his social circle expanded and book-length collections of his essays started to appear: *The Round Table* (1817) and *Characters from Shakespeare's Plays* (1817). He also embarked on a second lecture tour, which was a great success. On the other hand, he was subjected to increasingly virulent attacks in the Tory press, most notably in *Blackwood's Magazine*. In 1819, his marriage broke down. After a disastrous love affair with Sarah Walker, the daughter of his land-lady, he published an autobiographical narrative, *Liber Amoris* (1823), to near universal derision. The following year he married Isabella Bridgewater and moved to Paris. Hazlitt spent the later years of his career working on the monumental *Life of Napoleon*, of which he published the first two parts in 1828 and 1830. After his second wife left him, his health declined, and he died in 1830.

In his study of Romantic prose, Thomas McFarland describes Hazlitt as a brilliant prose stylist: 'No one has ever written like William Hazlitt; his style, sinewy, direct, and effortless, races along through all topics, those of the depths no less than those of the surface, with seemingly no premeditation or striving for effect' (McFarland 1987: 57–8). In one of his own disquisitions on style, 'On gusto', Hazlitt praises in painters qualities which can be found in his own writing. Gusto, for Hazlitt, is 'the power or passion defining any object', which, in a painter like Titian, communi-cates a sensuous vitality, 'stamped with all the truth of passion'.[1] In another essay, 'On familiar style', he describes the principles underpinning his approach to writing, advising of the need to write 'without affectation' but not 'at random', to search for 'the best word in common use', and to follow 'the true idiom of the language', to 'write as anyone would speak in common conversation' and thereby aspire to a universality of reference.[2] In his acclaimed biography, Stanley Jones (1991) writes that Hazlitt's style was something he honed over time.

Initially writing in the abstract manner fashionable at the time, he gradually developed the more personal, 'familiar' style which, in the end, says Jones, 'turned out to be in the mainstream of English prose' (ibid.: 105). For Jones, Hazlitt's style represents a Romantic rejection of the Enlightenment, associated with political radicalism. For Tom Paulin, who defines Hazlitt's style as distinctively republican, it is also deeply literary, containing a 'Shakespearean richness' of allusion (1998: 184), and Hazlitt was, of course, also a well-known reviewer of his literary contemporaries. Hazlitt is, then, a literary journalist in two senses: a 'literary' writer and a writer who discusses literature. In both senses, as I hope to demonstrate, his work raises questions concerning the status and function of literary journalism, questions which are, in many respects, particular to his time, but in others, remain significant. Moreover, in this essay, I want to suggest that Hazlitt's literariness is inflected by his sense of the marginal position of the literary journalist, marginal in relation to 'aristocratic' writers and to 'literature'. Indeed, I will suggest that, in this respect, Hazlitt's literariness is, like Keats's, intensely combative.

Expansion of print culture

The periodical press for which Hazlitt wrote was of relatively recent provenance. Its development was bound up with the expansion of print culture during the early modern period. At the beginning of the seventeenth century, printed materials existed, but they remained restricted. By the end of the century, a growing number of texts were available in print. Aside from improved techniques in printing, one of the main contributory factors to the expansion was the Civil War, which generated an increased demand for news. As Smith observes (1979), in the twenty years after 1640, roughly 30,000 news publications were produced. And in his study, Joad Raymond (1996: 15) observes that the content of seventeenth-century news publications was heterogeneous, embracing 'different kinds of reports and religious and cultural comment', especially after 1650.

By the early eighteenth century, a process of specialization was under way, with the rise of daily newspapers and the modern periodical press. Although they were not precluded from commenting on current affairs, the focus of periodicals such as the *Tatler* and the *Spectator* was on cultural matters. Culture was not restricted to 'art'. So, although there were discussions of the theatre, for example, and literary works such as *Paradise Lost*, and even aesthetic theory (*The Pleasures of the Imagination* is the best known), these periodicals also dealt with aspects of cultural life in general, such as coffee houses, duelling and even ill-natured husbands. Periodicals, as the noun suggests, appeared weekly, monthly or quarterly, and consisted of a mixture of essays, reviews, criticism and poetry. It was a field in which, as Brewer writes, it was possible to make a living as a professional writer (1997: 142). During the eighteenth century, it grew rapidly: by the 1760s, there were 30 London periodicals, but by the end of the century, there were more than 80 (ibid.).

Along with other forms of commercial writing, the eighteenth-century period-ical press was often the target of satire, the term hack writer originating in this period. In the most famous example, Pope's *The Dunciad*, Eliza Haywood, jour-nalist and author of numerous scandalous memoirs, who also established her own periodical, *The Female Spectator*, is attacked for her derivative and unscrupulous scribbling. It is a view that has persisted, for Virginia Woolf, echoing Pope, wrote of Haywood that 'she left behind her a mass of unreadable journalism which both by its form and by the inferiority of the writer's talent throws no light upon her age or upon herself' (1979: 93).

In her study of the eighteenth-century periodical, Iona Italia prefaces the intro-duction with Woolf's remark (2005: 1), and, throughout, addresses the issue of the periodical's status, or rather the lack of it. She treats the periodical as a literary genre in its own right, and identifies its distinctive features, which, it is suggested, owe more to the stage than to fiction, both in terms of its view of social life as performance and its interest in theatre. Part of the argument is that this literary newcomer is marked by a drive towards self-legitimization. The main strategy is gentrification. So, for example, contributors to the early periodicals, the *Tatler* and the *Spectator*, which became models for the rest, adopt highly genteel fictional personae, distancing themselves from the genre in which they work (ibid.: 22). By implication perhaps, literariness is a component of gentility, for, by addressing the public through a fictional persona, the real social identity of the writer remains intriguingly uncertain, and performative.

One of the claims made by the early periodical press is that it sought to enlighten its readers. In an early edition of the *Spectator*, the editor writes of its 'endeavour to enliven Morality with Wit, and to temper Wit with Morality', to bring 'Philosophy out of Closets and Libraries, Schools and Colleges, to dwell in Clubs and Assem-blies, at Tea-Tables and in Coffee-Houses'.[3] This view has informed modern eval-uations of the periodical press, in particular that of Jürgen Habermas, who argues that it helped to create a rationally debating 'public' (1989). Habermas's influential account of the development of an early modern public sphere rests on a theory of structural historical change. In the absolutist state, he writes, the king is the only public subject, the rest spectators. In the eighteenth century, a bourgeois public sphere develops, in which individuals gather together as equals, and, by engaging in rational debate, form public opinion, which checks excess authority. The literary public sphere forms part of this, by means of the epistolary format of the periodical press, producing a model of dialogue.

A debate has arisen over whether Habermas is describing an ideal or a reality, and over the accuracy of the time frame. Hohendahl (1982) argues that the model is actually an aristocratic one in origin, and took a long time to filter through to the middle class. Eagleton (1984) points out that it applies mainly to the cultural criti-cism of Steele and Addison, waning as the century progresses and periodical criticism becomes limited to reviewing books. He also notes the significance of the 'familiar style', which, theoretically including all readers, serves to assimilate rival ruling groups or old and new money (ibid.: 24–5). If there is disagreement over the details of Habermas's theory, there is consensus that this 'golden age', whether ideal or real, was over by the time the century closed. The catalyst was the French Revolution, which divided the country politically. As Klancher writes (1987: 18–46), after the 1790s, the notion of a general public would become impossible to sustain, and the aim of addressing such a public was all but abandoned by the press.

Fragmentation of the periodical press

By the time Hazlitt was writing, the periodical press had become fragmented, individual publications addressing particular constituencies of readers. As Marilyn Butler explains (1993: 131), with the launch of the *Edinburgh Review* in 1802, which aimed to address society's elite, a change began, and all the Reviews which followed 'visibly reacted'. Dominating the field for twenty years, the *Edinburgh* concentrated on those subjects judged to be of interest to its target readership: the natural sciences, moral philosophy and political economy. Literature figured only minimally, support pointedly given to writers felt to be in line with its Enlightenment agenda such as Edgeworth and Scott, while the early Romantics, Wordsworth, Coleridge, and Southey, were pilloried in its pages. The *Edinburgh*'s main rival, the *Quarterly Review*, had a slightly more literary focus, but was also hostile towards Romantic writers, condemning Byron and his circle for their aristocratic licence, the Keats school for its vulgarity. More sympathetic periodicals did exist, such as the *Examiner*, for which Hazlitt wrote, but they were produced very much against the grain.

It was not until the 1820s that the literary periodical would establish itself. As Butler writes, in the pages of the *New Monthly*, *Blackwood's* and the *London Magazine*, the literary culture we call 'Romantic' was born, ironically at the point when its major proponents were either dead or in 'decline' (ibid.: 143). The *London*, in particular, defined itself as literary not just by prioritizing works of literature, but also through the literary style of the contributors, who included Hazlitt, De Quincey and Lamb. Butler writes that the essays produced for the *London* were notable for their self-conscious literariness, and for creating a sense of shared experience through the idea of the commonplace 'to stand for that which is held in common' (ibid.: 146). Most importantly, this 'prose-poetry of modern urban life' came to be treated as literature (ibid.). The periodical press, Butler concludes, had reached the stage by which professional writers were treated as authors, themselves subject to the review process.

While it is the case that Hazlitt became well known and successful, his position as a writer was by no means settled, and was, indeed, intensely fraught. In 'The aristocracy of letters', published in 1822, he remarks at the prejudice that still exists against the professional writer: 'To be at all looked upon as an author, a man must be something more or less than an author – a rich merchant, a banker, a lord or a ploughman.'[4] Sanctioned by factors external to writing, chiefly 'birth, breeding or fortune', it is clear that this amounts to social hierarchy asserting itself. (The allusion to the poet John Clare, who was a ploughman, is surely the exception that proves the rule.) Staging a contrast between non-productive 'aristocratic' writers and mere 'Grub Street authors who write for bread and are paid by the sheet',[5] the picture Hazlitt paints of the latter's existence is of an intense insecurity coupled with constant exposure to potentially hostile criticism. Byron, he points out, because of his rank, can afford to ignore censure, while Keats, as an apothecary, is far more vulnerable to its effects.

In defence of the periodical press

Throughout his career, Hazlitt would defend the institution of the periodical press. In the most sustained example, an essay he wrote for the *Edinburgh Review*, he addresses the view that periodical criticism has a detrimental effect upon literature.[6] His main line of defence is that, as an engine of critique, it embodies the values of the Enlightenment, which 'suits the spirit of the times' and 'advances it'.[7] The more surprising undercurrent is the idea that periodical essays are also a form of literature, indeed, the intrinsically modern form. Early on, he applauds what he sees as the direction of literary energies into the periodical press: 'If literature in our day has taken this decided turn into a critical channel, is it not a presumptive proof that it ought to do so?'[8]

When it comes to evaluating contemporary literature, however, he is far less sanguine about its value. Overshadowing the essay is a theory of general literary decline, attributed to changes in literary production which mean that writers can no longer dedicate themselves to their art, but are perpetually distracted by modern life, not least by the pressures of being public figures, a role to which they are often ill-suited. The notion that each age has its own genre, each genre its own lifespan, whilst acknowledging that there will always be high points in cultural achievement, is ultimately subsumed within the overarching pattern. So, for Hazlitt as a critic, this involves placing emphasis on bringing to light the works of forgotten and neglected authors. As a writer, though, it brings profound self-doubt, for, as the quintessentially modern (literary) genre, the periodical press is therefore also exceptionally debased. The only hope lies in its absorption in the past.

The Romantic period is still regarded as a predominantly poetic age, indeed, one of the 'great' poetic ages. Perhaps not coincidentally, the poets of the time made great claims for poetry: Wordsworth, in the *Preface to Lyrical Ballads*, and Shelley, in the *Defence of Poetry*, assert that poetry offers a unique and privileged insight into the world. In both cases, poetry is defined sufficiently loosely to encompass any imaginative activity, and, certainly in Shelley's case, it is not divorced from prose (though the kind of prose he has in mind is Plato rather than, say, the contemporary novel). Hazlitt's position on poetry is complex. His most striking remarks are to be found in the essay on *Coriolanus*, in which he defines it, like Wordsworth and Shelley, as a language of the imagination, but also as 'fall[ing] in with the language of power'.[9] The essay foregrounds a conflict in values, for the imagination, he explains, 'is an exaggerating and exclusive faculty' which makes what is politically undesirable (monarchy/tyranny) aesthetically pleasing.[10]

Although the essay makes a clear distinction between poetry and prose, the latter associated with reason and republicanism, it enacts a negotiation, in which prose might be said to contain poetry through analysis. Elsewhere, Hazlitt explores more explicitly the possibility of a prose that not only dissects poetry but also resembles it. In *Lectures on the English Poets*, which echoes the celebratory line taken by Wordsworth and Shelley, he extends the remit of the poetic to prose in much stronger terms.[11] So, for example, in the introduction, we hear that the poetic is definitely not restricted to verse (Wordsworth changed his mind on this point). It also cites as poetic prose writers two literary journalists, Addison and Defoe.

Hazlitt is perhaps best known for his reviews of the Romantic poets, especially the Lake Poets, Wordsworth, Southey and Coleridge. As McFarland writes, Hazlitt's account, in which he presents the Lake School as having been inspired by the French Revolution into developing a 'revolutionary' poetry, casting aside convention in favour of poetic subjects and forms so 'singular' as to preclude any substantial engagement with the reading public, remains 'germane' today (McFarland 1987: 3). Yet, of as much interest as the content is the style of the reviews, which, as Butler and Eagleton remark, is highly poetic. While it is possible to see this as belonging to the post-revolutionary blurring of categories by which Hazlitt himself characterized contemporary literature, it is also revealing for what it tells us about the status and function of literary journalism. One element of Hazlitt's poetic style is its metaphorical quality. For example, when describing the (poetic) effect of hearing Coleridge's voice, his own language becomes highly metaphorical:

> Mr Coleridge has 'a mind reflecting ages past': his voice is like the echo of the congregated roar of the 'dark rearward and abyss' of thought. He who has seen a mouldering tower by the side of a chrystal lake, hid by the mist, but glittering in the wave below, may conceive the dim, gleaming, uncertain intelligence of his eye: he who has marked the evening clouds uprolled (a world of vapours), has seen the picture of his mind, unearthly, unsubstantial, with gorgeous tints and ever-varying forms.[12]

The relationship between Hazlitt and Coleridge is controversial, traditionally framed in terms of a (Romantic) paradigm of originality, in which Hazlitt is judged as secondary. While it has been important to rebut this view, the terms of the debate can be challenged. The above example can also be read in terms of Hazlitt proving his credentials as a critic by showing that he, too, can write in the medium he is writing about. In contrast to some of his contemporaries, he did not have another qualification to fall back on, such as a peerage, a profession or a university degree. In this sense, writing well, which involves writing imaginatively, authorizes his judgements. Hazlitt's metaphorical style can also be seen as an act of mediation, which contains a dangerously singular poetry in prose and provides it with the public it lacks. As Wellek writes (1955: 188–216; 197–8), Hazlitt's criticism both evokes the work and translates it into new terms. Hazlitt's mediation, the prose poem, is, then, a recreation which conveys the impression of the original and creates something new, which makes him a co-author.

Abundant use of quotation

Another feature of Hazlitt's literary style is the abundant use of quotation. As the edition of the *Selected Essays* helpfully highlights, Hazlitt's essays are liberally sprinkled with direct citations from literary texts (see Paulin and Chandler 2000). The essay on Coleridge, for example, contains more than 30 examples, sometimes a phrase or a couple of lines, sometimes even stanzas. In one sense, this forms part of a process of self-authorization, demonstrating Hazlitt's familiarity with a range of writers. In a general sense, it places the writer under review in the context of literary history. Especially interesting is the range: Hazlitt quotes a lot from 'established' authorities – the Old Testament, Milton and Shakespeare – but also makes space for more recent contenders like Collins and Lamb. If it is not quite the case of positing an equivalence, there is certainly an acknowledgement of the contributions made by 'minor' writers.

More specifically, in the essay on Coleridge, for example, quoting from authors whom Coleridge himself drew on, Milton and Shakespeare, Hazlitt indicates an expertise equivalent to that of his subject. By also quoting from authors Coleridge either rejected or did not acknowledge, Pope and Lamb, he suggests the greater breadth of his own. As well as authorizing his critical judgements, the use of literary quotation is part of Hazlitt's self-authorization as a writer, their presence enhancing the literariness of his own style. Again, viewed traditionally, this highlights Hazlitt's lack of originality as compared to, say, Coleridge, whose citations are mostly indirect. Yet, it can also be seen as part of a sociable strategy of self-authorization, which acknowledges the influence of other writers very directly. It brings to his essays a sense of writing in company, and contributes to what Tom Paulin (1998: 27) has identified as their multivoiced or bricolage effect. It enacts a collaborative model of authorship, which proceeds not through superseding other writers but by paying tribute to them.

One of the contemporary writers whom Hazlitt most admires is his friend and fellow literary journalist Charles Lamb. In 'Mr Lamb', he pays tribute to a writer whose observations 'are genuine and original', but whose 'sentences are cast in the mould of old authors'.[13] In this respect, it is the ephemeral productions of Lamb that stand as a locus of literary value for Hazlitt, not the pronouncements of his poetic contemporaries. One of the highest tributes Hazlitt pays to Lamb is to recall an occasion on which a friend who, struck by a phrase of Lamb's, but unable to recall where he had heard it, searched for it in the works of Ben Jonson and

Beaumont and Fletcher. The reason why this is such a tribute is that, in Hazlitt's personal canon, the genre that is most important to him is drama, specifically the drama of the sixteenth and seventeenth centuries.

Literary journalism as a form of creative spectatorship

As Stanley Jones writes, the theatre was tremendously important to Hazlitt. 'Playgoing', says Jones (1991: 85), 'had a unique sense for him: the privilege of inhabiting a special region of time arrested between past and future, the paradox of a real suspension of events bodied forth in an ideal succession of incidents; like novel-reading, but less solitary, more palpably related to concrete existence.' As 'bodied' and 'concrete' suggest, it is the corporeality of the theatre, and, I think, the embodied transmission of language, that are the sources of the attraction. For periods of time, Hazlitt made his living reviewing plays: he was made theatre critic at the *Examiner* in 1815, then at *The Times* in 1817, returning to the *Examiner* in 1828. The theatre provided the subject matter for several collections: *Characters of Shakespeare's Plays* (1817), *A View of the English Stage* (1818) and *Lectures on the Dramatic Literature of the Age of Elizabeth* (1820). It was also the focus for a series, Essays on the Drama, published in the *London Magazine* in 1820. So central was the theatre to Hazlitt's thinking that it informs all his work as a defining metaphor, or, as he defined it in 'On actors and acting', a 'bettered likeness of the world'.[14] In particular, it shapes his understanding of the practice of literary journalism, just as it had done for much earlier practitioners.

In spite of his enthusiasm, Hazlitt was conscious of writing in an age not renowned for drama. In an essay for the *London Magazine*, he concludes: 'The age we live in is critical, didactic, paradoxical, romantic, but it is not dramatic.'[15] As he goes on to point out, many of the major writers of the day tried their hand, but the results were either not intended for performance, or not commercially (or, in Hazlitt's view, dramatically) successful. The plays Hazlitt most admires date from the sixteenth and seventeenth centuries, his favourite playwright Shakespeare, whom he champions as a universal figure. As much an admirer of the age as the drama, Hazlitt applauded what he saw as the 'heroic and martial spirit' of the early modern period, in other words, its inherently dramatic quality, viewing the stage as 'a new thing' perfectly suited to the tendencies of its time.[16] Much of Hazlitt's career was spent reviewing contemporary performances of Shakespeare's plays. Throughout, he remains alert to the historical dimension of the exercise. In particular, he is conscious of the anomalies that result when the product of a dramatic age is reproduced in the very different conditions of a spectacular age.

Hazlitt is often thought of as a literary theatrical critic in the sense of privileging text over performance. It is true that in a notorious review of Kean as Richard II he wrote: 'The reader of the plays of Shakespeare is almost always disappointed in seeing them acted; and for our own parts, we should never go to see them acted, if we could help it.'[17] The view has, though, been overstated, and is the product less of a resistance to theatricality than of the excesses of the contemporary stage. In *Lectures on the English Poets*, Hazlitt reserves his highest praise for what he calls 'dramatic poetry', in other words, drama or poetry that is performed, and he makes it clear that performance is the decisive factor. Elsewhere, he expresses great admiration for actors, who, he suggests, living most fully in the imagination, are the truest artists, more so than poets.[18] In *A View of the English Stage*, he remarks that 'the player's art is one that perishes with him', later adding that, for this reason, acting is the most original of the arts.[19] While he was often critical of performances of Shakespeare, the exceptions, featuring Edmund Kean and Sarah Siddons, 'who have raised our imagination of the part they acted',[20] are highly significant ones. This is the tribute he pays to Siddons as Lady Macbeth:

> Her person was made to contain her spirit; her soul to fill and animate her person. Her eye answered to her voice. She wore a crown. She looked as if descended from a higher sphere, and walked the earth in majesty and pride. She sounded the full diapason, touched all chords of passion, they thrilled through her, and yet she preserved an elevation of thought and character above them, like the tall cliff round which the tempest roars, but its head reposes in the blue serene! Mrs Siddons combined the utmost grandeur and force with every variety of expression and excellence: her transitions were rapid and extreme, but were massed into unity and breadth – there was nothing warped or starting from its place – she produced the most overpowering effects without the slightest effort, by a word, a look, a gesture.[21]

He also says of Kean, in an earlier performance, that the character of Richard was 'perfectly *articulated* in every part'.[22] The main problem, for Hazlitt, is overacting, one symptom of a new system in which actors have become stars or celebrities. He notes a distinct change in Kean's acting style which he suggests can be attributed to overexposure at the hands of his London managers.[23] As a drama critic, Hazlitt typically responded to theatre as a spectator, not just as a reader. He was, indeed, highly attentive to the reactions of spectators, on one occasion relaying an anecdote about a Garrick performance of *King Lear* in which 'the whole pit rose up'.[24] Also alert to the element of social acting among spectators, he indicates, in this sense, that the spectator is an intrinsic element of the performance.

Like the early periodical writers, Hazlitt characterizes literary journalism by means of theatrical tropes, one of which is spectatorship. In 'On living to one's self', he describes the spectator as 'living in the world, as in it, not of it: it is as if no one knew there was such a person, and you wished no one to know it'.[25] This model of detachment is, by implication, an ideal rather than a reality, involving a mirroring between spectator and spectacle. In the context of the theatre, this is seen to have a civilizing effect, but, within literary journalism, this seems less certain. One example of Hazlitt's literary spectatorship is *The Spirit of the Age* (1825), a collection of contemporary portraits drawn largely from the literary world. The collection contributes to the cult of celebrity, but in a strongly demythologizing spirit. The portraits are far from flattering, the originals emerging as isolated and eccentric figures.

Those who, like Coleridge and Bentham, seem simply lost in abstract speculation are treated with greater sympathy than those who, like Wordsworth and Byron, seem, in their striving after originality, more confidently egotistical, though the distinction is not absolute. Of course, given that individuals are seen to exemplify the age, it is ultimately the age, which has produced these self-involved and self-promoting characters, that is the target. Most significant is the epigraph: 'To know another well were to know one's self.'[26] In a sense, the entire collection could be seen as an example of self-spectatorship, where scrutiny is turned inwards upon the self.

The Hazlitt who emerges is perhaps himself a withdrawn egotist, his indictments of others evidence of self-knowledge. Yet, there is at least one other Hazlitt who is insufficiently isolated or self-absorbed, too modest and uncertain to push himself forward, though he may wish to. It is interesting that, of all his contemporaries, unqualified praise goes to a Mr Knowles, an actor turned dramatist whose tragedy, *Virginius*, is identified as a 'perfect work of art'.[27] The key element is the author's personality; 'unconscious', 'unpretending' and 'artless', he is fully human, 'the only poet now that is a mere poet', and it is this that has shaped the play.[28] Hazlitt comments elsewhere that actors are both supremely human and the greatest artists, and one wonders if for him this is also so because they are not required to play themselves or perform their own words.

Literary journalism as a form of performance

If Hazlitt's literary journalism can be seen as a form of creative spectatorship, it can also be seen as a form of performance. The comments he makes about actors, their propensity to live in the imagination, their dedication to their profession, apply equally to him. Jones (op. cit.: 370–1) writes of his belief that 'life is lived through the imagination', and of his consummate professionalism when it came to writing. In 'On living to one's self', Hazlitt jokes that failed actors often find themselves joining the ranks of 'drawing-masters, picture-cleaners, or newspaper critics'.[29] His style, though it is undoubtedly poetic, is distinctively theatrical at times, or rather actorly. It often sounds spoken, rhetorical, immediate, and readers are addressed as if they were members of an audience. The opening of 'On living to one's self' sounds very much like a soliloquy in the scrupulously concrete details of its self-presentation:

> I never was in a better place or humour than I am at present for writing on this subject. I have a partridge getting ready for my supper, my fire is blazing on the hearth, the air is mild for the season of the year, I have but a slight fit of indigestion to-day (the only thing that makes me abhor myself), I have three hours good before me, and therefore I will attempt it. It is as well to do it at once as to have it to do for a week to come.

If the writing on this subject is no easy task, the thing itself is a harder one. It asks a troublesome effort to ensure the admiration of others: it is a still greater one to be satisfied with one's own thoughts. As I look from the window at the wide bare heath before me, and through the misty moon-light air see the woods that wave over the top of Winterslow,

'While Heaven's chancel-vault is blind with sleet', my mind takes flight through too long a series of years, supported only by the patience of thought and secret yearnings after truth and good, for me to be at a loss to understand the feeling I intend to write about; but I do not know that this will enable me to convey it most agreeably to the reader.[30]

Ironically, the essay as a whole complains of life on the public stage, and longs for a state of silent spectatorship, free from the desire to be a writer, to simply write. In some ways, though, the perils of authorship are kept at bay by writing as an actor. Perhaps the most important element of Hazlitt's theatrical style is that, like actors, it communicates through the words of others. Hazlitt's work, as I have noted, is made up of a tissue of quotations, many of which are from poetry or dramatic poetry, a substantial number from Shakespeare. So far, I have suggested that this use of citation enhances his poetic style, as well as authorizing his critical judgements. Yet, there is also a substantial performative element. In 'On living to one's self', Hazlitt implicitly defines himself as a failed actor, and there is a sense in which his literary performances are somehow secondary, screened by print. Yet, in thinking of himself as an actor, he offers up a way of reconceptualizing literary creativity as involving the transmission, expression or embodiment of words, not (just) their origination.

An alternative to the self-critical evaluation offered by Hazlitt might be to see him as a talented actor, with an immensely wide-ranging repertoire. In a marvellously whimsical essay on minor theatres, he recreates the feeling of being at the theatre as a child.[31] It could be argued that the cumulative effect of his essays is to recreate the plays themselves. By acting out key moments from a variety of dramatic and literary texts, he assembles a grand, fragmented and incomplete performance. Many critics have spoken of the bodily vigour of Hazlitt's prose. It is, in the sense I have been outlining, prose close to physical acting. If, in a real dramatic performance, words are embodied in the person of the actor, in the metaphorical performances of the periodical press, they are perhaps also embodied in Hazlitt's bodily prose.

Conclusion: the contesting paradigms of imagination

Hazlitt has always been difficult to place within the literary movement that has come to be known as Romanticism. If he is considered as a writer, his work seems too journalistic. Even one of his main defenders, Thomas McFarland, briefly speculates 'what Hazlitt might have been had he been liberated from the constant demands of putting his thoughts down almost as soon as they occurred to him' (1987: 57). Equally, if he is considered as a critic, his works seem too imaginative. For Rene Wellek, not unsympathetic to Hazlitt, his writing demonstrates 'an insufficient sense of the distinction between art and reality' (1955: 205). This indeterminacy results in part from the distinction between literature and criticism that has solidified over time, blurred though it was when Hazlitt was writing. Yet, it can also be attributed to the influence of a Romantic aesthetic that defines literary creativity as based on origination.

Romanticism is known for inaugurating the view that 'art' represents a special form of activity characterized by originality. When, for example, in the preface to *Lyrical Ballads*, Wordsworth writes of his 'experiment' in using 'the real language of men' to produce 'a class of Poetry' 'well adapted to interest mankind permanently', this is often taken as exemplary.[32] Persisting in the twenty-first century, the Romantic paradigm of creativity can seem clichéd, even complacent, part of a pervasive rhetoric. But its architects were not especially confident about the claims they made. In his influential study, Harold Bloom (1973) argued that the Romantics suffered from an 'anxiety of influence', striving to separate themselves from literary forebears such as Milton, the vocabulary of originality representing more a site of struggle than of confident assertion. Marlon Ross (1989) has written of a less heroic form of rivalry taking place in the literary marketplace between the canonical male poets and their commercially successful female counterparts, entailing the usurpation and conquest of the 'feminine' by male writers. There has, in addition, been a long-standing debate concerning the extent to which the Romantics can be considered as plagiarists, which has been taken up in a study by Tilar Mazzeo (2006).

Hazlitt is typically regarded as a significant contributor to the formation of a Romantic aesthetic, ironically so if this has contributed towards the marginalization of his own work. Ironic or not, much of his work champions originality as the main criterion for judging literary works. For example, in *Lectures on the English Poets*, he writes of 'the impassioned parts of Shakespeare's language, which flowed from the warmth and originality of his imagination, and were his own'.[33] Yet, as this chapter has suggested, Hazlitt puts forward an alternative model of creativity, which values performativity, the effective articulation of someone else's words. By implication, this represents a defence of the 'craft' of literary journalism as a valid form of 'creative' writing. Much of Hazlitt's work is concerned with how to present words to their best effect, that is to say with what makes a good performance. This brings to the fore questions not just of sensitivity, but of sincerity.

In 'Madame Pasta and Mademoiselle Mars', Hazlitt reflects on performance through the different acting styles of two well-known actresses, the one mannered and deliberate, the other spontaneous and unguarded. The essay defends the 'natural acting' of Madame Pasta, whose expression is 'noble' and 'natural', her movements 'simple' and 'graceful', her voice comparable to 'music'.[34] Central to its impact is the apparent erasure of the distance between performer and part: 'She gives herself entirely up to the impression of the part, loses her power over herself, is led away by her feelings ... and is transformed into the very being she represents. She does not act the character – she *is* it, looks it, breathes it.'[35] Though Madame Pasta was Italian, Hazlitt associates her natural style of acting with a tradition of heroic English liberty, with 'grandeur', 'manly strength' and 'breath and motion'.[36] Stilted, mechanical, and artificial, French acting, according to Hazlitt, belongs to the culture of the court, embodied in the image of the actor/courtier as puppet.

We might see Hazlitt's 'familiar style' as a form of 'natural acting'. It can be seen to negotiate the tensions inherent in his position as a literary journalist: the need to adopt a persona, whilst speaking honestly about the works under review, and the need to present authors' words to readers through the medium of print in a way that does justice to the original performance context. The idea of 'natural acting' makes a creative virtue out of tensions which are often seen purely as restrictions or constraints.

Notes

1 William Hazlitt, 'On gusto', *Examiner*, 26 May 1816, in *The Complete Works of William Hazlitt*, Howe, P. P. (ed.), 21 vols (London: Frank Cass, 1967), vol. IV, pp. 77–80 (p. 77).
2 Hazlitt, 'On familiar style', in Howe, vol. VIII, pp. 242–8 (p. 242).
3 Joseph Addison, *Spectator*, Monday 12 March 1711, in *Selections from the Tatler and the Spectator*, Ross, Angus (ed.) (Harmondsworth: Penguin, 1982), p. 210.
4 Hazlitt, 'On the aristocracy of letters', *Table Talk*, 1821–2, in Howe, vol. VIII, pp. 205–14 (p. 210).
5 Hazlitt, 'On the aristocracy', p. 205.
6 Hazlitt, 'On the periodical press', *Edinburgh Review*, May 1823, in Howe, vol. XVI, pp. 211–39.
7 Ibid., p. 212.
8 Ibid.
9 Hazlitt, *Characters of Shakespeare's Plays*, 1817, in Howe, vol. IV, pp. 170–361 (p. 214).
10 Ibid., p. 214.
11 Hazlitt, *Lectures on the English Poets*, 1818, in Howe, vol. V, pp. 1–168.
12 Hazlitt, 'Mr Coleridge', *The Spirit of the Age*, 1825, in Howe, vol. XI, pp. 28–38 (p. 28).
13 Hazlitt, 'Elia and Geoffrey Crayton', *The Spirit of the Age*, 1825, in Howe, vol. XI, pp. 178–84 (p. 182).
14 Hazlitt, 'On actors and acting', *The Round Table*, 1817, in Howe, vol. IV, pp. 153–60 (p. 153).
15 Hazlitt, 'The Drama: No. IV', *The London Magazine*, April 1820, in Howe, vol. XVIII, pp. 302–16 (p. 302).
16 Hazlitt, *Lectures on the Dramatic Literature of the Age of Elizabeth*, 1820, in Howe, vol. VI, pp. 169–364 (pp. 188–9).
17 Hazlitt, 'Mr Kean's Richard II', *Examiner*, 19 March 1815, in Howe, vol. V, pp. 221–4 (p. 222).
18 Hazlitt, 'The Drama: No. III', *London Magazine*, March 1820, in Howe, vol. XVIII, pp. 291–302.
19 Hazlitt, 'The Drama: No. I', *London Magazine*, January 1820, in Howe, vol. XVIII, pp. 271–80.
20 Hazlitt, 'Mr Kean's Richard II', p. 222.
21 Hazlitt, 'Mrs Siddons', *Examiner*, 25 May 1828, in Howe, vol. XVIII, pp. 406–10 (p. 408).

22 Hazlitt, 'Mr Kean's Richard', *Morning Chronicle*, 15 February 1814, in Howe, vol. V, pp. 180–2 (p. 181).
23 Hazlitt, 'Mr Kean's Richard', *The Champion*, 9 October 1814, in Howe, vol. V, pp. 200–4 (p. 201).
24 Hazlitt, *A View of the English Stage*, in Howe, vol. V, pp. 169–379 (p. 174).
25 Hazlitt, 'On living to one's self', *Table Talk*, 1821–2, in Howe, vol. VIII, pp. 90–101 (p. 91).
26 Hazlitt, *The Spirit of the Age*, 1825, p. 2.
27 Ibid. p., 184.
28 Ibid.
29 Hazlitt, 'On living to one's self', p. 94.
30 Ibid., p. 90.
31 Hazlitt, 'The Drama: No. III'.
32 William Wordsworth, 'Preface to *Lyrical Ballads*', in *Wordsworth: Poetical Works*, Hutchinson, Thomas (ed.) (Oxford: Oxford University Press, 1969), pp. 734–41 (p. 734).
33 Hazlitt, *Lectures on the English Poets*, p. 55.
34 Hazlitt, 'Madame Pasta and Mademoiselle Mars', in Howe, vol. XII, pp. 324–35 (pp. 324–5).
35 Ibid., p. 326.
36 Ibid., p. 329.

References

Bloom, Harold (1973) *The Anxiety of Influence* (Oxford: Oxford University Press).

Brewer, John (1997) *The Pleasures of the Imagination: English Culture in the Eighteenth Century* (London: HarperCollins).

Butler, Marilyn (1993) 'Culture's medium: the role of the review', in Curran, Stuart (ed.), *The Cambridge Companion to British Romanticism* (Cambridge: Cambridge University Press).

Eagleton, Terry (1984) *The Function of Criticism: From the Spectator to Post-Structuralism* (London: Verso).

Habermas, Jürgen (1989) *The Structural Transformation of the Public Sphere: An Inquiry into a Category of Bourgeois Society* (trans. Burger, Thomas) (Oxford: Polity Press).

Hodendahl, Peter (1982) *The Institution of Criticism* (Ithaca: Cornell University Press).

Italia, Iona (2005) *The Rise of Literary Journalism in the Eighteenth Century: Anxious Employment* (London: Routledge).

Jones, Stanley (1991) *Hazlitt: A Life* (Oxford: Oxford University Press).

Klancher, Jon P. (1987) *The Making of English Reading Audiences, 1790–1832* (Wisconsin: University of Wisconsin Press).

McFarland, Thomas (1987) *Romantic Cruxes: The English Essayists and the Spirit of the Age* (Oxford: Clarendon Press).

Mazzeo, Tilar (2006) *Plagiarism and Literary Property in the Romantic Period* (Philadelphia PA: University of Pennsylvania Press).

Paulin, Tom (1998) *The Day-Star of Liberty: William Hazlitt's Radical Style* (London: Faber).

—— and Chandler, David (eds) (2000) *William Hazlitt: The Fight and Other Writings* (Harmondsworth: Penguin).

Raymond, Joad (1996) *The Invention of the Newspaper: English Newsbooks, 1641–1649* (Oxford: Clarendon Press).

Ross, Marlon (1989) *The Contours of Masculine Desire: Romanticism and the Rise of Women's Poetry* (Oxford: Oxford University Press).

Smith, Anthony (1979) *The Newspaper: An International History* (London: Thames and Hudson).

Wellek, Rene (1955) *A History of Modern Criticism*, 4 vols (London: Jonathan Cape), II.

Woolf, Virginia (1979) 'A scribbling dame', in Barrett, Michele (ed.), *Women and Writing* (London: Women's Press).

Chapter 3

The personal is the political

George Sand's contribution to popular journalism

Jane Chapman

Born in 1804, Armandine Aurore Lucile Dupin grew up in the rural department of the Indre, in the Berry area of France. Her father was descended distantly from the King of Poland and Louis XVIII, but her mother's origins were humble. In 1830 she left her husband, Baron Casimir Dudevant, and moved to Paris. When she produced a novel, *Rose et Blanche,* with her lover, Jules Sandeau, she used the pseudonym 'Jules Sand' to avoid scandal. In 1832, she wrote her next novel, *Indiana,* alone, under the name 'George Sand'.[1] She would turn up at all-male newspaper offices sporting short hair and trousers: this androgyny offered her access to places and journalistic anonymity. A life-long commitment to republican socialism prompted her to address crucial themes in mould-breaking ways in her writings, such as property distribution, class relations, artisan communities and revolution. She faced disapproval over her relationships, some of them with well-known creative people, such as the Polish composer Frédéric Chopin, and she was regularly demonized by leading intellectuals such as Nietzsche and the famous anarchist thinker Proudhon. But the more she was hated, the more she was read.[2] George Sand's trials and tribulations as an editor/journalist are recorded in detail in her correspondence. She devoted much energy between 1841 and 1849 to launching four periodicals – a literary review, two local newspapers and a national republican political journal – with varying degrees of success. Her journalism reached a zenith during 1848, the year of revolutions in Europe. With 80 novels, 25 volumes of correspondence, ten volumes of autobiography and literary contributions to 47 periodicals and journals, she is still one of the most prolific authors in literary history. She died on 8 June 1876.

> For the aristocracy of the intellect she had always the deepest veneration, but the democracy of suffering touched her more ... Of all the artists of this century she was the most altruistic. She felt everyone's misfortunes except her own.
>
> (Oscar Wilde on George Sand)

Sand's contribution to the development of newspapers is twofold: first, by launching her own newspapers she helped to build the profile of the political press during a critical phase in the struggle for democracy in France – the issue that dominated nineteenth-century Europe. Second, the way she wrote in newspapers presented readers with a uniquely hybrid literary style. This journalistic inventiveness – what I call her 'flights of imagination' – increased as she became involved in the revolutionary events of 1848. I argue that this is because her literary strategy was motivated by a perceived political need to write in what she saw as the language of ordinary people.

Historical context and background

Current scholarship on Sand's political ideas, such as the work of Michelle Perrot (2004) and Bernard Hamon (2001), has examined the evolution of her principles as they emerge in her novels, letters and press articles, rather than contextualizing them as a developing journalistic form, which is the aim of this chapter. This lacuna may well stem from the fact that, although the word 'journalism' originated in France and was exported from about 1831 (Campbell 2000: 40), Charton's *Dictionnaire des professions* (1842) does not even mention the job of 'journaliste'.

It was not necessary to call oneself a journalist in order to collaborate in the publication of a newspaper; indeed, there was no clear separation between journalism and other forms of literature, or between journalists and other writers. The conventions of journalism – editing of copy, summarizing, quoting and interviewing – had yet to emerge. Similarly there was no attempt to differentiate between 'comment' and the factual reporting of events: the presentation of ideas about political morality, in whatever literary form, took precedence (Chapman 2005a: 7). Virtually every French author of any importance wrote press articles, although the rhetoric of newspaper writing was considered an inferior activity to novel writing.

Sand managed to achieve an interchange of ideas between novels and press articles, for as she put it: 'I have a violent and almost indestructible passion for the profession of writing' (1969, i: 807). She believed that experimentation was necessary in the communication of ideas and that this was more important than systems or ideology in order to achieve social transformation. From the standpoint of the history of journalism, we need to single out her press activities to examine her pioneering contribution as an editor/publisher who brought the creative flair of a novelist to many of her contributions. The evidence is plentiful: Sand was prolific, writing open letters with elements of reportage, open letters as opinion pieces, essays, informational bulletins and political discussions between imaginary characters.

Balzac, who studied the state of newspaper writing in France and advised Sand on how to write articles, was able by 1843 to characterize journalism as comprising two genres: publicity and criticism. Politicians were the publicists and literary people provided the critique (1965: 35, 207). Sand undertook both of these roles – in 1848 she wrote ministerial publicity for the revolutionary provisional government, but the bulk of her journalism falls within the category of criticism in that she saw her writing as providing an enlightenment role. Her aim was to provide political education about democracy and equality at a time when the majority of the population was still disenfranchized. However, Sand's publishing activities at local level were inhibited by many administrative and practical problems not of her making. Like newspapers in other countries, French journals had to pay stamp duty and postal costs for distribution in addition to a financial deposit ('caution money') required to launch in the first place. Anti-press legislation defined a range of offences such as criticism of the monarchy.

The influences on Sand

For Sand, personal and political first became intertwined in 1830, the year of an abortive revolution in France which led to the establishment of a new regime known as the July Monarchy, headed by the Orléanist, Louis Philippe. Sand broke away from her troubled marriage and declared herself a republican. She claimed to have inherited a progressive outlook from her father's egalitarian idealism and her mother's modest origins, but these influences were further enhanced by other personalities and events. The anti-clerical ideas of material, moral and intellectual well-being for working people propagated by the cult followers of the political philosopher Claude Henri de Rouvroy, Comte de St Simon (more commonly known as Henri de St Simon), greatly impressed Sand, and she endorsed their belief in non-violent principles of social reorganization, including the redistribution of private property. However, she stopped short of embracing St Simonian ideas of free love, which she considered were harmful to the cause of women (Hamon 2001: 8).[3]

By far the most significant influence on Sand's journalism during the first half of the 1840s came from the ideas of community, spirituality and love of the philosopher and political economist Pierre Leroux. He is credited with having introduced the word 'socialist' into France (Dayen 2006), and he attached great importance to education and morality, believing in painstaking, gradual persuasion. Leroux's ideas provided for a seductive egalitarianism that allocated time for the hearts and minds of the masses to be won over. Although Leroux is now considered to be one of the more influential and popular socialist thinkers of the period (Chastain 2004), his lasting contribution to early socialism in France centres mainly on the significance he attached to emotion and community. His Christian version of republicanism and socialism exalted the common man but rejected the institutional structures of Catholicism: journalism became a 'weapon' for the moral regeneration of society.

Likewise, Sand recognized the importance of journalism as a communication medium which could be used to win over hearts and minds (1969, v: 535–47). An emotional approach to social problems[4] is evident in both Sand's and Leroux's writings for *La Revue indépendante*, the Paris-based national journal they founded together in 1841 (Collins 1959: 91, 95). They chose its name to express their desired freedom of expression following Sand's legal problems with her publisher over the content of the novel *Horace*. The review provided an outlet for uncensored serialization, and also became a direct competitor to the leading literary review of the day, *La Revue des deux mondes*, that had rejected Sand's novels *Horace* and *Le Compagnon du tour de France* on political grounds.

In her novels, she began to explore how working people could achieve freedom and, at the same time, to develop a moral critique of what she called 'bourgeois' leadership. For instance, there is a dialogue in *Le Compagnon du tour de France* between the artisan, Pierre Huguenin, and the bourgeois professional agitator, Achille Lefort, who argues that it is not possible to change society without the leadership of educated, bourgeois men. He asks whether we should 'fold our arms and wait for people to liberate themselves?', for the common people need advice, guidance and order. Pierre responds that the people will evolve their own rules and considers that even the most outstanding leader will do well to listen to the people whom he presumes to lead. He should say to them: 'I realize that the most simple-minded among you has the right to curb my power if I abuse it, and the most obscure [of you] to reject my opinion if it is immoral; that I must prove my virtue and charity to be, in my own eyes and in yours, a great intellectual, a great leader, or a great poet' (Sand 1988: 276–7).

Thus Sand came to evolve a canon of socially aware literature by combining what she saw as the political action of republicanism, with the social and moral ideas of 'utopian socialism'.[5] Philosophically, she imagined that the gap between rich and poor could be bridged by a voluntary good sense and community of interests that would unite mankind. In the agricultural society of early nineteenth-century provincial France, Sand tended to see peasant life as an ideal which would provide a starting point from which better working conditions could be constructed: an approach also shared by the poet Alphonse de Lamartine, Balzac and many Christian socialists such as Leroux. In terms of how this ideal should apply to her writing, Balzac had told her: 'You look for man as he should be; I take him as he is. Believe me, we're both right. These two routes lead to the same destination' (Sand 1949: 302).

Gradually, Sand evolved a faith in the working class to achieve liberation themselves: hence she encouraged and even financed a number of working-class authors, helping them to get published. In addition, several of her own novels openly addressed political issues, such as *Le Compagnon du tour de France* (1840), *Horace* (1841), *Le Meunier d'Angibault* (1844) and *Le Péché de Monsieur Antoine* (1845). As the 1840s progressed, she became increasingly concerned about the underemployment and impoverishment of the working classes, and her novels became more overtly political, exemplified by *Consuelo* (1842) and *La Comtesse de Rudolstadt* (1843). Sand's collaboration with Leroux and others was deliberately aimed at the publication of working-class, oppositional, republican and socialist writing (Walton 2000: 130). Her politics may well have been more concerned with an abstract ideal than with institutions and power relations, but they were in tune with the progressive concerns and language of the time. The criticism of bourgeois leadership which emerged in her novels also provided the principal thrust in her journalism, especially the local newspaper *L'Éclaireur de L'Indre*.

Sand's first local newspaper

Sand deplored the weakness of the provincial press and what she saw as the destructive, centralizing influence of Paris, believing passionately in the need to reduce the gap between capital and provinces. Her goal was to achieve a united front editorially of all republican provincial papers to educate the public towards acceptance of greater decentralization from Paris, and more local democracy. In a letter to the poet Lamartine, who had launched a local paper in Mâcon, she commented: 'It is a great and important idea to make the provincial press both free and strong' (1879: 6).

Hence, in her Circular for the Foundation of *L'Éclaireur de L'Indre*, she refers to 'the strong awareness by all true patriots of the need to boost citizenship in the provinces, to place it on a footing of equality rather than rivalry with the metropolis' (ibid.: 2). This formidable task required extreme perseverance and motivation on the part of a local newspaper editor and owner (for the two were often synonymous during the early nineteenth century). Hence, when Sand embarked on establishing a provincial publication, she wrote: 'This venture is not merely speculative: the paper will only survive as a result of our devotion and sacrifices' (ibid.: 3).[6]

The first edition of Sand's *L'Éclaireur de L'Indre* was launched as a weekly journal with an annual subscription of 15 francs on 14 September 1844. Although she worked incredibly hard on the preparations, Sand was not officially on the board of directors. In her correspondence, it emerges that she was obliged to edit the paper herself for longer than she had wanted because a suitable editor could not be found. She suggested and approached various people, agonizing at length in her letters to Charles Duvernet, a former journalist on the Parisian national daily *Le National*, about the problem and feeling stressed by the pressure of her other commitments (Sand 1969, vi: 433, 448, 484, 501).

Sand's friends also tried unsuccessfully to find a local printer. Instead, they were obliged to print in Paris where craftsmen would take more risks in working on an oppositional paper because of business competition from a greater number of printers, which did not exist in the provinces. Sand and Leroux started their own printing firm, L'Imprimerie de Boussac, with money for the machinery and materials provided by George, whilst Pierre, as a trained printer and also with a brother who was a full-time typesetter, provided the knowledge and skills. The enterprise brought Sand into direct contact with an industrial workforce, but they voted against her idea of setting up a workers' cooperative (Rebéroux 1994: 92). Furthermore, Sand had disagreements with the *Éclaireur* editorial team over the use of printers and the political approach of the paper. She wanted the newspaper to become an organ for Leroux's ideas, to educate the provincial masses, but her colleagues from the Berry region were not so keen (Sand 1882, ii: 396).

Blaise Bonnin: the first flight of journalistic imagination

In 1843 Sand uncovered a story in her local area that was to mark her entry as a communicator into active politics and political journalism. It was the heart-rending story of a local girl (named 'Fanchette' by Sand) – a scandal that the writer wanted to communicate as widely as possible with maximum publicity, using all her literary expertise. Sand published the story during October and November 1843 in *La Revue indépendante* as 'Fanchette, letter from Blaise Bonnin to Claude Germain': this was the first time she had used a fictional character as pseudonym. Pierre Leroux recognized the potential of using the Fanchette story to mobilize local opinion: 'This is a gem of a campaigning issue,' he stressed (Perrot 2004: 64). And this prompted Sand to launch the regional newspaper *L'Éclaireur de L'Indre* to provide a vehicle for publicity of the case in the area.

A 15-year-old young girl who could hardly speak ('une idiote') had been discovered in a poor state after she had been roaming in the woods around Sand's rural locality of La Châtre, in the Berry area of the Indre. It was impossible to discover her real name, her family or where she had come from, but a doctor, who felt sorry for her, took her to a local convent. The nuns were reluctant to help, yet when the doctor made out a certificate indicating that the girl was sick, they had no choice but to take her in. She was soon 'farmed out' to another nun, from whom the girl ran away three times, finally returning to the convent where she had received support from the other children. Nevertheless, the mother superior organized for the girl to be taken and abandoned 24 kilometres away, somewhere between La Châtre and Aubusson. When local people started to gossip, the coachman was questioned and a search undertaken. By the time the girl was found, she had been raped and badly abused.

The story came at a time when Sand was becoming increasingly preoccupied with what she called the 'problème social' (1969, v: 826); therefore, she wrote about it in a way which would ellicit both compassion and indignation. Her literary style involved an imaginary correspondence between two characters: a Berrichon peasant (Blaise Bonnin), who represented the finer points of rural working-class common sense, and his godfather (Claude Germain). Blaise Bonnin's straight-talking appeared as a conversational style letter: 'Okay, so she doesn't deserve to die – but what sort of life does she deserve? Do you get me? I mean, what about food, clothing, somewhere to kip, some care and charity, for goodness sake? Either there's a government or there isn't. They should be answering me. I want to know the bottom line – what the law has to say' (Bibliothèque Nationale: 8 Lk7 326).[7]

Sand aimed to reveal the cruelty of the Catholic Church, the nonchalance, hypocrisy and inefficiency of the civil authorities. Conveniently, she could now have two or more voices: her fictional characters and her own as presenter of the story. Thus she added a note to the editor in her own name which allowed her to comment in *La Revue indépendante*: 'The entire population has been moved to the core by this horrendous story' (1969, vi: 264). There was certainly a public outcry, whilst the guilty parties accused Sand of 'making a novel' and threatened her with legal action (Winwar 1946: 270). She continued to expose the scandal by substantiating her allegations in further articles and also by publishing the story as a pamphlet, the proceeds being used to start a fund for the girl.

The refusal of local printers to print the Fanchette pamphlet forced her to conclude that public opinion deserved to have a stronger, freer means of communication. 'It's the same everywhere in the provinces: same position with printers, same reliance on the powers that be, same attempts by the authorities to paralyse the press' (BN 8 Lk7: 326). In effect, she had taken on the local 'bourgeoisie', who had closed ranks in defence of a challenge to part of their circle (Hamon 2001: 177), but she avoided prosecution because her facts were correct.

In journalistic terms she had passed the ultimate test by managing (in modern parlance) to 'stand up the story', backing up her articles with copies of the report of the police commissioner, a letter from the mayor and the convent doctor. Nevertheless, she risked imprisonment (ibid.: 177) and faced the possibility of intervention by the prefect, in addition to criticism from the establishment paper, *Le Journal de L'Indre*. At the time, prosecution in the law courts could represent the last straw for many provincial publications (Collins 1954: 281), so her tone had to be conciliatory but persuasive to avoid fines or closure of the newspaper (Sand 1882, ii: 317–21).

Further pseudonyms and campaigns

Sand followed up with a newspaper campaign to expose the exploitation of bakery workers and then with further writings by Blaise Bonnin on rural conditions, both of which were linked to the signing of petitions. First Sand used the cover of a letter to *L'Éclaireur* by 'G. bakery worker' (28 September 1844) to write about the working conditions in this industry in support of a 6,000-name petition by the employees calling for regulatory reforms that was ignored by the prefect of the Seine. Worker G. denounces the practices of employment bureaux which profited from worker unemployment during economic crises, and provides graphic descriptions of 'human slaughterhouses': unsanitary, humid, basement workplaces with water running down the walls, where workers slept on site in between 16- to 18-hour shifts for the daily sum of 4 francs plus two loaves of bread. 'You would imagine you were present at a final death scene' (1879: 28). Conditions were ignored by government inspectors, who had been bought off by employers.

Meanwhile Blaise Bonnin went on to develop a distinct range of views and literary character in the pages of *L'Éclaireur de L'Indre* with his own column: Letter from a Black Valley peasant, dictated by Blaise Bonnin (5–12 October 1844). The peasant complained about the onerous nature of taxes and of farming, about having to borrow at high rates and the inability of peasants to benefit from modern equipment. With all these regulations, 'with the local laws, with the law on hunting, with the law on vagrancy, I don't know if we've even got enough pennies left to buy a rope to hang ourselves with' (ibid.: 37–58). Bonnin espoused the cause of agricultural day workers whose situation had hardly improved since the Revolution, and in true Leroux fashion, suggested a communal way forward. The peasant justified this on the grounds that individuals were unable to borrow sufficient funds (at high interest rates of 15 to 20 per cent) to set up a business by themselves. But Bonnin pointed out that the cooperative approach would only work with a spirit of mutual understanding, respect and fraternity (Hamon 2001: 187).

Bonnin's complaints formed part of a bigger strategy for rural workers: *L'Éclaireur de L'Indre* was the first of about 50 provincial newspapers to back a petition and campaign by the radical politician Ledru-Rollin calling for a Chamber of Deputies enquiry into the condition of the working class (1969, vi: 485). Sand followed up by extending her all-inclusive sense of community: she was vocal in her opposition to a recent law which restricted the rights of vagrants, composing 'The Father Who Walks Alone', written for *L'Almanach populaire de France pour 1845*, and several articles in *L'Éclaireur de L'Indre* on the subject. The text of 'The Father Who Walks Alone' was supposed to have been sent to her by a traveller who had met an 80-year-old vagrant and written up a conversation he had observed. Sand's article is constructed as a conversation between the old man and a policeman, joined later by a priest and a lawyer.

Sand's first overtly political columns in her own name were published in *L'Éclaireur de L'Indre* on 16, 23 and 30 November 1844. Amongst the points she raised was the issue of women's rights: 'We don't recognize any innate superiority on the part of the opposite sex' (1879: 94). Significantly, Sand refers to the disenfranchized female sex collectively as 'we', but she also took the view that women's liberation was best achieved by the extension of civil liberties such as divorce and by the gradual achievement of economic independence before an extension of the vote which, in her view, should only come later. The class struggle came before the women's struggle.

Sand and the 'ugly' politics of 1848

During the momentous year of 1848 journalism offered Sand a crucial way of participating in republican politics. Now, more than ever before, she had a forceful and clear motivation – the desire to talk directly to French people through her writing, to contribute to the battle of ideas in whatever way she could, to win support for a consolidation and continuation of the new republic at the forthcoming elections. She spent time on the streets of Paris where, as she commented, one could see the life of France. Women were heavily involved in street politics, organizing themselves into groups, lobbying to defend their interests and putting up female candidates for the elections called by the provisional government for 23 April. The teacher at Leroux's commune in Boussac, Pauline Roland, turned down the opportunity for a nomination, then proceeded to announce Sand as a candidate for the women's paper, *Voix des Femmes* – without even asking Sand first. She refused the offer. Meanwhile, the conservative population of Nohant – Sand's village – elected George's 25-year-old son Maurice[8] as republican mayor. Villagers began to adopt the epithets 'citizen' and 'comrade' when addressing each other.

In Paris, she mixed in the new circles of power, knew the leading politicians well, hence was able to enlist the writer and poet Lamartine and the revolutionary leader Louis Blanc as collaborators for *L'Éclaireur de L'Indre*. In the provinces there was little if any support for the revolution. Sand was disturbed by the conservatism of the countryside: country people needed to be converted before the elections, yet the 'capacity for democracy' was sorely lacking: 'Berry produces patient and honest people, but the seeds of genius are not planted in our furrows,' as she wrote on 9 March (1969, viii, L3853: 334). Thus, once more, she assumed the pseud-onym 'Blaise Bonnin'.

The official return of Blaise Bonnin

After his debut as a rural day labourer, mouthpiece for the Fanchette scandal and vehicle for the complaints of the peasants in the Black Valley, the peasant was now rehabilitated with a higher social status: a voter and adjunct to the Mayor of Montgivray, the commune where Sand's stepbrother lived.

In Bonnin's brochure on the history of France since 1789 he addresses readers as 'Dear Parishioners', presenting a pointed analysis of contemporary history from a working-class perspective. He describes the 'social deception' which was respon-sible for the undermining of the first Republic, the weariness of the Napoleonic Empire and the fall of the July Monarchy. Now that people are calm, reasonable 'citizens', the task is to assess candidates wisely, that is, less for what they promise than for the way they conduct themselves, remembering 'how they treated us before the Revolution' (Perrot 2004: 257).

In La Châtre there was no popular enthusiasm for the Republic: people were feeling the bite of the provisional government's 45 centimes taxation measure. Thus Blaise Bonnin had a destiny: painstaking political education. His *Paroles de Blaise Bonnin aux Bons Citoyens* (*Message to All Good Citizens*) consisted of five brochures, written at the request of the Ministry for Public Education. Surprisingly, the title was suggested by Jean Reynaud, from the cabinet office who argued that this form of authorship would be 'both more respectable and simpler' (ibid.: 267). In other words, a government department wanted to support and legitimize Sand's fictional approach to journalism: recognition of the effectiveness of this idiosyncratic literary form. She produced the first two pamphlets within four days, then suggested that Agricol Perdiguier, the 'well known agricultural reformer', help her to write the third, which would be in the form of a dialogue between town and country: Blaise (Sand) as the peasant farmer, Claude (Perdiguier) as urban worker.

She corresponded regularly with Perdiguier and sponsored him; previously she had based the hero of *Le Compagnon du tour de France*, Pierre Huguenin, on Perdiguier and had collaborated with him on the *Livre du Compagnade* (1839). As a politically committed, self-educated literary artisan, he seemed to be the ideal role model for the job: he talked the language of 'real' workers, 'the sort that you want to hear' (ibid.: 267) – again, evidence of her concern with the style of language needed for democratic politics. Perdiguier did not respond, so Sand wrote the other brochures herself in April 1848. In these texts, she addressed economic problems in a characteristically Leroux-influenced way: countryside and town should unite against the common enemies of monopoly and financial speculation, since 'the best part of your production and profit lies under this powerful fist' (ibid.: 268).

In the first and second pamphlets, with what would now be considered a very modern argument, she defends progressive income tax as the fairest of systems, and she presents a portfolio of fiscal reforms for the future government. In the third pamphlet, Claude and Blaise compare their respective situations, and in editions four and five Blaise argues for the unity of the people, stating that Parisian issues are actually concerns for the entire population: 'You are Paris, it is France' (ibid.).

The launch of a national newspaper

In her attempt to reach the masses, Sand then launched a national newspaper, *La Cause du Peuple*. It only ran for three issues, all in the month of April 1848. The first two editions were written with the enthusiasm of her letters hailing the Republic, but the third and final issue showed despair at the waning of revolutionary support. Nevertheless, they acted as the vehicle for her eyewitness observations and commentaries, such as her support of moves to rid the provisional government of its conservative elements and her efforts to help organize a republican festival.

Sadly, when on 30 April she took stock of the number of subscriptions to her paper, she decided to 'suspend' the publication and to refund payments (1969, viii: 439). It was not commercially viable: she was too stretched financially. Instead, she reached an agreement immediately to write for Théophile Thoré, the owner of *La Vraie République*, who gave her total editorial freedom (Hamon 2001: 274). She provided him with 13 articles between 2 May and 11 June 1848.

More fictional conversations

As the political situation heated up, Sand's journalistic flights of imagination became more personalized. The results of the elections for the National Assembly were announced from the Hotel de Ville on the evening of 28 April. Sand was back in Paris, amongst the crowds waiting in anticipation outside for an announcement. She wrote a letter to Maurice, published by *La Vraie République* on 2 May 1848 as 'In Front of the Hotel de Ville', which consisted of detailed reportage about the waiting crowds and their conversations about politics: 'people aren't discussing, they are chatting'. After detailed descriptions of the mood of the 300,000-strong crowd, she comments on this historic experience of democracy in action, which she interprets as a wonderful example of popular education, consciousness-raising and self-discovery: 'What the People discover for themselves is better than anything that one can invent for them.'

However, reportage does not take priority: the descriptive passage is used merely to serve a didactic purpose as scene-setting for Sand's argument about popular democracy. She then switches to a 'verbatim' presentation of one typical conversation, between three workers, each a different character type, symbolized by their clothing: 'one in a shirt, one in a jacket, one dressed like a bourgeois'. A three-way discussion is used to present the measures needed as steps towards a more equal society.

On 15 May, Sand attended a rally for solidarity with Polish revolutionaries and marched alongside the leaders, Barbes, Blanqui, Raspail and Leroux, all of whom were arrested. The offices of *La Vraie République* were ransacked and the editor, Théophile Thoré, had to go into hiding. Sand's friends urged her to return to Nohant as she too was in danger of arrest. From the safety of distance she invented two new characters for a correspondence, a worker and his wife, who took over the former roles of Claude and Blaise. Antoine, a (horse-drawn) carriage-maker, was amongst the Parisian crowd as a witness to the troubles at the 15 May demonstration. In commenting on the events of the demonstration in terms of his own experience, Antoine is actually offering an interpretation of events on the controversial day, in defence of the activist leaders who were arrested.

Sand's aim is to show, via Antoine, that the crowd had been manipulated by right-wing *agents provocateurs* circulating rumours. He concludes defensively: 'We weren't preparing for anything, we weren't plotting, the only mistake we made was to behave noisily …. It wasn't a revolution, it wasn't even a riot – we didn't know what it was' (*La Vraie République*, 28 May). Antoine continues his eyewitness journalistic commentary: 'My eyes were full of tears when I saw these young children, already well-trained soldiers … fraternizing with the people … they didn't know any more than us what was going to happen' (ibid.).

More than ever, these two characters represented both sides of Sand's personality and lifestyle. On her return to her rural retreat of Nohant, Sand wrote: 'I think that I am returning to paradise' (1969, viii, L3947: 479). Fictional letter-writing style is used to contrast the politics of the revolutionary city with the politics of rural tranquillity. Antoine's wife Gabrielle is at home in the provinces, and writes to her husband about the political tensions amongst rural communities. Like Sand, she is a lover of nature and the countryside, who writes to her husband: 'I can no longer separate out ideas about man from ideas about nature' (*La Vraie République*, 5 June 1848).

Gabrielle witnesses inflammatory gossip about communism in the countryside, and her comments reflect a familiar theme of Sand's: 'Our country people have their heads so stuffed full of malicious stories and rumours by the bourgeoisie, and sometimes by the priests, that you could say they've all turned insane' (ibid.). Gabrielle's observations came at a time when people in the Berry area reacted violently to Sand's self-professed communism, demonstrating outside the walls of her estate, calling for death to all communists and shouting 'down with Mme Dudevant'.

The final attempt at a newspaper

In La Châtre the republican candidate was defeated during the May 1849 elections: Sand described the locals as 'voting like pigs' (1969, ix: 146). When further elections took place on 10 December 1849, the outsider presidential candidate, Louis Napoleon, obtained 74.2 per cent of the votes cast. Sand's journalism was now lower profile: she financed a new local newspaper – *Le Travailleur de l'Indre* – anonymously, leaving the writing and management to her Berrichon friends. Even this strategy proved difficult. Sand had wanted the paper to articulate 'pure and simple' democratic principles locally (ibid.: 294), but the editor, Victor Borie, was forced to flee in exile to Brussels. The first edition came out on 30 December 1849 with a new editor who was equally ill-fated: he was sentenced to three months in prison for reproducing an article from the Italian newspaper *L'Italia*, which challenged the position of Pope Pius IX [9]. The journal folded, exemplifying a bigger phenomenon – the collapse of the republican political press in the provinces. On 27 August 1850 Sand concluded in a letter to Louis Blanc, exiled in London: 'The provinces didn't understand and still don't understand.'

Conclusion

In December 1851, Louis Napoleon staged a coup to retain power before declaring himself emperor in the footsteps of his uncle. Sand now lived in daily expectation of arrest. The project of Louis Blanc (the man she once hoped would marry her daughter) – national workshops for the unemployed – had been closed and many of her friends and acquaintances died in fighting, were hanged or transported to distant penal colonies. She campaigned tirelessly for their release. The republican cause had suffered a serious setback. Sand continued her novels, but never again showed the same energy for political journalism.

Viewed historically, she was a female pioneer at a time of great social and political upheaval, contributing to the struggle for democracy as a participant, observer and political educator. Her prolific literary journalism brought to the process a mould-breaking combination of emotional commitment and imagination. Her radical newspapers had to struggle for survival, but Sand's commitment to political publishing by working people has survived to this day as journalism's most principled and important purpose.

Notes

1 She was not the only female writer in France to adopt a male *nom de plume*: the Countess of Agoult called herself Daniel Stern, writing essays, memoirs and a history of 1848, published by Soudie in 1853.
2 In 1848 street sellers in Paris were touting a pamphlet entitled 'The loves and intrigues of George Sand' (Adler 1979: 163).
3 Sand's status as a woman must remain a constant factor in any assessment of her journalistic contribution, and her position within the history of feminism has already been subject to much scholarly interest. The early feminist writers in France, producing

journalism exclusively by and for women, came from the ranks of St Simonian followers, but Sand gave priority to a universal class struggle, rejecting separatist gender campaigning for the vote (Adler 1979; Walton 2000).

4 For the correspondence between Sand and Leroux, see *Histoire d'une amitie: Pierre Leroux et George Sand, d'après une correspondance inédité*, 1836–66 by Jean-Pierre Lacassagne, reviewed by Robert T. Denomme in *French Review*, 48/3, pp. 628–9.

5 The phrase was used critically in Karl Marx's *Communist Manifesto* (1848) to denote idealized early socialist ideas that originated in France.

6 For more on the difficulties of survival for oppositional newspapers at this time, see Collins 1954, 1959; Sand 1969, ii: 279, 290–1; Chapman 2005b: 37.

7 Bibliothèque Nationale sources are henceforth referred to as BN.

8 Sand always claimed she had brought him up according to Leroux's philosophy.

9 It is possible that Sand translated the article in question (Hamon 2001: 311). Previously, she had translated Mazzini's writings, dedicated a novel to him, and kept in regular contact with the Italian revolutionary leader through correspondence.

References

Translations into English from the French original are the author's own

Adler, Laure (1979) *A l'aube du féminisme: les premières journalistes, 1830–1850* (Paris: Payot).

Balzac, Honoré de (1965) *Monographie de la presse parisienne* (Paris: Éd. Jean-Jacques Pauvert, Coll. Libertés).

Bibliothèque Nationale BN 8 Lk7 (Paris: *Éclaireur de L'Indre*) 5 et 12 Octobre 1844, reproduced in *Questions politiques et sociales*, 1879, pp. 37–58.

Campbell, Kate (ed.) (2000) *Journalism, Literature and Modernity: From Hazlitt to Modernism* (Edinburgh: Edinburgh University Press).

Chapman, Jane (2005a) 'Republican citizenship, ethics and the French revolutionary press', *Ethical Space: The International Journal of Communication Ethics*, 2/1 (Spring) pp. 7–12.

——— (2005b) *Comparative Media History* (Cambridge: Polity Press).

Charton, Édouard (1842) *Dictionnaire des professions et guide pour le choix d'un état* (Paris).

Chastain, James (2004) 'Pierre Leroux, 1797–1871'. Available online at www.ohiou.edu/~Chastain/ip/leroux.htm, accessed on 15 November 2006.

Collins, Irene (1954) 'The government and the press in France during the reign of Louis Philippe', *English Historical Review* (April) pp. 262–82.

——— (1959) *The Government and the Newspaper Press in France, 1814–1881* (Oxford: Oxford University Press).

Dayen, Daniel (2006) 'Pierre Leroux'. Available online at www.educreuse23.ac-limoges.fr/sand/leroux.htm, accessed 12 November 2006.

Hamon, Bernard (2001) *George Sand et la Politique: 'Cette vilaine chose ...'* (Paris: L'Harmattan).

Perrot, Michelle (2004) *Politiques et polémiques* (Paris: Belin).

Rebéroux, Michelle (1994) 'George Sand, Flora Tristan et la question sociale', in Michaud, Stéphanie (ed.), *Flora Tristan, George Sand, Pauline Roland: Les femmes et l'invention d'une nouvelle morale,1830–48* (Paris: Éditions Craphis) pp. 83–94.

Sand, George (1856) *Histoire de ma vie*, 10 vols (Paris: Lévy).

——— (1879) *Questions politiques et sociales* (Paris: Calmann Lévy Frères).

——— (1882–4) *Correspondance, 1812–76*, 6 vols, published between 1882–92 (Paris: Calmann Lévy Éditeur).

——— (1949) *Histoire de ma vie* (Paris: Éditions Stock).

—— (1969) *Correspondence*, Lubin, Georges (ed.) (Paris: Éditions Garnier Frères).

—— (1988) *Le Compagnon du tour de France*, Grenoble, Presses universitaires de Grenoble.

—— (1991) *Story of My Life: The Autobiography of George Sand* (Albany: State University of New York Press).

Walton, Whitney (2000) *Eve's Proud Descendants: Four Women Writers and Republican Politics in Nineteenth-Century France* (Stanford: Stanford University Press).

Winwar, Frances (1946) *The Life of the Heart: George Sand and Her Times* (London: Hamish Hamilton).

Chapter 4

Charles Dickens and the voices of journalism

John Tulloch

Better known as a novelist than a journalist, Charles Dickens (1812–70) became the first global literary celebrity. Biographers emphasize the dark side of his childhood – the social disgrace of a father imprisoned for debt, an interrupted education, a six-month spell working in Warren's blacking factory – and portray him as a driven, psychologically-wounded writer. But during his early years in rapidly changing London he enjoyed the support of a loving, if improvident, family – and he spent many happy hours voraciously reading the classics such as Smollett and Fielding. After mastering a version of shorthand, Dickens escaped from being a lawyer's clerk and entered journalism at 19 as a parliamentary reporter. He excelled in covering debates and published his first journalistic sketches of people and places in magazines and newspapers from 1833. These were collected in book form as *Sketches by Boz: Illustrative of Every-Day Life and Every-Day People* in 1836. At the same time, Dickens began work on *Pickwick Papers*, published monthly from March 1836. During the run of *Pickwick*, he started publishing *Oliver Twist*, inaugurating the mix of social campaigning and urban observation so distinctive of his fiction. Throughout his career, Dickens published his fiction in serial form, either in weekly episodes in magazines or monthly numbers. At roughly one third the price of a conventional novel, this ensured a mass audience for his fiction, and high circulations for magazines he edited and owned: *Household Words* (1850) and *All the Year Round* (1859). His journalism embraced virtually every genre, including campaigning articles, travel pieces, essays, reviews. Most memorable are his urban sketches – including a late series published from January 1860 onwards as *The Uncommercial Traveller*. From 1858 his public readings in England and the United States drew massive crowds. He died suddenly during the serialization of *The Mystery of Edwin Drood*.

Journalism's status anxiety

> I wrote a little something, in secret, and sent it to a magazine, and it was published in the magazine. Since then, I have taken heart to write a good many trifling pieces. Now I am regularly paid for them.
>
> (*David Copperfield*, Chapter 43)

Journalism in Britain has long been an activity of uncertain social esteem, lacking the secure role that in America is embodied in the First Amendment to the US Constitution, and more distant than its European neighbours from the world of literature. This insecurity of esteem is nowhere more marked than in the journalism of Charles Dickens.

In many accounts of Dickens, including his own, journalism is commonly presented as a sort of training for writing novels. For example, the critic Robert Browning asserts that 'Dickens was a press reporter; and whatever the deficiencies of his formal education, it is clear that he can hardly have had a better training for the craft of novel writing' (Browning 1962: 21). Although this customary judgment seems unproblematic – many journalists, indeed, 'graduate' to writing fiction – it has the effect of assigning the journalism to an inferior status.

Of course, as John Drew reminds us: 'Almost everything that Dickens published, by virtue of appearing in newspapers, magazines, or "numbers" could be technically classified as journalism – and frequently was by early reviewers – while its internal structure, narrative strategies, its very topicality gave it an intrinsically journalistic flavour' (Drew 1999: 305; and see 2003).

Many contemporary critics regarded Dickens's writing as inherently journalistic in both the positive and the negative connotations. The most celebrated formulation of this was by the English essayist, theorist of the British Constitution and editor of the *Economist*, Walter Bagehot. His 1858 essay on Dickens is frequently cited as brilliantly perceptive and approving. Bagehot singles him out as 'a special correspondent for posterity' and celebrates his power of vivid description; his rapid movement between different classes and locations; the speed, density and complexity of incident; the mimicry of a vast range of voices; his popularity from 'mistress to servant'; and a quality of modernity which Bagehot identified in a famous passage:

> London is like a newspaper. Everything is there, and everything is disconnected. There is every kind of person in some houses; but there is no more connection between the houses than between the neighbours in the lists of 'births, marriages, and deaths'. As we change from the broad leader to the squalid police-report, we pass a corner and we are in a changed world. This is advantageous to Mr Dickens's genius. His memory is full of instances of old buildings and curious people, and he does not care to piece them together. On the contrary, each scene, to his mind, is a separate scene – each street a separate street.
>
> (Bagehot 1858)

But a full reading of the essay reveals it as a patronizing hatchet job. Dickens's powers of reportorial observation are, for Bagehot, a signal about his low status, his fixation on externals rather than essences, and outlined in a series of limiting comments of extraordinary condescension. Dickens is

utterly deficient in the faculty of reasoning … [subject to] sentimental confusion … no writer less fitted for excursion to the imperative mood … nothing
less like the great lawyer … than the attorney's clerk who catches at small
points like a dog catching at fleas … he knows the dry arches of London Bridge
better than Belgravia … he excels in inventories of poor furniture, and is
learned in pawnbrokers' tickets … he describes the figs that are sold, but not
the talent that sells figs well.

(Ibid.)

It is only relatively recently, through the painstaking, scholarly identification of
hundreds of stories, sketches and fugitive pieces, and the publication of a magnifi-
cent four-volume collected edition edited by Michael Slater and John Drew
(Slater 1994, 1996, 1998; Slater and Drew 2000) that the scale and excellence of
Dickens's achievement as a *journalist* has become apparent. The journalism
reprinted before his death (in *Sketches by Boz*, *The Uncommercial Traveller*, *Reprinted
Pieces*) only constitutes less than half the canon. Altogether, Dickens published
about 350 articles – over a million words – in newspapers and magazines that can
be regarded as journalism: i.e. relatively short, expressly designed for periodicals
and mainly non-fiction (Drew 1999, 2003).

Journalism and the mass market

One obvious reason for the low status of English journalism has been its perceived
lack of creative control by the author compared to the control allegedly associated
with the 'artist'. Arguably one of the malign effects of Romanticism in British
culture was to define the 'true' artist's status as not having a patron but a soulful
relationship to the audience that precluded writing for anything as vulgar as the
market. Certainly the issues of creative control and his relationship to the mass
audience tantalized Dickens.

He strove to become a hugely influential editor and proprietor, and ultimately
succeeded, with his magazines *Household Words* and *All the Year Round*, in achieving a
position where he had complete creative control. And in a sense he created his own
market and audience. In this he was unique among Victorian journalists and
writers. Towards the end of his career he was able to celebrate his early years as a
young reporter covering elections and getting back in time for publication, despite
being 'belated on miry by-roads, towards the small hours, forty or fifty miles from
London, in a wheelless carriage, with exhausted horses and drunken postboys'
(speech to Newspaper Press Fund, 20 May 1865: Fielding 1960).

Dickens was also the prototype of the modern celebrity writer-journalist. Every
page of *Household Words* carries the assurance 'Conducted by Charles Dickens' – a
formulation which evokes, rather grandly, an orchestra of contributors being
brought into harmony and, rather more mundanely, a fare collector of an omnibus
in search of passengers. It also stands as an early example of deliberate celebrity
branding. Just as much as Paul Newman's face on a bottle of sauce, the name of

Dickens ensured both the popularity and the wholesomeness of the magazine's contents and its suitability for the entire family.

These early endeavours in creating a mass audience and building a community of readers around his magazines lacked the tangible interactivity he appears to have craved. A frequent performer of his own work to friends and family, from 1858 he began to criss-cross Britain and the US making public readings which were immensely lucrative and cemented his position as the most famous writer in the West. There were solid commercial reasons for undertaking readings, particularly in America, although some colleagues and friends, including John Forster, regarded them as vulgarly trading his status as a great writer for the role of a popular entertainer. Without speculating on deeper psychological motives, it is reasonable to suppose that a writer so concerned with his audience had a need for some frequent affirmation of its existence, and continued loyalty. One of the bleakest passages in his superb night-sketch, 'Night Walks', written soon after he began the public readings, is a contemplation of the *absence* of the audience, in an empty theatre:

> In one of my night walks, as the church steeples were shaking the March wind and rain with the strokes of Four, I passed the outer boundary of one of those great deserts, and entered it. I groped my well-known way to the stage and looked over the orchestra – which was like a great grave dug for a time of pestilence – into the void beyond. A dismal cavern of an immense aspect, with the chandelier gone dead like everything else, and nothing visible through mist and fog and space, but tiers of winding sheets. The ground at my feet where, when last there, I had seen the peasantry of Naples dancing among the vines, reckless of the burning mountain which threatened to overwhelm them, was now in possession of a strong serpent of engine-hose, watchfully lying in wait for the serpent fire, and ready to fly at it if it showed its forked tongue.
>
> (Slater and Drew 2000: 151–2)

Popularity – and critical condescension

Of course, most readers know their Dickens through the novels, and his fiction has never lost its popularity. Popularity itself is frequently accounted a critical crime in England, particularly by coterie writers such as the Bloomsbury set. His preeminent status as the most considerable novelist of the Victorian period was partially eclipsed for a period after his death in 1870 by critical condescension from the likes of Henry James and Matthew Arnold, later followed by Virginia Woolf, Lytton Strachey and E. M. Forster (Forster 1927).

But although Edwardian and inter-war critical opinion frequently treated his work with disdain, he retained enthusiastic critics as diverse as G. K. Chesterton (1906) and George Orwell (1940). Dickens enthusiasts formed one of the earliest fan clubs, with the foundation in 1902 of the Dickens Fellowship, which started its journal, *The Dickensian*, in the same year. And he always retained a considerable hold on the popular imagination – even the mass-readership *Daily Express* newspaper, fighting a circulation war in the 1930s, found it worthwhile to distribute sets of Dickens as inducements to subscribers. A continuing flow of film and television adaptations of the novels testifies to an enduring popularity (Sanders 2003: 196–206).

His reception into academic culture was more problematic. England's greatest literary critic of the twentiethth century, Dr F. R. Leavis, in his notorious afterword to *The Great Tradition* (1948), celebrated *Hard Times* as the only Dickens novel worth serious consideration and characterized him, with chilly condescension, as an 'entertainer'. The same trenchancy marked his reversal of this judgment, without visible *mea culpa* or apology, in his *Dickens the Novelist* (1970) where *Little Dorrit* is described as *the* Victorian novel, fit to rank with Tolstoy's *War and Peace*. A substantial body of critical opinion today now classes Dickens, alone with Shakespeare, in the pantheon of supremely gifted imaginative artists (see Ackroyd 1990).

Both *Sketches by Boz* and *The Uncommercial Traveller* (1860–9) have had their admirers, but they have always ranked low in estimations of Dickens's oeuvre. The *Sketches* are a mixture of descriptions of scenes from city life, short stories and semi-fictionalized portraits of 'types' or 'characters', observed by the persona of Boz. Frequently they are presented as a sort of training ground where Dickens develops the narrative and observational skills to be deployed with increasing confidence in *Pickwick* and the early novels, notably *Oliver Twist*. In contrast, *The Uncommercial Traveller* is often regarded as a relatively minor product of Dickens's final years when he produced some of his greatest work: *Tale of Two Cities* (1859), *Great Expectations* (1861) and *Our Mutual Friend* (1865).

Apart from being dismissed as merely a training ground in observational technique, Dickens's journalism can also be downgraded as a form of ephemeral commentary on social issues dealt with in a more profound way in the novels. Of course, the popularity of Dickens's novels derived, in part, from their combination of insistent topicality with a focus on some long-standing scandal: for instance, the operations of the Poor Law and child labour in *Oliver Twist* (Waller 2005: 14–15); Yorkshire schools in *Nicholas Nickleby* (1839) (Collins 1964: 98–123); industrial unrest and factory conditions in *Hard Times* (1854); the dilapidation of the English legal system in *Bleak House* (1853) (Butt and Tillotson 1968: 177–200).

The voices of journalism

Dickens's development as a journalist is very marked. John Drew (1999: 304–7) identifies three distinct phases in his journalistic career:

1   as newspaper reporter and sketch writer (1831–6);
2   as reviewer and commentator (1834–49);
3   as editor and essayist (1846, 1850–70).

Otherwise his career could be seen to embody a transition from the *flâneur* journalism of the early sketches – the relaxed, whimsical wanderer of the streets, at once 'cool, dandified, and masculine' (Zurier 2006: 91), observing urban life with a detached irony, fascination and satirical bite – to the mid-century social criticism of the morally engaged observer, whose thin-skinned capacity for outrage and anger and passionate campaigning prefigures the New Journalism of W. T. Stead and the American muckrakers (see Conboy 2004: 167–70). The final phase of essay and sketch writing in the 1860s is distinctively darker in tone. In part this development can be represented as a shift from the sketch writer to the serious editorial personage, from the young Boz to the institution of 'Charles Dickens', a mid-Victorian celebrity, social commentator and man of affairs.

But, just as in his novels, his journalism continues to return to, and rework, certain themes. The continuity is as remarkable as the growth, and the *flâneur* of the early *Sketches* may be fanciful but is not lightweight. He is morally engaged, and never a lizard-like transplant from the boulevards. The later wanderer of the city streets may be subject to existential doubts, but he retains an essential whimsicality and wit. What also remains constant between *Sketches by Boz* and *The Uncommercial Traveller* is a mobility of tone, a play of voices, a capacity for mimicry and a 'journalistic élan' well described by Gabriel Pearson as 'the pulse of energy, the extraordinary oscillation of moods and effects, the sheer density of stuff that remains our central experience of Dickens' (1962: xix). This stayed with him all his life and was already evident even before Dickens became a journalist:

> His first employer recalled that, at the age of fifteen 'His knowledge of London was wonderful, for he could describe the position of every shop in any of the West End streets'; and one of his fellow clerks at that time wrote, similarly 'He could imitate, in a manner I have never heard equalled, the low population of the streets of London in all their varieties, whether mere loafers and sellers of fruit, vegetables, or anything else. He could also excel in mimicking the popular singers of that day, whether comic or patriotic ... and imitate all the leading actors of that time'.
>
> (Collins 1973: 545)

Journalism presents itself as protean and many voiced, but Western print journalism deploys a comparatively limited repertoire of voices: around seven, which overlap in various ways and interact with the genres of content. Richard Keeble (2005: 109–10) lists 18 genres. They include: the sketch; the leader; the column; the essay; the news report; the eyewitness report; the gossip column; the investigative feature; the profile. Amongst the main voices are:

- the *telegraphic*, clipped voice appropriate for news and giving an illusion of objectivity;
- the *gossiper*, relaxed and malicious and sharing the same vocal space as the *diarist*;

- the *controversialist* dedicated to 'stirring things up', the personality prone to rant, prone to sarcasm, living in a column or, today, in a blog;
- the involved and *compassionate* voice of the social investigator;
- the *rational* voice weighing evidence appropriate for the leader;
- the detached ironic *observer* of the sketch;
- the *mimic*, reproducing by quotation or reported speech the voices of the people;
- the *campaigner*, marshalling evidence of abuses, in heavy ironic mode, for the prosecuting exposé.

Dickens pre-dated the telegraphic news style, which developed in the late nineteenth and early twentieth centuries (Schudson 1995: 53–71), but mastered a clipped, economical reporting style when required (for instance, 'Report on the Tory Victory at Colchester', *Morning Chronicle*, 10 January 1835; see Slater 1996: 13–14). He reserved the malicious gossipy voice for his letters. He also pre-dated the column, which evolved from the 1880s (Silvester 1997: Introduction), although both *Boz* and *The Uncommercial Traveller* adopt a consistent persona that could readily be mobilized in one. The ranting controversialist was a particular skill, but could display his most intolerant side, as in the sarcastic eloquence of this buttonholing, brutal racism:

> I beg to say that I have not the least belief in the Noble Savage. I consider him a prodigious nuisance, and an enormous superstition. His calling rum fire-water, and me a pale face, wholly fail to reconcile me to him. I don't care what he calls me. I call him a savage, a something highly desirable to be civilized off the face of the earth … cruel. False, thievish, murderous, addicted more or less to grease, entrails, and beastly customs; a wild animal with the questionable gift of boasting; a conceited, tiresome, blood-thirsty, monotonous humbug.
>
> (See 'The Noble Savage', *Household Words*, 11 June 1853, reprinted in Slater 1998: 147–8)

Otherwise he displayed an assured control of the remaining voices and an extraordinary ability to switch between them, moving between the detached, ironic observer, the involved and compassionate voice, the campaigner, and the mimic with consummate ease.

In Dickens's social investigations, the compassionate voice is tempered by his worldly alertness to having the wool pulled over his eyes – for example, in his 'perennial suspicion of mealy-mouthed "model prisoners"' (Collins 1962: 103), his shrewd watchfulness for the rogue, and a forensic concern to present social evidence. Moreover, there are numerous examples of the campaigning voice in heavy ironic or sarcastic mode. Dickens campaigned against capital punishment, publishing a series of letters in the *Daily News* (February–March 1846) calling for total abolition, although he later changed his line to the abolition of executions in public. A leading article in *Household Words* (17 May 1850 – Slater 1996: 350–6) sarcastically describes the hangman as The Finishing Schoolmaster:

> It was recently supposed and feared that a vacancy had occurred in this great national office. One of the very few public Instructors – we had almost written the only one – as to whose moral lessons all sorts of Administrations and Cabinets are united in having no kind of doubt, was so much engaged in enlightening the people of England, that an occasion for his services arose, when it was dreaded they could not be rendered. It is scarcely necessary to say who this special public instructor is. Our administrative legislators cannot agree on the teaching of The Lord's Prayer, the Sermon on the Mount, the Christian History; but they are all quite clear as to the public teaching of the Hangman. The scaffold is the blessed neutral ground on which conflicting Governments may all accord, and Mr John Ketch is the great state schoolmaster.

'Swiftian' is an overused adjective, but this voice plainly owes much to Swift – Dickens was an enthusiastic reader – and the balance between angry moral outrage and gentlemanly diction evident in 'A Modest Proposal'. Dickens's essay goes on to quote letters of application for the post of hangman.

The buzzing universe of things

Early observers of Dickens's journalism stressed its confident grasp of the sheer *thisness* of the material urban world, the buzzing universe of things – 'all the things that no-one had ever noticed before' (Ackroyd 1990: 167). It is evident, for example, in one of his earliest *Sketches*, on 'Brokers and Marine-store Shops', first published in the *Morning Chronicle*, 15 December 1834:

> On a board, at the side of the door, are placed about twenty books, all odd volumes; and as many wine-glasses – all different patterns; several locks, an old earthenware pan, full of rusty keys; two or three gaudy chimney-ornaments – cracked, of course; the remains of a lustre, without any drops; a round frame like a capital O, which has once held a mirror; a flute, complete with the exception of the middle joint; a pair of curling-irons; and a tinder-box. In front of the shop window are ranged some half dozen high-backed chairs, with spinal complaints and wasted legs; a corner cupboard; two or three very dark mahogany tables with flaps like mathematical problems; some pickle jars, some surgeons' ditto, with gilt labels and without stoppers; an unframed portrait of some lady who flour-ished about the beginning of the thirteenth century, by an artist who never flourished at all ...
>
> (Slater 1994: 177)

The list transfixes us with its seemingly random specificity, the eccentricity of the objects, the traces of their former owners not quite effaced, trying to convince us of the authenticity of the observation. But it bounces with élan and ironic pointers – the artist who never flourished, the chairs with inherited spinal complaints.

Dickens was also an inveterate traveller, and movement and travel were central to his journalism. He was fascinated by the railways, and some of his most powerful pieces concern the spatial and temporal changes in perception created by them:

> Bang! We have let another Station off, and fly away regardless. Everything is flying. The hop-gardens turn gracefully towards me, presenting regular avenues of hops in rapid flight, then whirl away. So do the pools and rushes, haystacks, sheep, clover in full bloom delicious to the sight and smell, corn-sheaves, cherry-orchards, apple-orchards, reapers, gleaners, hedges, gates, fields that taper off into little angular corners, cottages, gardens, now and then a church. Bang, bang!
>
> ('A Flight', *Household Words*, 30 August 1851, reprinted in Slater 1998: 26–35)

The recreation of popular speech

Dickens's capacity to observe, mirror and recreate popular speech was another element in his writing that astonished observers. His friend the historian Thomas Carlyle observed that mimicry was basic to human creativity.

> In its lowest phase, no talent can be lower (for even the Papuan and monkeys have it); but in its highest, where it gives you domicile in the world of a Shakespear [sic] or a Goethe, there are only some few that are higher … Dickens's essential faculty, I often say, is that of a first-rate Playactor.
>
> (Carlyle 1997: 368)

Above all, he captured the speech of London. F. S. Schwarzbach claims that 'Dickens is virtually the only English writer of any great stature to engage in a sustained effort to write about the city during the first two-thirds of the nineteenth century' (Schwarzbach 1979: 3). He writes as a resident of London, not a tourist, with an ear for the theatre of the streets – what Ackroyd (1990: 166) describes as an 'extraordinary mixture of display and directness, exterior irony and internal identification'. Ackroyd continues: 'What his contemporaries heard *were* the voices, and the prevailing admiration for Dickens's early work came from what was described as the "vivid" and "graphic" way in which he captured the speech of London.'

Many of Boz's sketches enact or refer to mini-fables of social decline and disgrace or urban change – the disappearance of a shop, imprisonment for debt. Dickens's Mr Bung, the Broker's Man – placed by second-hand dealers in a debtor's house to ensure no goods are removed before the broker can distrain them

(Slater 1994: 27) – is a 'shrewd, knowing fellow' who strikes the narrator with the 'power some men seem to have, not only of sympathizing with, but to all appearances of understanding feelings to which they themselves are entire strangers'.

> I wished again and again that the people would only blow me up, or pitch into me – that I wouldn't have minded, it's all in my way, but it's the being shut up by yourself in one room for five days, without so much as an old newspaper to look at, or anything to see out o' the winder but the roofs and chimneys at the back of the house, or anything to listen to but the ticking, perhaps, of an old Dutch clock, the sobbing of the missis now and then, the low talking of friends in the next room, who speak in whispers, lest 'the man' should overhear them, or perhaps the occasional opening of the door, as a child peeps in to look at you, and then runs half-frightened away – it's all this, that makes you feel sneaking somehow, and ashamed of yourself; and then, if it's winter times, they just give you fire enough to make you think you'd like more, and bring in your grub as if they wished it 'ud choke you – as I dare say they do, for the matter of that, most heartily.

Mr Bung goes on for six pages, but this serpentine, 191-word sentence captures the complexity and delicacy of popular speech, without parody or exaggeration.

Dickens's sketches struck observers, such as his friend and biographer John Forster, as profoundly original: 'The observation shown throughout is nothing short of wonderful. Things are painted literally as they are ...' (Forster 1872–4, Book 2, V), but they draw on a complex tradition. In essence, they presented themselves as spontaneous observations of 'ordinary life', caught in the streets of London. In English literature, the use of 'ordinary life' as a literary topic has diverse roots including: Jacobean city comedy, such as the work of Ben Jonson (*Everyman in His Humour* of 1601, *Bartholomew Fair* of 1614), traditions of pastoral poetry, composed in cities, that celebrate an idealized country life, opposed to the complexity and falseness of the court; and the mock heroic art of the eighteenth century, whose comedy joins the wretched incidents of vernacular life with the high style appropriate for the world of heroes. Its greatest exponent, Alexander Pope (1688–1744), who had translated Homer's *Iliad* into heroic couplets, constructed his *Rape of the Lock* (1712) around the theft of a lady's curl. Her anger parodies the rage of Achilles. His mock-heroic *The Dunciad* (1728) operates as a parody of the heroic *Iliad*, summoning brilliant comic images of mediocre writers diving into London sewers to win the favour of the goddess of Dullness.

If the ghost of these urban forms sits behind the sketches, there is also the presence of the great proto-journalists of the eighteenth century. The city sketch can be traced back to the early urban periodicals, notably the *Spectator* of Addison and Steele (1711–12, 1714), a publication addressed to gentlemen. The 'spectator' was a detached, ironic urban observer. The nineteenth century added to this the roles of reporters, urban investigators, cartoonists and travel writers who actively roamed the streets to write about incidents in the city.

Sketches of urban life

The simplest definition of a city is 'a human settlement in which strangers are likely to meet' (Sennett 1986: 39). The sketch as developed by Dickens is rooted in the nature of urban life – it is rapidly executed, witty, impressionistic, fidgety, provisional, speculative, prone to whimsy and therefore mobile in tone. Typically it wonders about the thoughts, feelings and lives of strangers, on the basis of external appearances. In all this it expresses much of the mystery of urban life, which depends on the willing cooperation of manifold strangers, a fabric of trust woven by people unfamiliar to each other at a personal level but daily negotiating a *modus vivendi*, a space in which all can live together with minimal conflict.

Ephemeral impressions of strangers are the basis of life in a modern city. Above all, the sketch added the idea of 'everyday life' or 'ordinary life' as a subject – explicitly addressed by Dickens in the title of his first book. The titles of the *Sketches* themselves baldly reflect this deliberate focus on the everyday though the names of the generic components of the city ('The Streets – Morning', 'The Streets – Night', 'Shops and their Tenants', 'Hackney Coach Stands', 'Brokers and Marine-store Shops', 'Gin Shops',` etc); specific references to places in London ('Scotland Yard', 'Seven Dials', 'Meditations in Monmouth Street'); and references to places of popular entertainment ('Astleys', 'Greenwich Fair', 'Vauxhall Gardens'). As Collins (1977) observes, the streets, shops, transport, crime, the law and popular amusements are the principal themes in *Sketches by Boz*. Bound together by the figure of the restlessly observant pedestrian, they were to remain recurrent concerns in his journalism.

The constancy of these preoccupations can be demonstrated by a comparison with one of his later sketches. Dickens spent the last ten years of his life editing *All the Year Round*, which carried his three last novels, *Great Expectations* (1861), *Our Mutual Friend* (1865) and the unfinished *Edwin Drood* (1870) – the first two generally considered among his finest achievements – as well as enduringly readable thrillers by his friend Wilkie Collins (1824–88) (*The Woman in White* of 1860, *Moonstone* of 1868). During this remarkable late flowering, he also created some extraordinary journalism in the persona of *The Uncommercial Traveller*, which the editors of his collected journalism claim as 'his greatest journalistic achievement' (Slater and Drew 2000: xxi). It is extraordinary for its range: the Traveller visits shipwrecks, pantomimes, workhouses, dockyards, city churches and 'shy neighbourhoods'. He retails the stories of tramps, Mormons, Italian radicals. He dissects the Medway towns, Liverpool's dockland, Paris and Gray's Inn chambers. He walks relentlessly, at night.

Journalism and the problem of authenticity

The journalistic methods employed by Dickens – the mimicry of voices mixed with direct quotation; the shifting personae and points of view of the writer; the narrative structures that are co-extensive with fiction – all raise issues of authenticity. That is, although his journalism insists with vivid clarity on his presence at the scene and the 'reality' of what he witnesses, the actual status of these truth claims is muffled or uncertain to the modern reader and his journalistic methodology concealed. Of course, the problem goes with the territory of Victorian journalism. Henry Mayhew's great portraits of Victorian street-life in *London Labour and the London Poor* (of 1851) (see Mayhew 1968) are based around superbly lively and evocative interviews, structured like urban sketches, with the dialogue dramatic, shaped and lengthy.

Dickens's piece 'On Duty with Inspector Field', published in *Household Words* on 14 June 1851, encapsulates these issues. The article is one of several in which Dickens celebrates the new detective police based at Scotland Yard. Field himself (1805–74) is frequently proposed as the basis for the sleuth Bucket in *Bleak House*. The piece demonstrates Field's mastery of the dangerous areas in London's East End – reassuringly for the middle-class readership of *Household Words* – and counterposes the imperturbable control of the police with the incipient chaos of criminal areas. The action is set at night, from 9 pm until 2 am, marked in the narrative by the recurrent device of the striking clock. During this time, narrator 'Dickens' roams with the police from New Oxford Street to Southwark, the London docks, Whitechapel and Holborn.

Dickens has been accused, in this piece and others, of naively hero-worshipping the new Metropolitan Police – contrasting them with the defunct Bow Street Runners, who were notoriously corrupt – and adopting an uncritical view that failed to reflect their marked shortcomings (see Collins 1965: 198–219). There is some evidence that this narrative is based on a number of excursions with the police, rather than one, and from interviews with Scotland Yard officers at the offices of *Household Words*. In fact, 'On Duty with Inspector Field' is constructed like a modern drama documentary and raises the same issues of authenticity: the narrative is constructed to assure us that 'the real' is witnessed and characterized by a hopelessly one-sided and prejudiced account of the material.

Despite these defects – hyperbole, prejudice and lack of transparency in its methods – it remains a remarkable piece of journalism. Dickens mimics the voice of Field, other police and various lodging-house keepers and figures, who are presented as belonging to criminal classes throughout the piece. The major structuring device is time – the text is punctuated by references and maintains a hectic pace, and a wild energy of observation, in a repelled (and repulsive) narrator:

> Clear the street there, half a thousand of you! Cut it, Mrs Stalker – none of that – we don't want you! Rogers of the flaming eye, lead on to the tramps' lodging house!
>
> A dream of baleful faces attends to the door. Now, stand back all of you! In the rear, Detective Serjeant plants himself, composedly whistling, with his strong right arm across the narrow passage. Mrs Stalker, I am something'd that need not be written here, if you won't get yourself into trouble, in about half a minute, if I see that face of yours again!

Saint Giles's church clock, striking eleven, hums through our hand from the dilapidated door of a dark outhouse as we open it, and are stricken back by the pestilent breath that issues from within. Rogers, to the front with the light, and let us look!

Ten, twenty, thirty – who can count them! Men, women, children, for the most part naked, heaped upon the floor like maggots in a cheese! Ho! In that dark corner yonder! Does anybody lie there? Me Sir, Irish me, a widder, with six children. And yonder? Me Sir, Irish me, with me wife and eight poor babes. And to the left there? Me Sir, Irish me, along with two more Irish boys as is me friends. And to the right there? Me Sir and the Murphy family, numbering five blessed souls. And what's this, coiling now, about my foot? Another Irish me, pitifully in want of shaving, whom I have awakened from sleep – and across my other foot lies his wife – and by the shoes of Inspector Field lie their three eldest – and their three youngest are at present squeezed between the open door and the wall. And why is there no one on the little mat before the sullen fire? Because O'Donovan, with wife and daughter, is not come in yet from selling Lucifers! Nor on the bit of sacking in the nearest corner? Bad luck! Because that Irish family is late tonight, a-cadging in the streets!

Racism, social disgust at the poor, anti-Catholicism, class prejudice, power worship – many questionable attitudes jostle for our attention in this narrative voice. But the energy and raw power of the observation are irresistible. This is journalistic writing of a high order, fully engaged, with a seamless blend of reported speech, mimicry and commentary. We may be repelled by the vision, and, at times, by its author, but this is a great journalist at the height of his powers.

Conclusion: Dickens's influence – and originality

As a writing journalist, editor and a proprietor, Dickens was extraordinarily influential on other journalists. He maintained close links with some of the leading writers and editors of the age, including Carlyle, Thackeray and Forster. In the 1850s he acted as a mentor and role-model to a generation of younger journalists, such as George Augustus Sala, Edmund Yates and Blanchard Jerrold, who became known as Dickens's 'young men' and went on to become highly influential figures (Edwards 1997: 3).

Dickens continued to be influential after his premature death in 1870. His magazine *All the Year Round* limped on until 1895 under the editorship of his son, Charles Dickens Jr. Alfred Harmsworth (later Lord Northcliffe), who, from the 1880s onwards, created a magazine empire followed by a daily newspaper empire, was a close student of his career: 'Dickens was for some years the chief object of Alfred Harmsworth's never obsessive capacity for hero-worship' (Pound and Harmsworth 1959: 98). He amassed an extensive collection of Dickensiana and regarded him as 'the greatest magazine editor of his own or any other age' (Johnson 1977: 367).

This is a relatively forgotten aspect of Dickens. The placing of him within progressively grander hardback editions effaced the purely journalistic aspect of his art – its openness and provisional quality, a living relationship with an eager readership, and the positive aspects of its journalistic qualities. Serial publication was always intrinsic to Dickens's creative work. Dickens always attempted to reach a larger audience by various forms of cheap publication. *Pickwick Papers* was published in the then unusual form of one-shilling monthly parts, made up of three or four chapters and several pages of advertisements in a paper cover, costing in total less than a third of a standard three-volume novel (Butt and Tillotson 1968: 13–14). The mode of publication was used for eight subsequent novels, including *Nicholas Nickleby*, *David Copperfield*, and *Little Dorrit*, published in nineteen monthly numbers, with the last part a double number.

This mode of production exerted complex demands on the writer.

> Writing in serial involved maintaining two focuses. The design and purpose of the novel had to be kept constantly in view; but the writer had also to think in terms of the identity of the serial number, which would have to make its own impact and be judged as a unit. Incident and interest had therefore to be evenly spread … Chapters must be balanced within a number in respect both of length and of effect. Each number must lead, if not to a climax, at least to a point of rest.
>
> (Ibid.: 15)

Apart from cheapness, the advantages to the reader were: the prolonging of narrative pleasure; the eager expectation of the next episode; a sense that the story was in the process of being formed or travelling through time; and the 'lifelike' characteristic of being open to surprise twists and influence, both from the audience and the incidents of the writer's life. Thus the readers became to some degree complicit in the text. This openness and provisional quality are the reverse of conceptions of high art, or high journalism for that matter. And this accounts for Dickens's startling modernity, and continuing ability to speak to us, in the context of the interactive newspaper and the universal blogger.

Of course, a limiting fact of journalism is that it is inevitably uneven – the demands of hourly, daily or weekly production strip even great writers of originality, force them to manufacture cliché, make them prone to padding. Journalism is always in a crisis of overproduction. Topicality may mean disposability. Dickens was less prone to the routine sins of wordsmithery than most, and even routine examples of what Carlyle deprecated as 'wordspinning' – efforts to fill his magazines – contain unexpected insights. But a substantial proportion of his million words of journalism are startlingly original, extend the possibilities of journalistic expression, and can stand alongside his finest fiction.

References

Ackroyd, Peter (1990) *Dickens* (London: Sinclair-Stevenson).

Bagehot, Walter (1858) 'Charles Dickens', *National Review*, 7 (October), reprinted in Bagehot, Walter (1911) *Literary Studies*, Everyman's Library (London: J. M. Dent).

Browning, Robert (1962) *Sketches by Boz*, in Gross, John, and Pearson, Gabriel (eds), *Dickens and the Twentieth Century* (London: Routledge & Kegan Paul).

Butt, John, and Tillotson, Kathleen (1968) *Dickens at Work*, University Paperback edition (London: Methuen) [first published 1957].

Carlyle, Thomas (1997) *Reminiscences, A New and Complete Edition*, Fielding, Kenneth J., and Campbell, Ian (eds) (Oxford: Oxford University Press) [first published 1881].

Chesterton, Gilbert Keith (G. K.) (1906) *Charles Dickens* (London: Methuen).

Collins, Philip (1964) *Dickens and Education* (London: Macmillan), second impression reprinted with alterations.

—— (1965) *Dickens and Crime* (London: Macmillan), second edition.

—— (1973) *Dickens and London*, in Dyos, H. J., and Wolff, Michael, *The Victorian City: Images and Realities*, vol. 2 (London: Routledge & Kegan Paul), pp. 537–57.

Conboy, Martin (2004) *Journalism: A Critical History* (London: Sage).

Crary, Jonathan (1990) *Techniques of the Observer: Vision and Modernity in the Nineteenth Century* (Cambridge, Mass: MIT Press).

Dickens, Charles (1854) *Household Words: A Weekly Journal*, vol. 9, 18 February–12 August (London).

Drew, John (1999) 'Dickens as journalist', in Schlicke, Paul (ed.), *Oxford Reader's Companion to Dickens* (Oxford: Oxford University Press), pp. 304–8.

—— (2003) *Dickens the Journalist* (Basingstoke: Palgrave Macmillan).

Edwards, Peter D. (1997) *Dickens's 'Young Men'* (Aldershot: Ashgate Publishing).

Empson, William (1962) 'The symbolism of Dickens', in Gross, John, and Pearson, Gabriel (eds), *Dickens and the Twentieth Century* (London: Routledge & Kegan Paul).

Hibbert, Christopher (1967) *The Making of Charles Dickens* (London: Longman Green).

Fielding, Kenneth J. (ed.) (1960) *Speeches of Charles Dickens* (revised edition 1988) (Oxford and New York: Oxford University Press).

Forster, Edward Morgan (E. M.) (1927) *Aspects of the Novel, The Clark Lectures* (London: Edward Arnold).

Forster, John (1872–4) *The Life of Charles Dickens*, 3 vols (London: Chapman & Hall) [one volume edition: Chapman & Hall 1892].

Johnson, Edgar (1977) *Charles Dickens: His Tragedy and Triumph*, one volume revised and abridged edition (London: Allen Lane) [previously published in two volumes 1952].

Keeble, Richard (2005) *The Newspapers Handbook* (London: Routledge), fourth edition.

Leavis, Frank Raymond (F. R.) (1948) *The Great Tradition* (London: Chatto & Windus).

—— and Leavis, Queenie (Q. D.) (1972) *Dickens the Novelist*, (Harmondsworth: Pelican Books edition) [first published Chatto & Windus 1970].

Mayhew, Henry (1968) *London Labour and the London Poor*, 4 vols, Dover edition – unabridged republication of original edition published by Griffin, Bohn & Company, 1861–2 (New York: Dover Publications).

Orwell, George (1968) 'Charles Dickens', in Orwell, Sonia, and Angus, Ian (eds), *The Collected Essays, Journalism and Letters of George Orwell*, vol. 1, An Age Like This 1920–40 (London: Secker & Warburg), pp. 413–60 [originally published 1940 in *Inside the Whale*, London: Gollancz].

Pearson, Gabriel (1962) 'Dickens: the present position', in Gross, John, and Pearson, Gabriel (eds), *Dickens and the Twentieth Century* (London: Routledge & Kegan Paul), pp. xvii–xviii.

Pound, Reginald, and Harmsworth, Geoffrey (1959) *Northcliffe* (London: Cassell).

Sanders, Andrew (2003) *Charles Dickens* (Oxford: Oxford University Press).

Schlicke, Paul (ed.) (1999) *Oxford Reader's Companion to Dickens* (Oxford: Oxford University Press).

Schudson, Michael (1995) *The Power of News* (Cambridge, Massachusetts, and London: Harvard University Press).

Schwarzbach, Fred (F. S.) (1979), *Dickens and the City* (London: The Athlone Press, University of London).

Sennett, Richard (1986) *The Fall of Public Man* (London: Faber) [first published in US and Canada, 1977].

Silvester, Christopher (ed.) (1997) *The Penguin Book of Columnists* (London: Viking).

Slater, Michael (ed.) (1994) *The Dent Uniform Edition of Dickens's Journalism*: vol. 1, *Sketches by Boz* and other early pieces 1833–39.

——— (ed.) (1996) *The Dent Uniform Edition of Dickens's Journalism*: vol. 2, The Amusements of the People and Other Papers. Reports, essays and reviews 1834–51.

——— (ed.) (1998) *The Dent Uniform Edition of Dickens's Journalism*: vol. 3, Gone Astray and Other Papers from *Household Words* 1851–59.

——— and Drew, John (eds) (2000) *The Dent Uniform Edition of Dickens's Journalism*: vol. 4, *The Uncommercial Traveller* and other papers 1859–70.

Waller, John (2005) *The Real Oliver Twist* (Cambridge: Icon Books).

Zurier, Rebecca (2006) *Picturing the City: Urban Vision and the Ashcan School* (Los Angeles and London: University of California Press).

Websites

www.usc.edu/dickens/index.html
www.dickensfellowship.org

Chapter 5

'A work and a purpose'[1]
Willa Cather's journalism

Charlotte Beyer

Willa Sibert Cather was born in 1873 in Virginia, America. Following her graduation from the University of Nebraska in 1895, she worked as a journalist for the *Nebraska State Journal* and *Lincoln Courier*, and became literary editor for the *Hesperian*. In 1896, she started editing the magazine *Home Monthly* in Pittsburgh, and later worked for the *Pittsburgh Leader*. Moving to New York in 1906 to join the staff on *McClure's Magazine*, she became managing editor in 1908. In 1911, Cather took leave of absence from *McClure's* to write fiction, although she still contributed to the magazine until the publication of her first novel, *Alexander's Bridge*, in 1912. Cather's journalistic career spanned more than 20 years. Her first novel was followed in 1913 by *O Pioneers!*, *My Ántonia* (1918), *The Professor's House* (1925), *My Mortal Enemy* (1926), *Death Comes for the Archbishop* (1927), *Shadows on the Rock* (1931) and *Sapphira and the Slave Girl* (1940), as well as short story and essay collections. Experiences of travelling in Europe, Canada and North America, as well as observations of the local and the specific, featured prominently in both her journalism and fiction. She became a well-known reviewer of drama, literature and the arts but also wrote about local life and communities. Cather died in 1947 at the age of 73.

Cather's 'submerged half'

> A reporter can write equally well about everything that is presented to his view, but a creative writer can do his best only with what lies within the range and character of his talent.
>
> (1988: 54)

With these words Willa Cather opens a discussion about the nature of talent, as it applies to two writing professions, both of which she occupied in her life, those of journalist and author. Talent is what sets the artist apart, she argues. However, as her journalistic work illustrates, writing good journalism also requires talent. The combination in Cather's journalism of talent and graft can be seen in the work explored here, as can the purpose she found within it.

This study examines what William Curtin calls 'the submerged half of the Cather canon' (1970: xvi), namely the journalism she produced before becoming an author. Critics have tended to favour her fiction instead, and as M. Catherine Downs notes: 'The scant attention paid to Cather's journalism is surprising, considering how much of it there is' (1999: 12). Recent years have witnessed a reappraisal[2] not just of Cather's journalism, but of the journalism written by other American women during this period, and their contributions to American journalism and cultural debates. The insights produced by such studies allow us, Curtin argues, to read Cather 'as a far more complex, innovative and universal artist than any ... had comprehended' (1970: xvi).

One of the challenges in a study of Cather's journalism is managing the sheer volume of her output and choosing focal points. During a career lasting from 1893, when she began writing regularly for the *Nebraska State Journal*, until she took leave from *McClure's* in 1911 to write fiction full time, Cather's journalism showcased her abilities as a writer within a number of differing areas, from social and cultural commentary to literature, art and drama reviews. Her thoughts and ideas about writing and the world are expressed in pieces discussing such wide-ranging topics as circus life, rural communities, religion, childhood and children, and education. This study brings out these diverse aspects of her journalism. As Cather's reviews of drama and literature have been discussed by critics elsewhere,[3] this study focuses instead on broader concerns in her journalism. Hence, this chapter explores selected central aspects of Cather's individual and idiosyncratic work, thereby foregrounding the ways it contributed to and energized American journalism.

Women in American journalism

Journalism was not an easy profession to break into for late nineteenth-century American women. Few professions were available for women, especially single women, as John Jakes describes (1969: 8). Women's lives were curtailed by social conventions, Jakes argues: 'Women could not vote, had only limited property rights, and were legally as much subject to their husband's authority as children today are subject to parental authority' (ibid.: 8–9). And this limited their employment opportunities, including within journalism. In their study of women in journalism, Deborah Chambers, Linda Steiner and Carole Fleming describe the profession during Cather's time as 'male-dominated and hierarchical' (2004: 15). The newsroom hierarchy meant that women journalists tended to be consigned to the 'society' pages, or as Chambers, Steiner and Fleming comment: 'a style of news writing confined to society news, reports on changing fashions and feature articles on domestic issues' (ibid.: 17). As long as women journalists conformed to those expectations of their writing, journalism offered a career possibility, they note: 'In an era when educational opportunities for women remained uneven, the relative openness of journalism meant that women who were reasonably well educated, middle class, confident and persistent could gain entry' (ibid.: 19). Journalism represented an alternative to domesticity, Downs argues: 'Writing for the newspaper or magazine was the way out of woman's sphere for many' (1999: 27).

Financial considerations played a part in Cather's journalistic ambitions.[4] Cather's choice of journalism as a professional occupation reflected her struggle to reconcile a 'calling' to write with financial necessity and the need to remain a self-reliant woman, independent of the institution of marriage and of her family. This study argues that Cather's work contributed to expanding the remit of the 'society' pages, and to challenging the perceived lesser importance and gravity of the concerns that those pages covered. Cather's journalism insists on the importance and validity of artistic endeavour, and on the integrity of those who engage with and discuss it. Her concerns were a reminder that, not so long ago, America had been a pioneering society, focused on practical concerns, where art and literature were regarded as less significant activities. Instead, Cather's journalism, in its preoccupation with art and culture, supported the developments of specifically American writing, earlier articulated in Ralph Emerson's call, in the essay 'Nature': 'Why should not we have a poetry and philosophy of insight and not of tradition, and a religion by revelation ... there are new lands, new men, new thoughts' (1836/2006: 1,582).

The notion of 'separate spheres' for the genders remained pervasive in American society during the period of the late nineteenth century. This ideology affected the working conditions of women journalists employed by newspapers, but also impacted, directly and indirectly, on how and what women journalists could write, as Downs comments: 'The concept of separate spheres for the genders was outdated but it still influenced what Cather could say in her public writings' (1999: 14). The pressure to conform led Cather to adopt a series of pseudonyms as a coping strategy, which allowed her to write more freely, and to experiment with a number of different 'observers', or perspectives, in her journalism. Listing the pseudonyms Cather used, Hermione Lee observes that: 'The number of her bylines (Helen Delay, John Esten, Charles Douglass, George Overing, Clara Wood Shipman, Gilberta S.Whittle, W. Bert Foster, Henry Nicklemann) shows how much these pseudonyms were common practice in American journalism' (1997: 48). The use of pseudonyms could be seen as a mechanism to shield herself from criticism, but also allowed Cather to explore discursive constructions of gender and perspective in journalism. It was, Downs argues, a strategy 'to articulate and explore her world, and to sell her columns' (1999: 66). This willingness to experiment shows an element of flexibility in her understanding of the role of a journalist, and the nature of journalistic writing, as fluid and open to definition and redefinition through differing perspectives.[5]

The profession of journalism was undergoing crucial changes during the latter part of the nineteenth century, as Phyllis Frus notes (1994: 68), and was becoming an influential force in society: 'Journalism seemed to shape the face of America' (Downs 1999: 121). Managing these changing conditions and expectations, Cather had to balance her ambition and drive to become successful in the profession, with the need to retain her professional and artistic integrity. She had a professional attitude to her work, and whilst she was well connected, she also possessed a significant degree of self-reliance. According to Lee, Cather's gestures of non-conformity in her personal life were a sign of her rebellion against the restrictions placed upon women and 'symptoms of a furious resistance to parochial narrowness and ... genteel conventions' (1997: 38). This resistance to conformity is evident in her journalism.

Literature and journalism

Despite her success, Cather often appeared modest, or pragmatic, about her journalistic achievements. This could be because she, according to Curtin, 'made an absolute distinction between her serious writing ... and the journalistic stint, the hundreds of thousands of words that she had to write to keep afloat' (1970: xiv). It is, however, apparent to the reader that, her own ambivalence aside, Cather applied craft as well as graft to her journalism. This view reflects Curtin's point that her journalism contains 'a glittering array of stories and articles and criticism, the products of conscientious craft' (ibid.). Such commitment from Cather towards her material would certainly seem to contradict the ambivalence she may have felt about her journalistic writing.

However, studies of Cather's journalism often essentially maintain the link to her literary oeuvre as a way of reading her journalism and of validating that activity. Commenting on her journalistic writings, Curtin maintains:

> Undeniably their chief interest to the general reader and their peculiar value to the scholar reside in their manifold and crucial connections with her later work and the unparalleled insight they afford into the process by which a gifted writer becomes a great artist.
>
> (Ibid.: xv)

In her discussion of O'Brien's biography of Cather, Downs notes that it 'does not address the effect of Cather's journalism on her prose, [but] believes Cather's years as a journalist were years of becoming' (1999: 12).[6] However, comparative studies of her journalism and fiction may involve problematic notions of 'value' in the evaluation of her work. In her discussion of 'literary journalism', Frus examines the relationship between journalism and fiction (1994: x), questioning the distinctions between 'high' and 'low' forms that describe and evaluate different kinds of writing in the academe (ibid.: xi).[7] Cather herself may well have been affected by those same standards Frus critiques and the hierarchical categories they inscribe, seeing her own work in those terms, and judging her journalism accordingly as of 'lesser' value. This study considers Cather's journalism as a separate body of work, although in a different context, as Downs demonstrates, it would be worthwhile examining 'what being a woman in an office, writing journalism, editing journalism, did to Willa Cather the author' (1999: 12).

Writing 'personal' journalism

What kind of journalism did Willa Cather write? Her style varied considerably, depending on context, but she drew boundaries to protect her professional integrity.

In 1896, Cather stated her position on the issue of 'personal journalism' at the Nebraska State Press Association conference, in a speech called 'How to Make a Newspaper Interesting'. She is reported to have said: 'The newspaper should be personal' (ibid.: 29). Downs concludes that in her writing for both the *Nebraska State Journal* and the *Journal*: 'Cather had the freedom to write on many subjects, and she expressed her modernity and freedom from party control by doing so. Cather would have known what personal journalism meant and what past practices had been' (ibid.).

In her journalism, Cather may have aimed at attaining objectivity as the ideal, Sawaya argues, but she nonetheless tended towards an individualist response (2004: 101). Broadly speaking, Cather's journalism could not be considered 'yellow journalism'. This style is defined by Chambers, Steiner and Fleming as 'new and emotional [and] used to appeal to a new market of unsophisticated readers', but which, however, examined matters of 'political affairs and public welfare' (2004: 20). This opinion echoes Lee: '[Cather's] interests were not political or reformist' (1997: 65), although Downs appears to differ, calling Cather's article on Brownville – discussed later in this chapter – a 'yellow' story (1999: 92). Rather than proving or disproving a particular point about Cather's journalism, these discussions perhaps illustrate the differences in critical opinion regarding how notions of 'political', 'yellow', 'emotional', 'personal' might be defined and applied.

During Cather's time, Downs explains, the role of the journalist had changed, and newspapers had generally become more independent of party politics (1999: 29). This trend benefited Cather's approach to 'personal' journalism, which involved adopting an individualized response, while, as Sawaya notes, struggling to maintain 'a notion of professional objectivity and impersonality' (2004: 81). In some ways the strategies Cather used mirrored those of 'literary journalism', as Norman Sims explains: 'Literary journalists write narratives focused on everyday events that bring out hidden patterns of community life [and] can reveal the structures and strains of real life' (1995: 3). This engagement is an important aspect of Cather's critical and journalistic work according to Stephen Tennant, who argues that 'her critical writing would have been powerless without the great range of her sympathies ... The wealth of her human warmth of feeling has been one of the great factors in the popularity of her books' (1988: viii).

Cather probed the meanings and purposes of 'personal' journalism. In her column, As You Like It, while discussing, amongst other things, the artist's role,[8] Cather rejects journalism which gets too 'personal', concluding: 'A paper's main object is to look out for itself, and not to mutilate people's feelings' (Curtin 1970: 123).[9] 'Personal', to her, did not equate to cruel or crude; however, it is clear she used differing positions in her journalism, as she experimented with perspectives, and with the possibilities that arose from using differing perspectives or 'observers'.

Cather's social and cultural critique

Cather's journalism reflected her active engagement with, and critique of, American society and culture, and her article 'Pittsburgh's Mulberry Street' (Curtin 1970: 870–4)[10] is an example of this. The title, as Curtin points out, contains a reference to Jacob A. Riis, a Danish-American journalist and reformer,[11] whose book *How the Other Half Lives* (1890) depicted life in New York slums (ibid.: 869).[12] Cather had reviewed Riis's sequel, *Out of Mulberry Street* (1898), Curtin notes, and praised his journalism (ibid.: 869). In her own article, Cather discloses that such sordid slums and depressing scenes can be found in Pittsburgh, where she was based at the time, and were not simply a big-city phenomenon. Cather writes under the guise of a male pseudonym in this article,[13] using the strategy to enable her to write about a deprived neighbourhood and its characters. She depicts an illegal poultry business as a means of reflecting on social deprivation and the costs to humans and animals (ibid.: 870). This allowed her Pittsburgh readers to see that 'Mulberry Street' was right under their noses, not someone else's problem.

Elsewhere, too, Cather's work reflects her social consciousness. As she writes in the article 'Under the White Tents', this time using her own name, about the world of circus women: 'One half the world never knows how remarkably like itself the other half is till it gets down and looks at it' (ibid.: 102).[14] Cather sets out to dispel the damaging notion that the circus represents a challenge to societal respectability, and that circus women are a threat to the domestic feminine ideal. She achieves this by exposing her own observer's assumptions, and inviting the reader to question them. Describing one of the circus women reading a recently published novel (ibid.: 101), she uses the observer's surprise at seeing the woman engaged in this activity as a means of exposing her unacknowledged prejudices about circus women and the environment they inhabit. Cather's conclusion stresses this may serve as a reminder 'that both halves came out of Eden originally, and both have wandered very far therefrom, and now of the two "Heavenly Twins" it is very hard to tell which is the less heavenly' (ibid.: 102). Cather's use of the religious motif reminds the reader of the framework of thought underpinning her position.

Cather's journalism showed readers that although Thomas Jefferson, in the 1776 Declaration of Independence, stated the values of 'life, liberty, and the pursuit of happiness' (2003: 728) as central to American experience, individuals and communities were sometimes in danger of being excluded by those very terms. In the article 'An Old River Metropolis',[15] Cather addresses these issues by analysing the plight of 'forgotten' places and individuals in her description of a visit to Brownville, a small town in south-eastern Nebraska. She deplores the material and spiritual decay in the town resulting from lacking 'a work and a purpose',[16] but also reminds the reader of the now forgotten role this place once played in American regional history: 'There are few people who know anything about the sleepy little town on the Missouri where the beginnings of Nebraska history were made' (Curtin 1970: 104).[17] Brownville has sadly become a backwater, left behind by the mainstream: 'Everything in Brownville is tired' (ibid.). Cather uses words such as 'tired', 'spiritless', 'creeps', 'rest', of the freight and the engineer himself, to illustrate this quiet despair and encourage the reader's involvement.

The key to the decay of Brownville, Cather suggests, is the spiritual apathy characterizing the place. One church is described with the terms 'ruin' and 'neglect'; another with the word 'decay', illustrated by the representation of a family of mice living in the church organ (ibid.: 107–8). The article reflects Cather's concern with exploring alternative ways of seeing and writing about history, away from official accounts of history and narratives about 'progress'. Such attention to the specifics of 'place' is especially important in America, Cather suggests, because the country does not have a long written history behind it:

> A country cares very little about its early history and traditions until it has had a great many trials and disappointments … until it settles down … then it has time to look back [and] to appreciate the talent and worth that it overlooked or pushed aside in its frenzied hurry to be great.
>
> (Ibid.: 103–4)

The role of religion

Religion is a recurring topic in Cather's writing, Curtin argues (ibid.: 4). An early series of columns by Cather, called One Way of Putting It, uses perspective in an interesting way, characteristic of Cather, to explore the subject and experience of religion. In the pieces referred to here, Cather uses an 'observer figure' positioned on the margins of unfolding events; is interested in individuals within communities and familial relations; and uses 'snapshots' to create a plurality of dimensions. Information regarding her personal opinion or faith is withheld to allow the reporting to unfold.[18] She zooms in on individual destinies in a way that foregrounds the role of language and her use of an observer in constructing characters. The discursive construction of religious engagement creates a link between feeling and corporeal reality: 'This enthusiasm of hers is a sort of afterglow that lights up her worn face where other fires have burned themselves out' (ibid.: 7).[19]

Foregrounding the nuances of words such as 'saved' and 'lost', Cather concludes that the qualities associated with such terms are not related to gender, education or class. The 'heavy-featured, coarse-looking man' is 'saved' (ibid.), whereas the 'professor of language … the product of life and development of intellect' is 'lost'. The 'coarse' man is, as Cather puts it, '"saved" not by knowledge, or capacity or righteousness, but by enthusiasm'. Vigour and faith drive humans forward towards productive creative expression: 'the men who know all about poetry but never write a line … lost eternally because of their frozen souls'. Likewise, Cather's exploration of a religious experience in a black church at Christmas time encourages the reader to empathize across racial, gender and faith divides (ibid.: 8).[20] Such divides, Cather shows, can be challenged by journalism and art.

Education and knowledge

In a piece featured in her column Utterly Irrelevant, Cather deplores the privileging of scientific knowledge over art, and definitions of what constitutes 'knowledge'. Privileging science is wrong, she argues, because: 'All the higher achievements of man, art, poetry, music, the drama, are the work of the creative mind; all the lower achievements, which minister only to the comforts of the body, are the work of the mathematical mind' (ibid.: 112).[21] Cather is resistant to what Josephine Donovan calls the 'scientific paradigm' because, Donovan explains, 'the pretensions to universality of scientific knowledge and its generalizing "mathematizing" character meant that differences and particularities were erased' (1989: 13). She calls for education that values art and emotional intelligence for both genders. Her journalism poses a series of rhetorical questions which have the effect of challenging the reader to consider their own position: 'Will there ever be a generation of teachers who will teach men how to feel and see?' (Curtin 1970: 113–14). Cather favours a less elitist approach to teaching the arts, and argues it should include 'the children of the people, the children who will probably be bound close to their workbench or plow all their lives' (ibid.: 113).

The education and reading habits of children attracted Cather's interest, a point also noted by Downs (1999: 75). In her column Observations, Cather wrote about the efforts to accommodate children as consumers of literature, and specifically as a readership group in public libraries. Cather expresses her concern about the 'dumbing down' of writing that she observed as resulting from these initiatives: 'The enthusiastic librarians have conceived a gigantic plan of reducing all literature to the kindergarten dimension' (Curtin 1970: 853).[22] This process of omission denies children essential experiences and insights, Cather argues: 'To keep from the child the knowledge that the world is a hard place to live in, and that he will have to do many difficult and distasteful things before he gets through with it, is as disastrous as to keep him out of the reach of those childish diseases which are ten times as dangerous if contracted when he is older' (ibid.: 853).

Children and childhood

In Cather's journalism, discussions of children and childhood sometimes act as vehicles for social and cultural critique. In parts of her vignette 'One Way of Putting It' and 'The Hotel Child' (ibid.: 874),[23] the figure of 'the child' is portrayed as vulnerable, an 'other' patronized by adults, but also strangely feared. The observer in the pieces, on the other hand, appears to empathize, describing the plight of children sympathetically but without being overly sentimental (ibid.: 8–9).[24] Cather's observer describes seeing a young girl, standing outside the toyshop window with a friend, gazing longingly at a doll she yearns to have. In portraying the young girl's vernacular speech, Cather makes the child's emotional response 'real' to the reader.[25]

The treatment of children by adults is also the subject of 'The Hotel Child'. This article, as Curtin notes, was signed by Cather herself, and explores the phenomenon of 'the hotel-bred child' (ibid.: 874).[26] Cather uses the setting of 'the hotel' to scrutinize the concept of 'home', questioning the foundations of 'family' when removed from that locale, associated with images of 'the American Dream' and popular cultural mythology since J. Hector St John de Crèvecoeur's *Letters From an American Farmer*.[27] The 'hotel child' is an inconvenience to adults: 'his mere existence is denounced, resented, concealed and even denied' (ibid.: 875).

However, Cather's observer suggests, the human imagination will always provide an outlet and an escape: 'their fanciful powers thrive under their imprisonment' (ibid.). The use of the word 'imprisonment' merits attention because of its ambiguity. 'Imprisonment' suggests that being a child equals being a criminal who is justly punished for misdemeanours. On the other hand, it implies that the child is innocent but punished, imprisoned, purely for being a child. Cather's use of language foregrounds the double standard, making the reader question the commitment of American society to its young and its vulnerable, and query the values that support childrearing and education, and society's commitment to individual fulfilment.

In an article in her column As You Like It, Cather addresses a question central to working women then and now – how to reconcile the need to work and a calling towards art with caring for children.[28] The article describes Madame Réjane who has come to America to perform, but has had to leave behind her four-year-old son whilst bringing her older daughter.[29] Cather represents Réjane as a loving maternal woman, forced by the circumstances dictated by her art to be parted from her young child for a long period of time. Her exploration of this dilemma deflects negative judgement passed on Réjane's mothering, and draws attention to the validity of women's need for 'a work and a purpose': 'It is almost as much to Madame Réjane's credit that she is so good a mother as that she is so great an artist' (ibid.: 200). Cather foregrounds the role of language in creating and promoting positive images of working (artistic) mothers: 'There is one hour in the day when the great French actress Madame Réjane is not at home to anyone … Then she is busy writing letters to a little yellow-haired boy who roams dolefully about his lonely nursery over in Paris' (ibid.: 199).

Writing and art as a vocation

This study argues that Cather's journalism was driven by a need for direction in, and engagement with, the world through the medium of journalism and language. Writing, to use Cather's own phrase, had to have 'a work and a purpose'; furthermore, if language and writers were deprived of fluidity and energy, stagnation might result, a destructive condition that Cather explored, as we have seen, in her article on Brownville. Cather was inspired by a work ethic which was specifically 'American', according to Downs: 'America's work ethic ... said that if one worked hard enough, starting at the bottom, one could make it to the top. Cather expressed her admiration for this ethic throughout her journalistic career' (1999: 35).

This wholehearted involvement was also an element of professional and artistic activity which she recognized in the work of others, as is evident in her reviews and articles. In her column The Passing Show, Cather describes the writer's effort towards expression as a journey, the purpose of which is truth itself and she quotes Shakespeare's *King Lear*: 'Thy truth then be thy dower' (Slote 1966: 417)[30] – writing, in other words, offers its own reward simply through the act of articulating a vision through words. Cather's view of the centrality of language itself in the making of art is crucial, and reflects the consciously crafted expression of her own written work: 'Art is not thought or emotion, but expression, expression, expression' (ibid.).

In a regular column, Utterly Irrelevant, Cather highlights the importance of immediacy in the writer's relationship with language and readership and audience. In discussing the critic's position in timing the writing of reviews, she argues that the critic 'must take his impression as he gets it and rush it upon paper. He must take it before it becomes an opinion or freezes into a deduction; while it is an emotion, a feeling, imperfect and half formed perhaps, but living' (ibid.: 258).[31] To Cather, art should be taken seriously, because it mattered in the world at large. She was determined to give her best in her writing, Downs argues, and to demonstrate to readers what was involved: 'Cather used her newspaper pulpit to teach her readers just how hard writing was – to professionalize it and make it into a career which one earned by study and hard work' (1999: 60).

Conclusion: 'be wide awake and not afraid to work'

Cather's journalism insisted on the validity of subjective perspectives, as she herself embodied what Lee calls 'a refusal to be enlisted' (1997: 12). She did this even though by the late nineteenth century an increasingly money-orientated newspaper environment meant that 'fading rapidly then was the model of "personal journalism", in which the editor and his experience, insights, and intellect infused the newspaper with distinctive character and voice'.[32] Cather's answer was to attempt to redefine or reinvent herself in response to these pressures within the profession, but ultimately to leave it behind, although writing remained her 'work and purpose'.

Cather did not limit herself to one particular area of journalism, but used her talent and skill for writing to illuminate many diverse areas of American life, and to create debate, reflecting de Crèvecoeur's earlier assertion that: 'The American is a new man, who acts upon new principles; he must therefore entertain new ideas and form new opinions' (2003: 660). It is clear from her references to the significance of religion that her journalism can be seen as existing within, and influenced

by, the parameters of her beliefs. This idea echoes Slote: 'She linked art and religion, but art that praised by its own being, and religion that was neither stiff-
necked nor solemn' (1966: 45).

Cather often called for a recognition of the role of writing and the arts in shaping
American life. In an interview, she had the following reflections to offer, which also
relate to her own time as a journalist: 'There are many young people who like good
literature and go to work on a magazine or newspaper with the idea of reforming it
and showing it what to print ... They must be wide awake, adaptable and not
afraid to work' (ibid.: 452). This last quotation in many ways sums up Willa
Cather's unique approach to journalism.

Notes

1 The phrase is Cather's, taken from 'Cather', in Curtin, W. (ed.) (1970) p. 106.
2 See Curtin (1970), Slote (1966), Downs (1999), Frus (1994) and Lee (1997).
3 Slote (1966). See also Stout, Janis P. (1999) 'Willa Cather's early journalism: gender,
   performance, and the "manly battle yarn"', *Arizona Quarterly*, 1999, 55/3: 51–82.
4 According to Downs, '[Cather's] preoccupation with the money theme stems from her
   employment ... she was in her office, performing an activity that was not well-defined
   for a woman – earning money, holding power' (1999: 15).
5 Downs (ibid.) discusses Cather's use of pseudonyms and the differing journalistic
   discourses that resulted, and the relevance of these for Cather's development of narrative perspective in her fiction.
6 Downs refers to O'Brien, S. (1987) *Willa Cather: The Emerging Voice* (New York: Oxford
   University Press).
7 Frus's study refers to 'texts by canonical American writers who have published journalism as well as fiction' (1994: x).
8 See Curtin (ed.) (1970) p. 978.
9 *Nebraska State Journal*, 16 December 1894, p. 13.
10 *Pittsburgh Gazette*, 8 December 1901, p. 5.
11 www.bartleby.com/people/Riis–Jac.html, accessed on 23 October 2006.
12 Riis's book, according to Downs, 'made his horror and disgust at the lives of "the other
   half" into good copy, an income, and ultimately, laws' (1999: 78).
13 Henry Nicklemann; the name Cather uses in 'Pittsburgh's Mulberry Street', according
   to Curtin (see 1970: footnote 15, p. 870).
14 *Nebraska State Journal*, 27 May 1894, p. 13.
15 *Nebraska State Journal*, 12 August 1894, p. 13.
16 This article contains the phrase 'a work and a purpose' which is used in the title of this
   chapter.
17 In her discussion of the article, Downs focuses on what she perceives as Cather's manip-
   ulation of fact to get a good story, by 'shocking readers' (1999: 53).
18 Curtin notes: 'Herself a Protestant in a predominantly Protestant city, Cather seems
   equally at home in the Catholic cathedral, under a Salvation Army tent, in the Negro
   church, and at a service at the Nebraska State Penitentiary' (1970: 4–5).
19 *Nebraska State Journal*, 5 November 1893, p. 13.
20 Ibid., 17 December 1893, p. 17.
21 Ibid., 14 October 1894, p. 13.
22 *The Courier*, 17 August 1901, pp. 2–3.
23 *Pittsburgh Gazette*, 10 August 1902, p. 4.
24 *Nebraska State Journal*, 17 December 1893, p. 17.

25 Downs (1999: 71) notes 'the age's fascination with childhood ... the moment when imagination was especially alive and when the human creature's play was innocent'.
26 F. Scott Fitzgerald published a short story in 1931 entitled 'The Hotel Child' (see Websites).
27 Baym et al. (2003) p. 660.
28 *Nebraska State Journal*, 21 April 1895, p. 13.
29 Cather's 'Portrayal of Réjane and the problems for women of reconciling career and family' is also discussed by Slote (1966: 70).
30 *Nebraska State Journal*, 1 March 1896, p. 9.
31 *Nebraska State Journal*, 21 October 1894, p. 13.
32 Campbell, W. J., CBS News, 12 October 2006.

References

Baym, N. et al. (eds) (2003) *The Norton Anthology of American Literature*, vol. A, sixth edition (London: W. W. Norton & Company).

Campbell, N. and Kean, A. (1997) *American Cultural Studies: An Introduction to American Culture* (London: Routledge).

Cather, W. (1922) 'The novel démeublé', in Cather, W. (1988) *On Writing: Critical Studies on Writing as an Art* (Lincoln: University of Nebraska Press), pp. 33–43.

—— (1925) 'The best stories of Sarah Orne Jewett', in Cather, W. (1988) *On Writing: Critical Studies on Writing as an Art* (Lincoln: University of Nebraska Press), pp. 47–59.

—— (1988) *On Writing: Critical Studies on Writing as an Art* (Lincoln: University of Nebraska Press).

—— (1988a) *Not Under Forty* (Lincoln: University of Nebraska Press).

Chambers, D., Steiner, L. and Fleming, C. (2004) *Women and Journalism* (London: Routledge).

Crèvecoeur, J. Hector St John de (1782) *Letters from an American Farmer*, in Baym, N. et al. (eds) (2003) *The Norton Anthology of American Literature*, vol. A, sixth edition (London: W. W. Norton & Company), pp. 657–82.

Curtin, W. M. (ed.) (1970) *The World and the Parish: Willa Cather's Articles and Reviews, 1893–1902* (Lincoln: University of Nebraska Press).

Donovan, J. (1989) *After the Fall: The Demeter-Persephone Myth in Wharton, Cather, and Glasgow* (University Park: Pennsylvania State University Press).

Downs, M. C. (1999) *Becoming Modern: Willa Cather's Journalism* (Selinsgrove: Susquehanna University Press).

Emerson, R. (1836) 'Nature', in Lauter, P. et al. (eds) (2006) *The Heath Anthology of American Literature*, vol. B, edition 5 (New York: Houghton Mifflin Company), pp. 1582–609.

Frus, P. (1994) *The Politics and Poetics of Journalistic Narrative: The Timely and the Timeless* (New York: Cambridge University Press).

Hockett, E. M. (1966) 'The vision of a successful fiction writer', *Lincoln Daily Star*, October 1915, in Slote, B. (ed.) (1966) *The Kingdom of Art: Willa Cather's First Principles and Critical Statements, 1893–96* (Lincoln: University of Nebraska Press), pp. 450–2.

Jakes, J. (1969) *Great Women Reporters* (New York: G. P. Putnam's Sons).

Jefferson, T. (1776) 'The declaration of independence', in Baym, N. et al. (eds) (2003) *The Norton Anthology of American Literature*, vol. A, sixth edition (London: W. W. Norton & Company), pp. 726–32.

Lauter, P. et al. (eds) (2006) *The Heath Anthology of American Literature*, vol. B, edition 5 (New York: Houghton Mifflin Company).

Lee, H. (1997) *Willa Cather: A Life Saved Up* (London: Virago Press).

Sawaya, F. (2004), *Modern Women, Modern Work: Domesticity, Professionalism, and American Writing, 1890–1950* (Philadelphia: University of Philadelphia Press).

Sims, N. and Kramer, M. (eds) (1995) *Literary Journalism: A New Collection of the Best American Non-fiction* (New York: Ballantine Books).

Slote, B. (ed.) (1966) *The Kingdom of Art: Willa Cather's First Principles and Critical Statements, 1893–96* (Lincoln: University of Nebraska Press).

Tennant, S. (1988) 'The room beyond: a foreword on Willa Cather', in Cather, *On Writing: Critical Studies on Writing as an Art* (Lincoln: University of Nebraska Press), pp. v–xxiv.

Websites

The Willa Cather Archive. Available online at www.cather.unl.edu/life/chronology.html, accessed on 11 November 2006.

The Columbia Encyclopedia, sixth edition, 2001–5. Available online at www.bartleby.com/people/Riis-Jac.html, accessed on 23 October 2006.

Campbell, W. J. (2006) 'On lessons for American journalism from another tumultuous time', CBS News, 12 October 2006. Available online at www.cbsnews.com/blogs/2006/10/12/publiceye/entry2086287.shtml, accessed on 13 October 2006.

Scott Fitzgerald, F. (1931) 'The Hotel Child', *Saturday Evening Post*, 31 January 1931. Available online at www.gutenberg.net.au/fsf/THE%20HOTEL%20CHILD.txt, accessed on 15 Ocotber 2006.

Chapter 6

'The dangerous third martini'

Graham Greene, libel and literary journalism in 1930s Britain[1]

David Finkelstein

Graham Greene was born on 2 October 1904 at St John's, Berkhamsted, Hertfordshire, to Charles Henry Greene, teacher, and Marion Raymond, a distant relative of Robert Louis Stevenson. Educated at Berkhamsted School, where his father was headmaster, he went on to study history at Balliol College, Oxford. There he met and fell in love with Vivienne (later Vivien) Dayrell-Browning, whom he married in 1927. They were to have two children before separating after the end of the Second World War. On graduating in 1925 with a second-class degree in history, Greene began a career as a journalist, starting as an unpaid sub-editor at the *Nottingham Journal*, later moving to London and sub-editing at *The Times*, then working as book and film critic for the *Spectator*, *The Times*, *Sight and Sound* and other publications. He published his first novel, *The Man Within*, in June 1929. A historical romance set on the Sussex coast in the early 1800s, the swashbuckling work proved a commercial success. It was followed by two less well received works in similar vein. In 1932, however, Greene produced *Stamboul Train*, a narrative of political intrigue set on the Orient Express. Its critical success would start Greene on a peripatetic literary journey that lasted until his death in 1991, where powerful pieces of film criticism, book reviews, non-fiction and literary journalism – *Journeys Without Maps* (1936), chronicling a journey through Liberia; *The Lawless Roads* (1939) set in Mexico; *Getting to Know the General* (1985) on the Panamanian general Omar Torrijos – were overshadowed by an impressive number of novels including *Brighton Rock* (1938), *The Power and the Glory* (1940), *The Heart of the Matter* (1948), *The End of the Affair* (1951), *Our Man in Havana* (1958), *Travels with my Aunt* (1969) and *The Honorary Consul* (1973). In all Greene was to produce more than two dozen novels, numerous plays, essays and short stories, two volumes of autobiography, a history of drama and a literary biography of the poet Lord Rochester. He was also to engage actively, though with some feelings of ambiguity, in screenwriting, adapting several of his works for the cinema, including *Brighton Rock* (1947), *The Fallen Idol* (1948), *The Third Man* (1949) and *The Comedians* (1967). From the 1960s onwards he based himself in Antibes, but spent the last year of his life in the small village of Corseaux, near Vevey, Switzerland, where he died on 3 April 1991.

Greene – the forgotten film critic

When Graham Greene died aged 87 in 1991, his obituaries declared him one of the greatest writers of the twentieth century, with works such as *The Honorary Consul, Our Man in Havana* and *The Third Man* acknowledged as classics. Less recognized was his early career as an influential film critic between 1928 and 1941, writing for *The Times*, the *Spectator, Sight and Sound* and the short-lived literary journal *Night and Day*, among others. Greene was one of the finest film critics of his generation, described by the documentary film-maker John Grierson as 'the best critic we ever had' (quoted in Sherry 1989: 588). His engagement with film was for a time as complete and as thorough as could be expected of someone who had grown up entranced by the silent movies shown at his local cinema. As Basil Wright, film-maker and fellow film critic put it, Greene had been born 'a child of the film age', his teenage years in particular dominated by frequent visits to cinemas in his home town of Berkhamsted (Wright 1974: 94).

Greene's earliest film memory was of attending a screening of Anthony Hope's *Sophy of Kravonia* in Brighton at the age of 12, later taking in work by D. W. Griffith, Von Stroheim and Charlie Chaplin (Parkinson 1993: xii–xiii). Absorbing the language of film from such viewings, and reading journals for insights into cinematic structures, narrative conventions, camera angle and cutting effects, left Greene feeling, as one commentator has noted, 'destined to produce worthwhile literature' (ibid.: xv). After taking his degree at Oxford in 1925, he moved into journalism work, sub-editing first on the *Nottingham Journal* and then at *The Times*, where he began contributing short film reviews to the Entertainments section. He would leave this as his writing career developed, only to return seriously to film criticism when he took on the role of chief critic for the *Spectator* in 1935. 'The idea of reviewing films came to me at a cocktail party after the dangerous third martini,' he wrote, tongue-in-cheek, many years later, adding his output eventually covered 'more than four hundred films – and I suppose there would have been many, many more if I had not suffered during the same period from other obsessions …' (Greene 1980: 58–9).

Over the next six years, in work for the *Spectator, Sight and Sound*, and later for the journal *Night and Day*, Greene produced serious, insightful and rigorous appraisals of contemporary film releases. Dilys Powell, the legendary *Sunday Times* reviewer, would later comment that Greene's work was inspiring and also enviable:

> I well remember when I was beginning as a film critic reading with the most passionate envy the writings of Graham Greene in the *Spectator* and various other periodicals; it struck me that this was the kind of thing that film criticism should be … One was terribly grateful that somebody of his literary genius should care so much and with such deep and original feeling about a medium that was not literary, which is partly visual and partly literary.
>
> (Quoted in Parkinson 1993: xx)

Greene was preoccupied with film's power as entertainment: though not against popular culture, he was wary of works that hid ideological agendas beneath a thin veneer of populist, historical truth. Not for him the heavily adulterated film biographies of Rhodes, Pasteur, Zola, Parnell and others that passed for 'respectable' depictions of contemporary history. Rather, treating cinema's populism 'as a virtue', Greene saw value and honesty in films whose main aim was *precisely* pure entertainment. 'I preferred the westerns, the crime films, the farces, the frankly commercial' (Greene 1980: 47). Or, as he would put it, while film as a representative of ideological and political interests needed to be treated carefully, the power of mass culture films to move and bind audiences together was something worthy of appreciation: 'I admire a film like *Song of Ceylon* more perhaps than anything else I've seen on the screen, but I would rather see the public shouting and hissing in the sixpenny seats' (quoted in Adamson 1990: 46).

Greene was not the only critic at the time to acknowledge the potential of films to move individuals emotionally, to entertain as well as convey aesthetic truths. As novelist and essayist Elizabeth Bowen commented, like many she returned time and again to watch movies for particular reasons: 'I slough off my preoccupations there … I judge the film as I judge the bottle of wine in its relation to myself, by what it does to me' (Davy 1938: 205, 207). Immersion and sensation, as poet Louis MacNeice agreed, were key to a film's power and critics' reactions to it:

> the stars would return and the huge Cupid's bows of their mouths would swallow up everybody's troubles – there were no more offices or factories or shops, no more bosses or foremen, no more unemployment and no more employment, no more danger of disease or babies, nothing but bliss in a celluloid world where the roses were always red and the Danube is always blue.
>
> (MacNeice 1965: 138)

Immersed as he was in aesthetic judgements, Greene had little time or sympathy for those who merely paraphrased and rewrote studio handouts. Of his contemporaries, 'the simpering of Sydney Carroll [*Sunday Times* critic] and the snobbery of C. A. [Caroline Alice] Lejeune [film critic for the *Observer* from 1928–60] incurred his special wrath' (Parkinson 1993: xxi). He believed it was not the job of a critic to act as a publicity agent for film studios or to praise films for upholding contemporary moral values; more to the point, reviewers had a duty to judge and discuss films based on their innate strengths and weaknesses. As Greene commented: 'What I object to is the idea that it is the *critic's* business to assist films to fulfil a social function. The critic's business should be confined to the art' (ibid.: 405). Greene's most positive reviews in this sense invariably drew attention to the art of the film-maker, the sharpness of focus and sophisticated use of cinematic techniques such as flashbacks, time dissolution, and the taut but evocative dialogue found in the best films he viewed during his time as a critic.

Equally prevalent, though, were trenchant commentaries on US studio practices and the 'star' system, of Hollywood studios and their production-line system of film making, and of the ethics on display in popular film. He could be blunt about quality: in his first eleven months as *Spectator* critic, for example, Greene later wrote that from the countless films he sat through, 'only 13 conveyed any kind of aesthetic experience and another 48 were reasonably entertaining: the other 63 films were trash' (ibid.: 108). As Philip French commented later, such uncompromising views as developed in Greene's film columns were 'the most ferocious I've ever come across' (ibid.: xxiv), while Neville Braybrooke complained that the excesses of Greene's film criticism amounted to 'slickness and cruelty' (ibid.: xxiv). In 1937, however, Greene's trenchancy caught up with him when a short review about a child star brought on damaging litigation and the closure of an emerging London literary periodical.

The child star

The child star in question was Shirley Temple, and the story of how and why she sued Graham Greene for libel highlights how far a Hollywood studio was prepared to go to protect the reputation of its most valuable commodity. It is also a salutary example of what happens when literary journalists cross the line between fair comment and libel, and an early example of the entanglement between media practices and moneyed interests. To understand the issues at stake, it is useful to recap Temple's early film career and examine the film that drew Greene into trouble.

Shirley Temple was born in 1928 in Santa Monica, USA, a stone's throw from the big Hollywood studios that dominated the area. Her showbiz training started early when she was enrolled at Mrs Meglin's Dance Studio at the age of three. Her talent was to take her to the top of the entertainment business in an extraordinary life that spanned several careers as movie and television star, politician and diplomat. Shirley Temple made her film debut in 1931 in a kiddie parody of *The Front Page* called *The Runt Page*, produced by the Educational Films Corporation, a firm that, despite its name, specialized in low-budget, 'skid-row' comedies. The firm's dubious exploitation of children began at the audition, where Shirley was required, along with other wannabe child actors, to undress and act coquettishly: 'We all ran around in our panties ... I had to stand in front of the camera ... and smile, and wink my eye, and shake my shoulder two or three times' (Edwards 1988: 33). In the following year, Temple starred in a series of eight one-reel shorts ('Baby Burlesks') that parodied contemporary cinema themes, from the western (*Pie Covered Wagon*) to boxing (*The Kid's Last Fight*) and exotic adventure films (*Kid 'in' Africa*).

More films followed, as well as transfers to major studios, first to Paramount and then to Twentieth Century Fox. Shirley's film image also shifted from mocking, worldly comedienne to sprightly, virtuous, self-confident innocent. Her appeal, particularly during the low public mood of the US Depression of the Thirties, was captured by President F. D. Roosevelt when he wrote: 'it is a splendid thing that for just 15 cents, an American can go to a movie and look at the smiling face of a baby and forget his troubles' (Edwards 1988: 76). Not all agreed: her 1934 picture *Baby Take a Bow* was banned in Nazi Germany where the official legal gazette, *Reichsanzeiger*, complained that it was full of gangsters and guns. It is worth noting, however, that in the same year, Leni Riefenstahl's documentary *Triumph of the Will* received rave reviews from the same journal. Also that year, the sheet music of 'The Good Ship Lollipop', from the Temple movie *Bright Eyes*, sold 400,000 copies, smashing the record previously held by Bing Crosby.

In 1935, a national juvenile survey of girls rated Shirley Temple top of an 'I-want-to-be' list. (Second and third places went to Amelia Earhart and Mrs Eleanor Roosevelt.) By 1936, Shirley Temple had, according to *Time* magazine, become the world's 'most photographed person', featuring in an average of 20 mass-media journals per day. She was the mascot to the Chilean Navy, a captain of the Texas Rangers, and her fan club base numbered in the hundreds of thousands, including the Kiddies Club of England, whose 165,000 members had pledged themselves to 'imitate' her 'character, conduct and manners' (Anon., 'Peewee's Progress', 1936: 37).

She had also become Twentieth Century Fox's most valuable commodity. Of Fox's $8,000,000 corporate profit that year, almost 90 per cent was due to earnings from Temple's last four movies. Her annual salary during this time reflected her status as Hollywood's biggest earner. In 1937, while Fox's studio head Darryl F. Zanuck was paid an annual salary of $265,000, and MGM's top three stars Clark Gable, Greta Garbo and Spencer Tracy drew $272,000, $270,000 and $212,000 respectively, Temple was pulling in $307,014 (Ginger Rogers could only manage $208,767, James Cagney $243,000 and Errol Flynn a paltry $181,333) (Edwards 1988: 93–4).

Wee Willie Winkie

Temple's career at this stage was being carefully managed under the Hollywood studio system. She was contracted exclusively to Fox, who refused to lend her out to other studios for films not under their control. Thus Temple was initially considered for the part of Dorothy in *The Wizard of Oz* but lost out to Judy Garland when it began shooting at rival MGM studios in 1938. In 1936, however, Fox were deep into planning for her next blockbuster, *Wee Willie Winkie*. Fox chairman Zanuck wanted to follow MGM's lead of creating more substantial roles for their child stars (MGM's Freddie Bartholomew and Mickey Rooney had succeeded in improving their studios takings in lavishly produced films such as *Captains Courageous* and *The Devil is a Sissy*). Another factor in this decision was the effect of the full implementation in 1934 of the infamous Hays Office Production Code, adopted by the industry under pressure and threat of boycott from religious and civic groups. All films released in US cinemas had to have the Hays Office seal of approval, and the code strictly regulated the type of language, sexual nature, situations and plot stratagems that could be shown in films.

In the face of such internal industry censorship, flamboyant and sexually risqué female characters (characterized in particular by Mae West, for example) quickly receded in favour of more 'family-friendly' subject matter and personalities. As one contemporary critic noted, the move from Mae West (box office leader in 1933) to Shirley Temple (leader in 1935) was a move from adult knowledge to energetic innocence, with 'something rude and rowdy in [Temple's] characteristic expression [that] is positively boisterous, a sort of hoot at the pomposity of the entire grown-up world' (Seldes 1935: 86). To put it more bluntly, the licence granted to Temple as a child innocent of the world allowed her films greater licence and leeway than was the case for more mature stars: 'precisely because she was young – and not a sexual being to control or fear, she could dictate her needs, act on her whims, and meddle in the business of all concerned' (Rosen 1973: 183). Temple would be portrayed as a uniting force in Tinsel Town's oblique reflections on the Depression era. The result was that in her most popular films, crafted between 1934 and 1937, plots were designed for her principal function, 'to soften hard hearts (especially of the wealthy), to intercede on the behalf of others, to effect liaisons between members of the opposed social classes and occasionally to regenerate'(Eckert 1974: 17–20).

Zanuck demanded veteran Hollywood director John Ford be brought on board. Ford had been in the business since 1917, and his output had ranged from classic westerns (*The Iron Horse*, 1924) to powerful human dramas (*Arrowsmith*, 1931; *Judge Priest*, 1934). In 1935 he had won the Best Director Oscar for *The Informer*. Ford was already under contract to Fox, but was wary of working with Zanuck, considering him lacking in artistic integrity and interested mainly in making safe commercial pictures. Direct pressure from Zanuck eventually led Ford to accept, and filming began in late 1936.

Set in colonial India, and taken from a Rudyard Kipling tale, *Wee Willie Winkie* was a sepia-toned British Empire reimagined through Hollywood sensibilities. The plot centred on Temple, the granddaughter of a Scots Highlander general, reconciling troubled Indian 'natives' and stalwart British imperial armed forces. The pedigree cast included Victor McLaglen (a stalwart of John Ford's films and Best Actor Oscar winner for *The Informer*), C. Aubrey Smith and Cesar Romero (who years later would gain cult fame as The Joker in the 1960s *Batman* television series). Ethnic matters in the plot were often brushed over or utilized for dramatic purposes: McLaglen's Scottish character perished halfway through the film but was so likeable that, on seeing the rushes, Zanuck asked Ford if they could keep him in. Ford replied his death was integral to the plot. Not one to waste resources, Zanuck replied: 'Well, we have all those bagpipes. Can you give him an impressive military funeral?' (Edwards 1988: 104–5). It was duly noted and done.

Given *Wee Willie Winkie's* pedigree of Hollywood's top star, director, producer and a stellar supporting cast, it is not surprising that the movie opened in the US to positive notices. The reviews reflected different perspectives on Temple's widespread appeal. Writing in her newspaper column, the President's wife, Eleanor Roosevelt, also a friend of Shirley Temple, was moved to comment: 'I wonder how many people seeing *Wee Willie Winkie* will get the main lesson from it. It took a little child's faith and logic to bring a dangerous tribal chief in India to an understanding with his ancient enemy, the Soldier of the Queen' (Black 1990: 182). More evident to some critics, however, was Temple's growing maturity as a performer. The *New Yorker* critic likened Temple to another American film icon:

> Under John Ford's expert hand, Shirley has become something more than just a pretty puppet. The child is growing up, seems to understand the emotions she is portraying and there is a definite expansion of personality. She is developing the same appeal, puffed sleeves, the ability to smile-through-tears, that made Mary Pickford 'America's Sweetheart'.
>
> (Edwards 1988: 105)

But not all were bowled over by the Shirley Temple juggernaut. The *Literary Digest* stuck to the traditional view of Temple as the Eternal Child, writing: 'The strength of this film is as much in the yarn as in the girl. Now her drooling is less evident' (Black 1990: 182). More cruel jibes were to emanate from a small literary journal in London a few months later.

Graham Greene enters the picture

By the time of *Wee Willie Winkie*'s release in 1937, Greene had authored nine novels and, as noted already, had spent several years watching and reviewing films. His unique critical talents, and his unrelenting and rigorous scrutiny of the popular films of his day, marked him out from his contemporaries. On the strength of his *Spectator* reviews, Greene was invited to edit a brand-new literary magazine – *Night and Day* – due to launch in spring of 1937. Greene clearly had high hopes for the magazine, and threw himself into the role of literary editor. He set about recruiting the cream of London's literary society, securing, among others, the talents of Evelyn Waugh as drama critic on six guineas a week. Waugh's view was that *Night and Day* would become the English equivalent of the *New Yorker*. Greene also enlisted poets Stevie Smith and John Betjeman, and ultimately brought on board a veritable who's who of contemporary literary London, including Christopher Isherwood, V. S. Pritchett, Malcolm Muggeridge, Elizabeth Bowen, A. J. A. Symons, William Empson and Anthony Powell. If the talent on display was outstanding, even more impressive was the list of writers rejected, a roll call that included Henry Miller, Marghanita Laski, Nancy Mitford and H. E. Bates.

Wee Willie Winkie gets the bullet

Night and Day was launched on an unsuspecting London in July 1937. Three months into the magazine's run, the 28 October issue opened innocently enough with droll remarks on news and current issues ('Mr. Neville Chamberlain held out the hand of friendship to Mussolini last night …'). Elizabeth Bowen's *Letter from Ireland* advised: 'The small town hotels in Ireland are brightening up, and are now

perfectly possible to stay in …'. Stevie Smith's latest poetic offering, 'Steriliza-
tion', declared:

> But the great Dostoievsky the Epileptic
> Turned on his side and looked rather sceptic.

Graham Greene's contribution – the movie review of *Wee Willie Winkie* – sat
innocuously on the last page of the issue. It was not the first time Greene had
reviewed Temple's films. In May 1936 he had written positively for the *Spectator*
on her performance in *The Littlest Rebel*, nevertheless pointing up a theme he
would return to in later reviews. 'I had not seen Miss Temple before,' he noted,
'as I expected there was the usual sentimental exploitation of childhood, but I
had not expected the tremendous energy which her rivals certainly lacked'
(quoted in Sherry 1989: 618). In August 1936 he wrote a more barbed assessment
of her unchildlike, mature performance in *Captain January*: 'Shirley Temple acts
and dances with immense vigour and assurance, but some of her popularity seems
to rest on a coquetry quite as mature as Miss [Claudette] Colbert's and on an
oddly precocious body as voluptuous in grey flannel trousers as Miss Dietrich's'
(ibid.: 619).

By 1937 Greene had had enough of the studio's managed presentation of the
pre-pubescent Temple. Acerbic, insightful and all too candid, Greene's short
Night and Day piece savaged Temple's image and her core audience, implying that
her appeal was carefully cultivated to capitalize on the forbidden, sexual allure
between child and adult. It is worth quoting at length:

> The owners of a child star are like leaseholders – their property diminishes in
> value every year. Time's chariot is at their back; before them acres of
> anonymity. What is Jackie Coogan now but a matrimonial squabble? Miss
> Shirley Temple's case, though, has peculiar interest: infancy with her is a
> disguise, her appeal is more secret and more adult. Already two years ago she
> was a fancy little piece (real childhood, I think, went out after *The Littlest Rebel*).
> In *Captain January* she wore trousers with the mature suggestiveness of a
> Dietrich: her neat and well-developed rump twisted in the tap-dance: her eyes
> had a sidelong searching coquetry. Now in *Wee Willie Winkie*, wearing short
> kilts, she is a complete totsy. Watch her swaggering stride across the Indian
> barrack-square: hear the gasp of excited expectation from her antique audi-
> ence when the sergeant's palm is raised: watch the way she measures a man
> with agile studio eyes, with dimpled depravity. Adult emotions of love and
> grief glissade across the mask of childhood, a childhood skin-deep.
>
> It is clever, but it cannot last. Her admirers – middle-aged men and cler-
> gymen – respond to her dubious coquetry, to the sights of her well-shaped
> and desirable little body, packed with enormous vitality, only because the
> safety curtain of story and dialogue drops between their intelligence and

their desire … 'Why are you making my Mummy cry?' – what could be
purer than that? And the scene when dressed in a white nightdress she begs
grandpa to take Mummy to a dance – what could be more virginal? On
those lines her new picture, made by John Ford, who directed *The Informer*, is
horrifyingly competent.

(Hawtree 1985: 204)

The case unfolds

Later Greene would elide over his intended meaning, explaining coyly in his
memoir only that 'I had suggested that she had a certain adroit coquetry which
appealed to middle-aged men' (Greene 1980: 60). But the effect of this literary dart
was beyond anything he or *Night and Day* staff could have imagined. The major
British news retailer W. H. Smith immediately refused to stock the offending issue.
Anxious *Night and Day* publishers sought legal counsel on the matter, and D. N. Pritt,
King's Counsel, assured them unequivocally that the article was not libellous and
could be published without risk. The editors remained cautious about matters:
Stevie Smith subsequently received proofs of her latest poem in which the poetry
editor drew her attention 'to the fact that we have discovered there is a Mr.
Montague Cohen living in Golders Green. This unfortunate coincidence would
make it highly dangerous to publish the poem as it stands' (Hawtree, 1985: xiii).
Stevie Smith replied, tongue-in-cheek: 'I'm so sorry about Mr. Montague Cohen,
and agree, from a quick glance at the telephone directory, that what you say is probably an understatement. I have therefore altered his suburb to Bottle Green' (ibid.).

If the editors were cautious, the publishers were less so: in the wake of the
controversy, seeking to boost sales (which at the time were languishing well below
the 30,000 an issue needed to make a profit), they produced publicity posters for
display in shops emblazoned with the headline 'SEX AND SHIRLEY TEMPLE'.
Sales did not rise as hoped. Instead, notice was taken of the matter across the
Atlantic. While no copy of the *Night and Day* review had been released in the US,
the newspapers there exclusively (but erroneously) revealed that Greene had
described Temple as a midget with a seven-year-old child of her own. This scoop
was not confined to America. It had been a persistent rumour even in the Vatican.
When the reporter for its official newspaper *Osservatore Romano*, Father Silvio
Massante, shared the rumour with Shirley and her mother, Mrs Temple exploded:
'Why don't they *stop* it! All those letters calling you a thirty-year-old midget with a
seven-year-old child, and now a Priest!' To add insult to injury, she added, they
were getting other important health matters wrong: 'And I *do* wish people would
stop saying she has *all* her adult teeth! She only has *eight*!' (Black 1990: 266).

Within a month of the offending article being published, Twentieth Century Fox
(enlisting Temple's parents as co-plaintiffs) had hauled Greene and *Night and Day* into
the High Court in London. The Statement of Claim narrated that Greene had
accused Twentieth Century Fox of 'procuring' Temple 'for immoral purposes'. The
Lord Chief Justice immediately sent the papers in the case for the consideration of

the Director of Public Prosecutions (thus placing Greene's name permanently on the files of Scotland Yard). Greene and his publishers consulted their lawyers.

The financial state of *Night and Day* was already precarious. By 1 November 1937, within a week of Greene's review being published, the magazine's board was informed that the publication could not continue without a substantial injection of capital. Frantic efforts were made to salvage the journal. Evelyn Waugh wrote in his diary for 18 November: 'Greene rang up to say that *Night and Day* is on its last legs; would I put them into touch with Evan Tredegar [2nd Viscount Tredegar], whom I barely know, to help them raise capital. They must, indeed, be in a bad way' (Hawtree 1985: xiii). Backers did not materialize, and the final issue of *Night and Day* was published on 23 December 1937.

In January 1938 Greene left for Mexico to prepare a book on the Mexican Revolution and the Catholic Church, later published as *The Lawless Roads*, and to finish correcting proofs of *Brighton Rock*. He could not, however, escape the legal action. As he wrote to author Elizabeth Bowen from Mexico: 'I found a cable waiting for me in Mexico City asking me to apologize to that little bitch Shirley Temple' (Sherry 1989: 621). But apologize he did, as did the publishers. The case was settled before reaching the trial date in May. The matter had to be put before the judge so that he could approve the terms of the settlement. The case appeared before the High Court of Justice on 22 May 1938, and a day later it appeared in the Law Reports section of *The Times* (as Greene recalled in his 1980 memoir *Ways of Escape*, reproducing the entire item as proof) (Greene 1980: 61).[2] The Lord Chief Justice, in awarding £3,500 plus legal costs of £1,500 to Fox, pronounced sententiously: 'This libel is simply a gross outrage, and I will take care to see that suitable attention is directed to it. In the meantime I assent to the settlement on the terms which have been disclosed, and the record will be withdrawn' (ibid.: 63).

Fox (and Temple) had emerged victorious, with an apology and a cash settlement from the now defunct *Night and Day* magazine and the absent Greene. Temple had little need for the money, so the settlement was invested on her behalf in British War Loan Bonds, 'to help arm sorely pressed England against a troubled Europe'. More importantly, the case put to rest rumours about Temple's actual age (nine), confirmed she was childless, and helped raise takings at the box office. 'The saucy publicity tweaked British box-office interests,' Temple commented. '*Wee Willie Winkie* prospered gloriously' (Black 1990: 270).

Greene's view on the libel case betrayed light-handed bitterness. Later he would claim that he kept the offending statement of claim on his bathroom wall 'until a bomb removed the wall' (Greene 1980: 60). Some commentators have suggested the libel case had been brought on because Greene had made a collective enemy of the American studios through his constant criticism of the US film industry. In the view of the critic John Atkins, Greene was targeted. 'One false step and they would move heaven [and] earth ... to put an end to it ... He would certainly go too far, if not next week, then the week after' (Atkins 1969: 86).

Greene was not paranoid enough to think the entire industry wanted him silenced. He did, however, believe that Twentieth Century Fox subsequently went out of its way to stop him writing further reviews, and reported angrily to a colleague in 1938: 'The Fox people went round to Gaumont-British to try and get them to withdraw all tickets [free tickets to see previews] from me, thus breaking me as a critic, but G.B. told them to go to hell' (quoted in Sherry 1989: 624). Later he would write that 'Twentieth Century Fox went beyond the limits for an ordinary action for libel by writing to an editor and trying to get [my] criticisms stopped in future'. The editor in this case was the *Spectator*'s Derek Verschoyle (ibid.: 624). The results were negligible, and it did not stop him subsequently joining the industry he had once disparaged, working in the 1950s and '60s on such classic screen adaptations of his works as *The Third Man* and *Brighton Rock*.

The blurred line 'between childlike innocence and knowing worldliness'

Greene's comments on Temple's precocious sexual appeal were jarringly at odds with those of contemporaries such as the American broadcaster Walter Winchell, who noted in 1936: 'Sex can't be important in films ... Remember, the world's leading film attractions remain Charlie Chan, Boris Karloff, and Shirley Temple' (Black 1990: 152). Greene's friend and colleague Anthony Powell commented more perceptively that such contemporary critical responses to Temple were naïve at best: 'Even at that distant period, the notion that children neither had nor could express sexual instincts was, to say the least, an uninstructed one' (Hawtree 1985: xiii).

In retrospect, however, Greene's criticisms are strikingly modern in attitude. As many critics now point out, the line between childlike innocence and knowing worldliness is one often blurred in today's youth-orientated markets, films and advertising. Greene's mistake was to suggest *Wee Willie Winkie* might encourage Temple's admiring audience of middle-aged men and clergymen to forget such a line existed. It is unlikely that Greene's acerbic thumbs-down review, printed in a literary journal struggling for subscription survival, was ever going to drive down *Wee Willie Winkie*'s box-office sales. In the end, this proved to be a classic case of strong moral opinion versus big-money interests. To protect the reputation of its biggest earner, a film studio with clout wielded libel laws to silence a needling critic. They got what they wanted – a Shirley Temple cocktail that was made pure again, ready for the next paying customer.

Notes

1 This chapter derives from research undertaken in conjunction with my colleague Ross Macfarlane for a long-standing project on libel and slander. I am grateful to him for allowing me to develop the material further as a piece for this volume. Some of the arguments here have previously appeared in *Ethical Space*, 2/1 (2005). I am grateful to the editor and publisher for permission to revise and reutilize the relevant material for inclusion here.

2 An edited version follows here:

HIGH COURT OF JUSTICE
King's Bench Division
Libel on Miss Shirley Temple: 'A Gross Outrage'
Temple and Others *v.* Night and Day Magazines,
Limited, and Others
Before the Lord Chief Justice

A settlement was announced of this libel action which was brought by Miss Shirley Jane Temple, the child actress ... , Twentieth Century-Fox Film, Limited, of Berners Street, W., against Night and Day Magazines, Limited and Mr Graham Greene, of St. Martin's Lane, W.C. ... in respect of an article written by Mr Greene and published in the issue of the magazine *Night and Day* dated October 28, 1937. ...

Sir Patrick Hastings [for the plaintiffs], in announcing the settlement, by which it was agreed that Miss Shirley Temple was to receive £2,000, the film corporation £1,000, and the film company £500, stated that the first defendants were the proprietors of the magazine *Night and Day*, which was published in London. ...

The plaintiff, Miss Shirley Temple, a child of nine years, has a world-wide reputation as an artist in films. The two plaintiff companies produced her in a film called *Wee Willie Winkie*, based on Rudyard Kipling's story.

On October 28 last year Night and Day Magazines, Limited, published an article written by Mr Graham Greene. In his (counsel's) view it was one of the most horrid libels that one could well imagine. Obviously he would not read it all – it was better that he should not – but a glance at the statement of claim, where a poster was set out, was quite sufficient to show the nature of the libel written about this child.

This beastly publication, said counsel, was written, and it was right to say that every respectable distributor in London refused to be a party to selling it. Notwithstanding that, the magazine company, with the object no doubt of increasing the sale, proceeded to advertise the fact that it had been banned.

Shirley Temple was an American and lived in America. If she had been in England and the publication in America it would have been right for the American Courts to have taken notice of it. It was equally right that, the position being reversed, her friends in America should know that the Courts here took notice of such a publication.

SHOULD NOT BE TREATED LIGHTLY

Money was no object in this case. The child had a very large income and the two film companies were wealthy concerns. It was realised, however, that the matter should not be treated lightly. The defendants [*Night and Day* and Graham Greene] had paid the film companies £1,000 and £500 respectively, and the money would be disposed of in a charitable way. With regard to the child, she would be paid £2,000. There would also be an order for the taxation of costs.

In any view, said counsel, it was such a beastly libel to have written that if it had been a question of money it would have been difficult to say what would be an appropriate amount to arrive at.

Miss Shirley Temple probably knew nothing of the article, and it was undesirable that she should be brought to England to fight the action. In his (counsel's) opinion the settlement was a proper one in the circumstances.

Mr Valentine Holmes [for the defendants] informed his Lordship that the magazine *Night and Day* had ceased publication. He desired, on behalf of his clients, to express the deepest apology to Miss Temple for the pain which certainly would have been caused to her by the article if she had read it. He also apologised to the two film companies for the suggestion that they would produce and distribute a film of the character indicated by the article. There was no justification for the criticism of the film, which, his clients instructed him, was one which anybody could take their children to see. He also apologised on behalf of Mr Graham Greene. So far as the publishers of the magazine were concerned, they did not see the article before publication.

His Lordship – Who is the author of this article?

Mr Holmes – Mr Graham Greene.

His Lordship – Is he within the jurisdiction?

Mr Holmes – I am afraid I do not know, my Lord … .

His Lordship – Can you tell me where Mr Greene is?

Mr Mathew – I have no information on the subject.

His Lordship – This libel is simply a gross outrage, and I will take care to see that suitable attention is directed to it. In the meantime I assent to the settlement on the terms which have been disclosed, and the record will be withdrawn.

References

Adamson, Judith (ed.) (1990; 1991) *Reflections* (London: Reinhardt).

Anon. (1936) 'Peewee's progress', *Time*, 27 April, pp. 36–44.

Atkins, John (1969) *Graham Greene* (London: Calder & Boyard).

Black, Shirley Temple (1990) *Child Star* (Bath: Chivers Press).

Davy, Charles (ed.) (1938) *Footnotes to the Film* (London: Lovat Dickson).

Eckert, Charles (1974) 'Shirley Temple and the house of Rockefeller', *Jump Cut: A Review of Contemporary America*, 2/1: 17–20. Available online at www.ejumpcut.org/archive/onlineessays/JC02folder/shirleytemple.html, accessed on 20 November 2006.

Edwards, Anne (1988) *Shirley Temple: An American Princess* (London: Collins).

Greene, Graham (1937) 'The Films', *Night and Day*, 28 October; in Hawtree, Christopher (ed.), *Night and Day* (London: Chatto & Windus).

—— (1980) *Ways of Escape* (London: The Bodley Head).

Hawtree, Christopher (ed.) (1985) *Night and Day* (London: Chatto & Windus).

MacNeice, Louis (1965) *The Strings are False: An Unfinished Autobiography* (London: Faber & Faber).

Parkinson, David (ed.) (1993) *Mornings in the Dark: The Graham Greene Film Reader* (New York and London: Applause Books and Carcanet Press).

Rosen, Marjorie (1973) *Popcorn Venus: Women, Movies and the American Dream* (New York: Coward, McCann & Geoghegan).

Seldes, Gilbert (1935) 'Two great women', *Esquire*, July, p. 86.

Sherry, Norman (1989) *The Life of Graham Greene, vol. 1: 1904–39* (London: Jonathan Cape).

Stimson, Blake (2001) 'Andy Warhol's red beard – influence of Ben Shahn and Shirley Temple on Warhol', *The Art Bulletin*, September. Available online at www.findarticles.com/p/articles/mi_m0422/is_3_83/ai_84192648, accessed on 20 November 2006.

Wright, Basil (1974) *The Long View* (London: Paladin).

Chapter 7

The lasting in the ephemeral

Assessing George Orwell's As I Please columns

Richard Keeble

George Orwell, author of the world famous *Animal Farm* (1945) and *Nineteen Eighty-Four* (1949), was also one of the greatest journalists of the last century. Born Eric Arthur Blair in Motihari, Bengal, in 1903, he won a scholarship to Eton but in 1921 left the college 138th out of 167 candidates in final-year exams. Confounding the expectations of his family, he sailed for Rangoon, Burma, to become a probationary assistant district superintendent of the Imperial Police. But he grew disillusioned with British imperialism and in 1927 resigned 'on medical grounds'. That winter he went 'down and out' in London's East End and the following year moved to a cheap hotel in Paris. He adopted the pseudonym George Orwell in November 1932, and *Down and Out in Paris and London* was published during the following year. The novels *Burmese Days* (1935), *A Clergyman's Daughter* (1935) and *Keep the Aspidistra Flying* (1936) followed in quick succession. In 1936 he travelled through northern England, the West Midlands, Lancashire and Yorkshire researching the working class, and in December delivered the manuscript of *The Road to Wigan Pier* before leaving for Spain, which was in the grip of civil war. Here he fought for the Republicans against the fascists led by General Franco and was wounded, his experiences (and his conversion to socialism) being captured in *Homage to Catalonia* (1938). After two unhappy years working for the BBC's Eastern Service, in February 1943 he became literary editor of *Tribune*, writing the weekly As I Please column. In 1945 he served as a war correspondent on the Continent for David Astor's *Observer*. The same year also saw the publication of *Animal Farm*, which secured massive sales in Britain and the United States, and he began spending part of every 12 months in a cottage on the remote Scottish island of Jura, Inner Hebrides. While his health continued to deteriorate he worked on completing *Nineteen Eighty-Four*. He died in 1950 aged just 46, soon after marrying his second wife, Sonia.

In November 1943 George Orwell, with great relief, quit his job at the BBC and began working as literary editor of *Tribune*. In the process he took a substantial wage cut – from £720 a year to £500 – and started on the novel which was to secure his international reputation, *Animal Farm*. Launched in 1937 by Sir Stafford Cripps and George Strauss (both Labour MPs), *Tribune* had become the leading voice of the left wing of the Labour Party. By the time Orwell joined the staff, Aneurin Bevan was editor (controlling its political position and writing most of its leaders) with Jon Kimche, who had worked with Orwell in 1934 as an assistant at Booklover's Corner, Hampstead, doing most of the editing and commissioning.[1]

One of Orwell's main contributions to *Tribune* as literary editor was the As I Please column. A similar title had been used by Raymond Postgate in *Commentary* in 1939, while Walter Duranty, foreign correspondent for the *New York Times* (1913–39), had written a book, *I Write as I Please* (1935). But Jon Kimche told Peter Davison, editor of the 20-volume series of Orwell's collected writings (1998a: 3), that he had suggested the title for the series. In all, Orwell contributed 80 As I Please columns, his last one appearing on 4 April 1947, by which time Michael Foot MP (later leader of the Labour Party) had become managing director.

After his unhappy two years as talks producer at the BBC, where he was increasingly annoyed by the censorship and bureaucracy, Orwell clearly loved the freedom at *Tribune*, all the more so because it was a journal with which he could totally identify. In his As I Please column on 31 January 1947 he wrote: 'It is the only existing weekly paper that makes a genuine effort to be both progressive and humane – that is, to combine a radical socialist policy with a respect for freedom of speech and a civilised attitude towards literature and the arts.'

Between February 1945 and November 1946 there is a gap in Orwell's As I Please contributions, with Jennie Lee (who married Aneurin Bevan in 1935 and was first minister for the arts from 1967 to 1970) taking over the role. For the first three months of this period he served as war correspondent for the *Observer* and *Manchester Evening News* on the Continent. His 19 articles represent the only time Orwell worked to strict deadlines as a reporter for mainstream newspapers. And yet these pieces have been either ignored or usually damned as dull (Crick 1980: 480; Ingle 1993: 67; Meyers 2000: 232 – but see Keeble 2001).[2]

Orwell's distress over 'ephemeral journalism'

In contrast, commentators are virtually unanimous in ruling his columns outstanding examples of his journalistic style. Yet until Paul Anderson's edited collection of Orwell's *Tribune* writing (published in 2006) there was no academic study of all the 80 columns. And Anderson concentrates on Orwell's politics as expressed through the columns rather than his journalistic strategies and writing styles.[3] Paradoxically, Orwell shared many of the academy's prejudices against journalism. Throughout his career he constantly downgraded his own writing as mere journalism or pamphleteering and looked up to literature which he thought of as a higher form. In his celebrated 'Why I Write' essay of 1946 he confessed: 'In a peaceful age I might have written ornate or merely descriptive books and might have remained almost unaware of my political loyalties. As it is I have been forced into becoming a sort of pamphleteer' (Orwell and Angus 1968, vol. 1: 26). Hilary Spurling, in her affectionate biography of Orwell's second wife, Sonia, records how Orwell confided to her, just before he died, how dissatisfied he felt with his overall output, feeling he had wasted too much time on 'ephemeral journalism' (Spurling 2002: 100).

Raymond Williams places this elevation of the aesthetic by Orwell in a social and historical context. He argues that, with his 'categorical confusions' (and belief in the simple dualities – form versus content, 'art for art's sake' versus writing about something) Orwell was typical of the writers from the 1880s onwards who emerged from the commercial middle class, concerned to offer their writing as above the commodity system (Williams 1984: 29–40; see also Dentith 1998: 205).

Orwell and the tradition of 'personal journalism'

For Christopher Silvester (1997) Orwell's columns have to be considered in the context of a tradition of 'personal journalism' which emerged out of the nine-teenth-century's Romantic movement and its focus on the contemplation of the self. In addition Silvester stresses the financial pressures on the new mass-selling newspapers in the United States and Britain which needed to vary their diet of straight, hard news with 'human interest' news, features and comment to main-tain reader interest. In the mid-1880s T. H. White's Lakeside Musings for the *Chicago Tribune* and the twice-weekly columns by J. M. Barrie, the creator of Peter Pan, in the *Nottingham Guardian* created a new genre of regularly appearing, well-crafted columns of commentary – both serious and whimsical.

In the early years of the twentieth century – with the role of editor and propri-etor now completely separated – editorials took on a more formal tone while the column could become the site of vigorous, splenetic opinion, sometimes even going against the editorial line of the title in which it ran (ibid.: xiii). By the 1930s columnists such as Walter Lippman (whose thrice-weekly political analyses were syndicated out of the *New York Herald Tribune*) and the Broadway diarist Walter Winchell (syndicated out of the *New York Daily Mirror*) were becoming media celebrities. In Britain syndication never caught on. But, as Silvester stresses, the 1930s proved to be a golden era for columnists in the mainstream press – with Tom Driberg's William Hickey gossip column and J. B. Morton's Beachcomber column in the *Daily Express*, D. B. Wyndham Lewis's witty columns in the *Daily Mail* and the anti-fascist rhetoric of Cassandra (William Connor) in the *Daily Mirror*.

But Gordon Bowker (2003: 306) rather highlights the way in which Orwell's columns follow in the long tradition of Hazlitt, Lamb, Stevenson, Belloc and Chesterton. 'It was a form of good-humoured prose rumination practised in Orwell's day at Eton in the *College Chronicle* and in Butler's *Written Sketches* which he so enjoyed.' According to Orwell's biographer Jeffrey Meyers (2000: 226): 'His column transformed a humble genre into significant literary works. He not only promoted socialist ideas and put contemporary political events in historical perspective but also (gloomy as he was) cheered people up with entertaining subjects and – in an intimate tone of voice – combined public issues with personal feelings.' And for Scott Lucas (2003: 70), the column was crucial in establishing Orwell as 'an English cultural icon'.

Orwell: making the personal political

According to Colin Sparks (1992: 39–40), the media's stress on the personal 'becomes the explanatory framework within which the social order is presented as transparent ... [T]he "personal" obliterates the "political" as an explanatory factor in human behaviour.' And he argues that the media's highly personalized representations of reality deny consumers the means to recognize the structural basis of power relations in society. In many ways, the current obsessions with sex, celebrity, randy royals and reality TV stars reflect a profound depoliticization of the culture. Yet in his As I Please columns, Orwell showed how the personal does not necessarily obliterate the political. He did not cover the normal beat of a political columnist: elections, the personal squabbles of politicians, ministerial changes, legislation, parliament. But as Paul Anderson stresses (2006: 3): 'It would be wrong to suggest that his columns were not political. They were intensely so – even, paradoxically, when they appeared to have nothing to do with politics.'

Orwell's writing bursts with original ideas and yet is *distinctly journalistic* in that it is never obscured by abstraction and endless referencing.[4] The 'I' voice of the column was perfectly suited to his style, even though he felt typically ambivalent about this subjectivity. At the end of 'Why I Write' (Orwell and Angus, vol. 1: 29–30) he asserted: 'One can write nothing readable unless one constantly strives to efface one's own personality. Good prose is like a window pane.' Yet, as Orwell's long-time friend and literary editor Cyril Connolly said of him: 'He was a man ... whose personality shines out in everything he said or wrote.' Richard Filloy (1998: 49) resolves this apparent paradox by suggesting that self-effacement was the important persuasive strategy for Orwell.

> By making his reports those of an ordinary person rather than those of a great man, he allowed his audience to put themselves in his position without imagining the impossible ... By offering us a character who is ordinary, Orwell not only allows the reader to share the perceptions of the writer, he also disarms our suspicion of an ethos which is so good and so intelligent that our training tells us to mistrust it. After all, we are not in the presence of an especially superior person, merely another poor soul like ourselves.
>
> (Ibid.: 52)

His 'persuasive rhetoric of personality' (ibid.: 47–63) is most apparent in the columns which feature surprisingly idiosyncratic, 'ordinary' subject matter, deliberately far distant in tone and style from the heavy diet of political polemic and policy analysis that filled the rest of the pages of *Tribune* (Anderson 2006: 26). His column of 28 January 1944 (Davison 1998a: 80–3) is typical of the genre in blending together four very different topics drawn imaginatively from four contrasting sources: a news item, a letter from a reader, a barmaid's comment and a book he had just reviewed for the *Manchester Evening News*. In the first section, Orwell responds with argumentative gusto to a news item about an Indian journalist being arrested for refusing military service. 'By behaviour of this kind you antagonise the entire Indian community in Britain – for no Indian, whatever his views, admits that Britain had the right to declare war on India's behalf or has the right to impose compulsory service on Indians.'

Next he answers a correspondent defending Ezra Pound, the American poet who had become a fervent propagandist for Mussolini in Rome. Basing his judgement on a concept of 'ordinary decency', Orwell argues that any writer's political opinions should not interfere with the critical assessment of their work. 'Personally I admire several writers (Céline, for instance) who have gone over to the Fascists and many others whose political outlook I strongly object to. But one has the right to expect ordinary decency even of a poet.' And he ends succinctly. Agreeing with the correspondent that the Americans should not shoot Pound, he quips: 'It would establish his reputation so thoroughly that it might be a hundred years before anyone could determine dispassionately whether Pound's much-debated poems are any good or not.'

His next section is a particularly idiosyncratic one as he expands on a passing comment by a barmaid (an archetypically 'ordinary' source) that 'if you pour beer into a damp glass it goes flat much more quickly'. From seemingly nothing Orwell conjures a fascinating list of 'those superstitions which are able to keep alive because they have the air of being scientific truths'. For this he draws on his childhood memories of fallacies taught to him 'not as an old wives' tale but as a scientific fact'. His favourites included that a swan can break your leg with a blow of its wing, that bulls become furious at the sight of red and that powdered glass is poisonous. He ends drolly: 'As for the third, it is so widespread that in India, for instance, people are constantly trying to poison one another with powdered glass, with disappointing results.' And in the final section he argues the case for a new international language.

In another quirky column on 4 February 1944 (Davison 1998a: 89) Orwell responds to a Board of Trade announcement ending the ban on turned-up trouser-ends. He sees a tailor's advertisement, hailing this as 'a first instalment of the freedom for which we are fighting'. Orwell's close identification with his readers is sealed as he addresses them as 'we'. He continues: 'If we were really fighting for turned-up trouser ends, I should be inclined to be pro-Axis. Turn-ups have no function except to collect dust and no virtue except that when you clean them out you occasionally find a sixpence there.' From this specific news-driven point he moves on to make a general political and social comment about 'clothes snobbery'. 'The sooner we are able to stop food rationing the better I shall be pleased but I would like to see clothes' rationing continue till the moths have devoured the last dinner jacket and even the undertakers have shed their top hats.'

Orwell's factional voice

The As I Please column (No. 22) of 28 April 1944 (see Anderson 2006: 130–3) captures many of the elements of Orwell's style. At the start he focuses on the 'when', 'who' and 'what' of the typical introductory section (the 'intro' in the jargon) of a news article, together with a stress on his personal involvement in the event:

> On the night in 1940 when the big ack-ack barrage was fired over London for the first time, I was in Piccadilly Circus when the guns opened up, and I fled into the Café Royal to take cover. Among the crowd inside a good-looking, well-made youth of about twenty-five was making somewhat of a nuisance of himself with a copy of *Peace News*.

While rooted in news-writing routines, the column has no specific newsiness (the event happened four years earlier). Orwell is more concerned about the issues raised in his conversation with the youth. He says his account is not completely accurate (it 'went something like this') and with the 'youth' remaining anonymous Orwell's 'factional' strategy leaves him free to blend fact and fiction. The 'youth' claims that a necessary 'compromise peace' with the Germans will help him 'remain alive' and allow him to get on with his work as a painter. In response, Orwell argues it is a fallacy 'to believe that under a dictatorial government you can be free *inside*' (his emphasis). And so emerges the central theme (the fate of the individual's spirit in the face of the Big Brother, totalitarian state) which is later to dominate his novel *Nineteen Eighty-Four* (1949).

Orwell moves from a snatch of conversation four years ago to an exploration of major political, cultural, philosophical issues: the importance of freedom of speech, the survival of creative inspiration and the threats posed by 'totalitarianism', which, he says, is 'on the up-grade in every part of the world'. 'Out in the street the loudspeakers bellow, the flags flutter from the rooftops, the police with their tommy guns prowl to and fro, the face of the Leader, four feet wide, glares from every hoarding …'. But take away freedom of speech 'and the creative faculties dry up'. Anticipating Winston Smith with his secret diary in *Nineteen Eighty-Four*, Orwell here argues that 'little worth-while writing of any kind – even such things as diaries, for instance – has been produced in secret under the dictators'.

Orwell as proto-blogger: building the community of the Left

Tim Holmes (2006: 160–8) has identified four categories in a practical taxonomy of column writing: community building, oppositional viewpoint, unofficial extension of predominant ideology and commercial advantage.[5] Most writers fulfil one of these categories. Orwell somehow managed to achieve all of them in his columns.

According to Holmes (ibid.: 162), 'Ever since 1693, when John Dunton [founder of the *Ladies' Mercury*] identified the market for a title aimed specifically at women, magazines have flourished on building communities around particular interests and offering particular approaches to those interests.' Holmes stresses that within the mainstream, 'community' is a 'commercial concept not a social ideal'. But for Orwell, deliberately working away from the mainstream, his enormous commitment was towards the social ideal of building up the community of the Left. After he travelled to Spain in 1936 to fight alongside the Republicans against Franco's fascists and witnessed both socialism in action and the ruthless attempts by the communists to suppress it (graphically captured in *Homage to Catalonia*), Orwell's commitment to the Left was sealed. As Taylor comments (2003: 201): 'Spain, it can be safely said, was the defining experience of Orwell's life.' Significantly, Orwell stressed in his famous essay 'Why I Write', published in the totally obscure journal *Gangrel* in the summer of 1946 (Orwell and Angus 1968, vol. 1: 23–32): 'Every line of serious work that I have written since 1936 has been written, directly or indirectly, against totalitarianism and for democratic socialism as I understand it.' This might suggest an emphasis on the rhetorical, propagandistic, 'journalistic' aspects of writing. Yet Orwell goes on to assert that he wanted to 'make political writing into an art', thus resolving the aesthetics-versus-politics dilemma by combining the two.

Orwell used essentially two strategies to promote his notion of 'the community of the Left': firstly through columns focusing on political, cultural, social or literary issues; and secondly, and most imaginatively, through developing a close relationship with his readers. This relationship was crucial to the flowering of Orwell's journalistic imagination. While he realized mainstream journalism was basically propaganda for wealthy newspaper proprietors, at *Tribune* he was engaging in the crucial political debate with people who mattered to him. They were an authentic audience compared with what Stuart Allan (2004: 85) calls the 'implied reader or imagined community of readers' of the mainstream media.

Often Orwell speaks directly to fellow socialists. For instance, in his fourth column, of 24 December 1943, he moves from commenting on the influence of T. E. Hulme (1883–1917) on many of the writers grouped around the journal *Criterion* (such as Wyndham Lewis, T. S. Eliot, Aldous Huxley, Malcolm Muggeridge, Evelyn Waugh and Graham Greene) to a gentle warning to the 'socialist movement' not to ignore the influence of this 'neo-reactionary school of writers'.

In the close relationship he instinctively developed with his readers, Orwell can, in many ways, be seen as a proto-blogger, responding to letters sent to him directly or addressed to *Tribune*; inviting letters, asking readers to answer queries or to point him towards a book, pamphlet or quotation he is looking for; running a competition for a short story or giving them a quirky brain teaser to answer.[6] Not only did Orwell respond to letters but also, as Peter Davison's *Collected Works* show, his columns often provoked correspondence, both critical and supportive, from readers. For instance, following his criticisms of newspapers carrying pictures of French Nazi collaborators on 8 September 1944 a reader wrote: 'How much longer must your readers be affronted by the quite patently pro-Fascist, neo-Jesuit posturing of George Orwell. He writes in the wrong periodical.'

Oppositional viewpoint (licensed contradiction): Orwell as socialist dissident

According to Holmes (2006: 165), a newspaper may wish to be seen to encourage debate and hire columnists who are licensed to disagree with the dominant editorial line. 'Culturally this establishes a tone of diversity, and commercially it hedges its bets with the readership.' Orwell performed this role perfectly – promoting socialism and yet, in his *Tribune* columns and elsewhere, constantly raising questions about the movement's ideas and strategies.

For the historian E. P. Thompson, Orwell betrayed the Left with his constant critiques. While discussing Orwell's *Inside the Whale* of 1940 (in which he examines the writings of Henry Miller in the context of the main literary tradition of the 1920s and 1930s), Thompson says: 'He is sensitive – sometimes obsessively so – to the least insincerity upon his left, but the inhumanity of the right rarely provoked him to a paragraph of polemic' (cited in Hitchens 2002: 26). Scott Lucas (2000) also argues firmly that 'Orwell was not a socialist'. His socialism 'consisted primarily of bashing other socialists' (ibid.: 49). 'Orwell banged away in a negative key, his positive melody reduced to vestiges of Englishness – the perfect cup of tea, the consummate pub, the common toads – and the mantra of "freedom".'

In contrast, Rodden stresses (1998: 177–8):

> his criticism was almost always directed at social*ists*, not social*ism*: he railed at socialists because he wanted socialist intellectuals to be worthy of socialism. A 'conscience of the Left' does criticize from within; and though Orwell may sometimes have been guilty of being the excessively scrupulous 'wintry conscience of his generation', he flayed the Left intelligentsia in order to fortify it, not to weaken or abandon it.

A typical Orwellian 'imaginative provocation' appears in his column on 21 January 1944 (Davison 1998a: 76–9). Responding to a correspondent who reproaches him for being 'negative', he says he, in fact, likes praising 'things'. After an opening section on the pros and cons of the BBC output, he suddenly shifts focus and writes in praise of the Woolworth rose. The following week a reader accuses Orwell of 'bourgeois nostalgia'. Michael Foot later wrote that Bevan was 'the only editor who, in those days before Orwell's reputation was sure, would have given him complete freedom to offend all readers and lash all hypocrisies, including socialist hypocrisies' (see Taylor 2003: 326).

Thus, on 10 December 1943 he moves from discussing a pamphlet, *The Negro: His Future in America*, to highlighting the problems of securing class solidarity across racial lines. And he is quick to criticize fellow socialists for failing to confront the issues (Davison 1998a: 23–4).

> An English working-man spends on cigarettes about the same sum as an Indian peasant has for his entire income. It is not easy for socialists to admit this, or at any rate to emphasise it … In Asiatic eyes the European class struggle is a sham. The socialist movement has never gained a foothold in Asia or Africa, or even among the American Negroes: it is everywhere side-tracked by nationalism and race-hatred.

Significantly, Alok Rai (1988: 63) suggests that the anti-imperialism which lay at the core of Orwell's critique of contemporary socialists emerged from his years in Burma (1922–7) as a member of the Imperial Indian Police. 'The history of Orwell's relations with that highly differentiated entity, the "Left" is determined and bedevilled by a variety of factors: but it is clear at any rate that his colonial experience gives Orwell an air of superiority which he is often not greatly at pains to conceal.'

In a similar vein, on 11 February 1944, Orwell uses his column to criticize the Left's weak response to anti-Semitism (Davison 1998a: 91–2). Reporting on how his recent *Observer* review of books dealing with the persecution of Jews in Europe had provoked 'the usual wad of anti-Semitic letters', he suggests the Left's response is too rationalistic. 'The official Left wing view of anti-Semitism is that it is something "got up" by the ruling classes in order to divert attention away from the real evils of society. The Jews, in fact, are scapegoats. This is no doubt correct, but it is quite useless as an argument. One does not dispose of a belief by showing that it is irrational.' Instead, he calls for a detailed inquiry into the causes of anti-Semitism and the main charges made against the Jews, whether anti-Semitism is actually on the increase and to what extent it had been aggravated by the influx of refugees since 1938. And it is difficult for him to avoid making a jibe at fellow writers. 'Without even getting up from this table to consult a book I can think of passages in Villon, Shakespeare, Smollett, Thackeray, H. G. Wells, Aldous Huxley, T. S. Eliot and many another which would be called anti-Semitic if they had been written since Hitler came to power.'

In his column of 3 March 1944 (ibid.: 111–15) he takes up the criticisms of a Catholic correspondent to explore, with rhetorical panache, the relevance of flying saints to socialism, linking this to the Left's inadequate response to the decline in the belief in personal immortality. He achieves the shift to metaphysical, ethical debate with ease, mixing vernacular slang with erudite argument. One moment he is talking about the 'wishy-washy metaphorical sense' of Christian doctrine; at another time he criticizes the Catholic intellectual for playing a 'sort of handy-pandy game, repeating the articles of the Creed in exactly the same terms as his forefathers, while defending himself from the charge of superstition by explaining that he is speaking in parables'.

Along with criticism of socialists went a critique of Left-wing newspapers. For instance, on 10 December 1943 while examining the 'horrors of the colour war', he criticizes the Left press for using insulting nicknames:

> It is an astonishing thing that few journalists, even in the Left wing press, bother to find out which names are and which are not resented by members of other races. The word "native" which makes an Asiatic boil with rage, and which has been dropped even by British officials in India these ten years past, is flung about all over the place.

On 17 January 1947 (Davison 1998d: 18–19), the *Daily Herald*, 49 per cent of its shares owned by the Trades Union Congress, came under attack from Orwell for describing Indians who broadcast on German radio as 'collaborators'. Highlighting his own contacts with Indians in London, he argues: 'They were citizens of an occupied country, hitting back at the occupying power in the way that seemed to them best.' And he deplores a serious inaccuracy in a caption to a photograph. 'And this happens not in the *Daily Graphic*[7] but in Britain's sole Labour newspaper.'

Unofficial extension of predominant ideology: Orwell and Marxism

According to Holmes (2006: 166), comment pieces also allow a publication to run articles which express more extreme versions of its own ideology. Significantly Orwell's columns fulfilled this role too. Orwell's politics, literary criticism and social observations were never Marxist in the strictest sense and he maintained a long-standing suspicion of leftist ideological abstractions. Terry Eagleton (2003: 8) is blunt when he says: 'Orwell's commitment to decency makes him a mainstream English moralist like Cobbett, Leavis and Tawney; where the Continentals had Marxism, we English had moralism. Outside Catalonia, Orwell's contact with Marx did not extend much further than his poodle, who was named after him.' Yet Orwell did occasionally extend beyond *Tribune*'s predominant radical socialist ideology in his columns to embrace Karl Marx's theories.

For instance, in his column of 24 December 1943 (Davison 1998a: 34–5), he highlights the refusal of 'pessimists' such as Pétain, Sorel, Berdyaev, or the columnist 'Beachcomber delivering side-kicks at Beveridge in the *Express*' to believe that human society can be 'fundamentally improved'. The real answer, he argues, is to dissociate socialism from Utopianism. And with his argument flowing concisely and elegantly, he concludes:

> any thinking socialist will concede to the Catholic that when economic justice has been righted, the fundamental problem of man's place in the universe will still remain. But what the socialist does claim is that the problem cannot be dealt with while the average human being's preoccupations are necessarily

economic. It is all summed up in Marx's saying that after socialism has arrived, human history can begin.

Again, on 25 February 1944 (see Davison 1998a: 103–5), discussing Chesterton's comment 'There are no new ideas' in his introduction to Charles Dickens's *Hard Times*, he writes:

> Where your treasure is there will be your heart. But before Marx developed it what force had that saying? Who had paid attention to it? Who had inferred from it – what it certainly implies – that laws, religions, and moral codes are all a superstructure built over existing property relations? It was Christ, according to the Gospel, who uttered the text but it was Marx who brought it to life.

And on 17 November 1944 (ibid.: 463–9), in responding to a correspondent who has sent him a copy of a pamphlet by a reactionary Conservative MP, he is keen to defend Marx against misrepresentation. According to the pamphleteer, Marxism regarded individual acquisitiveness as the motive force of history. But Orwell stresses: 'Marx not only did not say this, he said almost the opposite of it.'

Orwell and *Tribune*'s survival

Holmes argues that newspapers often use star columnists strategically as circulation boosters (2006: 163–4). As a newspaper of the Left, *Tribune*'s primary concerns were political agitation and education and not profit: hence its appeal to Orwell. Yet the contribution of Orwell to the survival of *Tribune* was significant. Under the editorship of H. J. Hartshorn, from 1938 to 1940, *Tribune* adopted the pro-Soviet line of the Communist Party of Great Britain, opposing the war as an imperialist adventure (Anderson 2006: 13–16). But this had disastrous consequences for the newspaper. As circulation dipped, Hartshorn was sacked and in February 1940 journalist Raymond Postgate became editor with a new policy to back the war and take the paper upmarket to compete against the *New Statesman*. And so the revival of the newspaper began. Then under Bevan, with Orwell controlling a third of *Tribune*'s pages and occupying its most prominent bylined space, it at last 'found real success despite a doubling of price to sixpence' (ibid.: 23). While it would be wrong to say Orwell single-handedly rescued *Tribune* from oblivion, his contribution to the journal at a time when its survival appeared under threat was crucial.

The range of subject matter

According to Stephen Glover, founding editor of the *Independent* and currently media commentator on the same paper, the columnist's skill is 'in writing about matters of which one is ignorant' (1999: 290–1). Orwell demonstrates the opposite, gliding confidently over a vast range of subjects: shifting tone from the polemical, the subversively witty, the campaigning, the poetic, the belligerent, the socially compassionate, the intellectually discursive, the analytical, to the personally intimate and revealing. One moment he is generalizing provocatively; the next he is virtually inventing cultural studies, examining in precise details the front page of a newspaper or the advertisements in a women's fashion magazine. As Paul Anderson (2006: 27) comments: 'The columns reverberate with reflections on the relationship between politics and literature and with observations of public opinion and political culture – the unreported rise of popular anti-Americanism, the impact of official pro-Russia propaganda, the effects of rationing and shortage, the influence of the flying bombs on morale, attitudes to the treatment of war criminals.' For George Woodcock (1984: 18), too, 'he rarely failed to find a subject – a popular song, an aspect of propaganda, the first toad of spring[8] – on which there was something fresh to say in prose that, for all its ease and apparent casualness, was penetrating and direct'.

Here is an overview of his subjects: views on writers and writing (86); critiques of the mainstream press (17); war effort (12); language (10); personal reminiscence and experiences (10); media censorship/promotion of free speech (9); idiosyncratic likes and dislikes (9); BBC (8); post-war reconstruction (8); racism/anti-racism/anti-Semitism (7); love of nature (5); socialism (4); critiques of socialism (5); ruling classes (5); social issues (5); social observations (4); handling of collaborators (3); promotion of *Tribune* competition (3); capitalism/anti-capitalism/imperialism (3); critique of foreign media (2); critiques of pessimists (2); nationalism (2); women's issues (2); critiques of left-wing press (2); training of journalists (2); architecture (1); national anthem (1); nature of history (1); problems of geography (1); definition of fascism (1); globalization (1); British intelligentsia (1); plight of the writer (1); jingoistic ballad (1); costs of books (1); the poor (1); superstition (1) and the law of libel (1).

Keith Waterhouse, the eminent *Mirror* columnist, advised (1995): 'Every columnist needs a good half-dozen hobby horses. But do not ride them to death.' Orwell's hobby horse was clearly literature and the range of his reading was very broad, particularly given that at the same time he was writing the column he was acting as literary editor of *Tribune*, contributing regular columns to the American-based *Partisan Review* and reviewing for the *Observer* and *Manchester Evening News*. His reading was eclectic: pamphlets, novels, journals, philosophy, newspapers, a book of cartoons, biographies and autobiographies, literary criticism, history, memoirs, children's stories, a preface to a play – from *Chronological Tablets, exhibiting every remarkable occurrence from the creation of the world down to the present time* (printed by J. D. Dewick of Aldersgate Street in 1801 which pronounced the creation of the world as happening in September 4004 BC) to *Old Moore's Almanac*.[9]

Orwell and the journalistic imagination

Yet Orwell's journalistic imagination is so rich he never ceases to surprise in his columns. For instance, on 8 November 1946 (Davison 1998c: 471–2) he examines an American women's magazine sent to him, and goes on to explore its representation of beauty: 'One striking thing when one looks at these pictures is the over-bred, exhausted, even decadent style of beauty that now seems to be striven after. Nearly all of these women are immensely elongated.' But Orwell doesn't simply stay with what's presented; he highlights what's missing:

> A fairly discreet search through the magazine reveals two discreet allusions to grey hair but if there is anywhere a direct mention of fatness or middle age I have not found it. Birth and death are not mentioned either: nor is work except that a few recipes for breakfast dishes are given. The male sex enters directly or indirectly into perhaps one advertisement in twenty and photographs of dogs and kittens appear here and there. On only two pictures out of about three hundred, is a child represented.

This is hardly the writing of a typical anti-feminist!

Orwell is often linked with pessimism and defeat and gloom. For instance, according to Raymond Williams, Orwell was, like George Gissing, a spokesman of despair born of social and political disillusion (cited in Hitchens 2002: 35; see also Rai 1988). D. S. Savage (1983: 143) comments: 'From childhood onwards an embittered fatalist, Orwell yet struggled fitfully against his crippling despondency in vain attempts to escape into some freer, happier ambiance.' But in these columns it is his playfulness, optimism and lightness of spirit that so impress. He appears to be a man at the peak of his powers, playing with the genre, switching subject matter and tone effortlessly; one moment he is deconstructing the front page of a morning newspaper, the next he is constructing a mini-play about a family determined to drink their tea in the face of a V-bomb attack, recounting a racist conversation overheard in a Scottish hotel, campaigning for communal washing-up service or admitting a mistake over the authorship of a poem.

Elsewhere Orwell used his column to chew over ideas touched on in book reviews or later developed into longer essays and books. For instance, his obsession with language, which culminated in the essay 'Politics and the English Language' (in Cyril Connolly's *Horizon* of April 1946) and in his depiction of newspeak, oldspeak and doublethink in *Nineteen Eighty-Four* (1949), was reflected in many of his As I Please columns. Here his optimistic, campaigning stance is particularly striking.

Humour is always around the corner. For instance, on 7 January 1944 (see Davison 1998a: 55–8), he writes:

> Looking through the photographs in the New Years Honours List I am struck (as usual) by the quite exceptional ugliness and vulgarity of the faces displayed

there. It seems to be almost the rule that the kind of person who earns the right to call himself Lord Percy de Falcontowers should look at best like an overfed publican and at worst a tax-collector with a duodenal ulcer.

Conclusion: the redefinition of radical politics

After Eric Blair adopted the pen name George Orwell in 1932, writing became the means for creating this new personality. But while he constantly sought to represent his own personality as 'ordinary', his feelings, actions and writings, such as his As I Please columns, were far from commonplace. As Filloy argues (1998: 59): 'They were the result of an exceptionally astute and sensitive observer of wide experience bringing a sophisticated intellect to bear on the situation ... It took all of Orwell's literary craftsmanship to bury his Eton education and intellectualism and to render his perceptions and thoughts ordinary.'

Orwell was, in effect, through his contributions to *Tribune* from 1943 to 1947, defining a new kind of radical politics. It involved reducing the power of the press barons, facing up to racial intolerance, defending civil liberties. Yet it also incorporated an awareness of the power of language and propaganda, a celebration of the joys of nature and an acknowledgement of the cultural power of Christianity. Above all, in the face of the vast political, cultural, economic factors driving history, it recognized the extraordinary richness of the individual's experience – summed up in his idiosyncratic columns.

According to Andrew Marr (2004: 369), 'Writing a column is easy ... But writing a *good* column is not easy. It is fantastically difficult and only a handful of people at any one time are able to manage it.' Orwell certainly managed it.

Acknowledgements

The author wishes to thank Paul Anderson, John Gilliver, Nol van der Loop and John Tulloch for their excellent critical comments on a draft of this chapter (though he remains entirely responsible for the final copy).

Notes

1 See www.en.wikipedia.org/wiki/Tribune_%28magazine%29, accessed 1 September 2006.
2 In 1945–6, Orwell's essays were presented as discrete features and not as As I Please columns. Paul Anderson suggests that Jennie Lee 'who was notoriously touchy, had nabbed the title while Orwell was away and refused to give it back'. Between March and November 1946, Orwell took refuge on the remote island of Jura, 'supposedly to write what became *Nineteen Eighty-Four* (though, in fact, he spent most of his time fishing and mucking about)'. Paul Anderson in an email to the author, 10 October 2006.
3 Bernard Crick contributes an introduction to *Unwelcome Guerrilla* (1980), an anthology of Orwell's writing in the *New Statesman*, published by the magazine, but again only briefly covers Orwell's reviewing style. For instance, he describes Orwell as a 'working journalist': 'he tries to have something lively, amusing and provocative to say, even in unlikely contexts'.

4 Indeed, it could be argued that Orwell's greatness as a writer is largely due to his never having had to endure a university education.
5 Holmes includes a fifth category, 'Elite reinforcement of preferred message' (ibid.: 164–5), but this only applies to editorial columns.
6 'George Orwell: journalist and proto-blogger', by Richard Keeble. Available online at www.fifth-estate-online.co.uk/comment/georgeorwell.html, accessed on 26 December 2006.
7 The *Daily Graphic* was owned by Lord Kelmsley, proprietor of *The Sunday Times* and a vast chain of provincial morning and evening titles.
8 Woodcock erred here. Orwell's essay 'Some thoughts on the common toad' was printed on 12 April 1946, but not as part of the As I Please series. See Anderson (2006), pp. 306–9.
9 In a review of *The Complete Works of George Orwell*, Peter Davison (ed.) (*Observer*, 23 August 1998), Paul Foot comments: 'He says somewhere he had 900 books, but he seems to have read seven or eight times that many.'

References

Allan, Stuart (2004) *News Culture*, second edition (Maidenhead: Open University Press).
Anderson, Paul (2006) *Orwell in Tribune* (London: Politico's).
Bowker, Gordon (2003) *George Orwell* (London: Little Brown).
Bromley, Michael (2003) 'Objectivity and the other Orwell: the tabloidisation of the *Daily Mirror* and journalistic authenticity', *Media History*, 9/2: 123–35.
Carter, Michael (1985) *George Orwell and the Problem of Authentic Existence* (London/Sydney: Croom Helm).
Crick, Bernard (1980) *George Orwell: A Life* (Harmondsworth: Penguin).
Davison, Peter (ed.) (1998a) *I Have Tried to Tell the Truth 1943–4: The Complete Works of George Orwell* (London: Secker & Warburg).
—— (ed.) (1998b) *I Belong to the Left 1945: The Complete Works of George Orwell* (London: Secker & Warburg).
—— (ed.) (1998c) *Smothered under Journalism 1946: The Complete Works of George Orwell* (London: Secker & Warburg).
—— (ed.) (1998d) *It is What I Think 1947–8: The Complete Works of George Orwell* (London: Secker & Warburg).
Dentith, Simon (1998) 'Orwell and propaganda', in Holderness, Graham, Loughrey, Bryan, and Yousaf, Nahem (eds), *George Orwell: Contemporary Critical Essays* (Houndmills, Basingstoke: Macmillan Press), pp. 203–27.
Eagleton, Terry (2003) 'Reach-me-down romantic', *London Review of Books*, 19 (June): 6–9.
Filloy, Richard (1998) 'Orwell's political persuasion', in Holderness, Graham, Loughrey, Bryan, and Yousaf, Nahem (eds), *George Orwell: Contemporary Critical Essays* (Houndmills, Basingstoke: Macmillan Press), pp. 47–63.
Glover, Stephen (1999) 'What columnists are good for', in Glover, Stephen (ed.), *Secrets of the Press: Journalists on Journalism* (London: Allen Lane/Penguin Press) pp. 289–98.
Hitchens, Christopher (2002) *Orwell's Victory* (London: Allen Lane).
Holmes, Tim (2006) 'Creating identities, building communities: why comment?', in Keeble, Richard (ed.), *Print Journalism: A Critical Introduction* (London: Routledge), pp. 159–68.
Hunter, Lynette (1984) *George Orwell: The search for a voice* (Milton Keynes: Open University Press).
Ingle, Stephen (1993) *George Orwell: A political life* (Manchester: Manchester University Press).

Keeble, Richard (2001) 'Orwell as war correspondent: a reassessment', *Journalism Studies*, 2/3: 393–406.

—— (2005) 'Journalism ethics: towards an Orwellian critique?', in Allan, Stuart (ed.), *Journalism: Critical Issues* (Maidenhead: Open University Press), pp. 54–66.

Lucas, Scott (2000) 'The socialist fallacy', *New Statesman*, 29 May, pp. 47–50.

—— (2003) *Orwell* (London: Haus Publishing).

Marr, Andrew (2004) *My Trade: A Short History of British Journalism* (London: Macmillan).

Meyers, Jeffrey (2000) *Orwell: Wintry Conscience of a Generation* (New York/London: W. W. Norton & Company).

Newsinger, John (1999) 'The American Connection: George Orwell, "Literary Trotskyism" and the New York intellectual', *Labour History Review*, 64/1: 23–43.

Norris, Christopher (ed.) (1984) *Orwell: Views from the Left* (London: Lawrence & Wishart).

Orwell, Sonia, and Angus, Ian (eds) (1968) *The Collected Essays, Journalism and Letters*, vol. 1: *An Age Like This 1920–40*, vol. 2: *My Country Right or Left*, vol. 3: *As I Please*, vol. 4: *In Front of Your Nose* (Harmondsworth, Middlesex: Penguin).

Patai, Daphne (1984) *The Orwell Mystique: A Study in Male Ideology* (Amherst: University of Massachusetts Press).

Rai, Alok (1988) *Orwell and the Politics of Despair: A Critical Study of the Writings of George Orwell* (Cambridge: Cambridge University Press).

Rodden, John (1989) *The Politics of Literary Reputation: The Making and Claiming of 'St George' Orwell* (Oxford: Oxford University Press).

—— (1998) 'Orwell and the London Left Intelligentsia', in Holderness, Graham, Loughrey, Bryan, and Yousaf, Nahem (eds), *George Orwell: Contemporary Critical Essays* (Houndmills, Basingstoke: Macmillan Press), pp. 161–81.

Savage, D. S. (1983) 'The Fatalism of George Orwell', in Ford, Boris (ed.), *The New Pelican Guide to English Literature*, vol. 8: The Present (Harmondsworth: Penguin Books), pp. 129–46.

Shelden, Michael (1991) *Orwell: The Authorised Biography* (London: Heinemann).

Silvester, Christopher (1997) *The Penguin Book of Columnists* (London: Penguin).

Sparks, Colin (1992) 'Popular journalism: theories and practice', in Dahlgren, Peter, and Sparks, Colin (eds), *Journalism and Popular Culture* (London: Sage), pp. 24–44.

Spurling, Hilary (2002) *The Girl from the Fiction Department: A Portrait of Sonia Orwell* (London: Penguin Books).

Stansky, Peter, and Abrahams, Williams (1972) *The Unknown Orwell* (London: Constable).

Taylor, D. J. (2003) *Orwell: The Life* (London: Chatto & Windus).

Waterhouse, Keith (1995) 'Talking of which …', *Guardian*, 6 March.

Williams, Raymond (1984) *George Orwell* (London: Fontana).

Woodcock, George (1984) *The Crystal Spirit: A Study of George Orwell*, second edition (London: Fourth Estate).

Website

www.herodote.info/orwell/biblio_orwell.htm – contains a massive bibliography of 500 Orwell-related texts

Chapter 8

An unscathed tourist of wars
The journalism of Martha Gellhorn

Deborah Wilson

Better known now as a pioneering war correspondent, during her lifetime Martha Gellhorn yearned for personal satisfaction and critical appreciation as a novelist. Gellhorn was born in 1908 in St Louis, Missouri. After studying one year at Bryn Mawr College, Pennsylvania, she decided to become a journalist and so never graduated. She worked briefly for the *New Republic* and the New York-based *Times Union* but then, in 1930, left the United States on a speculative mission to research and write in Europe, paying for her transatlantic passage by writing an article on the shipping line's service. In Paris she worked for a number of journals, including *Vogue* and the *St Louis Post-Dispatch*, and began a controversial affair with the married journalist and author Bertrand de Jouvenal. She returned to the States, and her first, highly autobiographical, novel *What Mad Pursuit* (1934) had mixed reviews but her second book, *The Trouble I've Seen* (1936) – based on her reports for the Federal Emergency Relief Administration on how people were surviving the Depression across America – was well received. In all she published six novels between 1934 and 1967. Gellhorn established herself as a war correspondent by filing reports from the Spanish Civil War during 1937–8 for the American magazine *Collier's Weekly*. While reporting from Madrid she worked alongside the celebrated American novelist Ernest Hemingway whom she married on 21 November 1940. Hemingway dedicated his famous novel about the Spanish Civil War, *For Whom the Bell Tolls* (1940), to Gellhorn – but the marriage was to last just five years. Gellhorn went on to report on World War Two, including the D-Day landings and the liberation of the Dachau concentration camp.[1] She later reported from Vietnam in 1966 (for the *Guardian*) and from the 1967 Arab/Israeli Six-Day War. Her final war assignment – at the age of 81 – was the 1989 invasion of Panama by the US. Collections of Gellhorn's journalism were compiled as *The Face of War* (1959) and *The View From the Ground* (1988). Her sole overtly autobiographical work, and the only piece in which she wrote in the first person, was *Travels With Myself and Another* (1978), which includes the account of a trip to China in 1941, with Hemingway referred to throughout as 'UC' – Gellhorn's Unwilling Companion. She died on 15 February 1998, aged 89.

Gellhorn the war correspondent

Gellhorn's career as a journalist began as a reporter on a small local paper in the US. But she had been on family holidays in Europe and had developed a keen interest in working there. She took a passage on a ship, writing an article on the service in exchange for her fare. The writing of her first novel, *What Mad Pursuit* (1934), which was based on her experiences in Paris where she became active in the pacifist movement, was funded by the fashion articles she sent back to the US and a number of brief jobs. This set a pattern which would form a central theme to her working life: Gellhorn the author supported by Gellhorn the journalist.

In 1936 Gellhorn was in Stuttgart, working in a library on the background research for a novel. It was there that she read in the German press about the beginning of the Spanish Civil War: 'I read the newspapers, coarse and belligerent in tone, which is how I learned of the war in Spain, described as the revolt of a rabble of "Red Swine Dogs". Those few weeks turned me into a devout anti-fascist' (Gellhorn 1992). In her introduction to the selected articles written in Spain and reprinted as a collection in *The Face of War* (1959), Gellhorn describes her transformation from pacifist and liberal-reformer:

> I stayed some months in Germany discussing, with anyone who still dared to discuss, the freedom of the mind, the rights of the individual, and the Red Swine dogs of Spain. Then I went back to America, finished my novel, shoved it forever into a desk drawer, and started to get myself to Spain. I had stopped being a pacifist and become an anti-fascist.[2]

She was determined to back the Republicans against General Franco's forces and made her way to Madrid via France carrying a letter from *Collier's* but no formal accreditation.

> This letter was intended to help me with any authorities who wondered what I was doing in Spain, or why I was trying to get there; otherwise it meant nothing. I had no connection with a newspaper or magazine, and I believed that all one did about a war was go to it, as a gesture of solidarity, and get killed, or survive if lucky until the war was over ... I had no idea you could be what I became, an unscathed tourist of wars.[3]

At first Gellhorn spent her time learning from the experience of the established war correspondents, absorbing what she could of the language and the conflict whilst working with the aid stations, and she was urged to write about the situation in Madrid. But she was initially reluctant, unsure that any reporting from a more domestic, possibly *female*, perspective carried any validity as war reportage. When she was eventually persuaded to send a piece to *Collier's Weekly*, an illustrated magazine which carried both articles and short stories (and welcomed the human interest angle), it was published, 'and all of a sudden I was a war correspondent' (Gellhorn 1990).

Gellhorn's contribution to the reporting of that time was to describe for the reader the daily life of Madrid citizens living in a city under siege: snapshots of the devastating impact of military conflict.

> Later, you could see people around Madrid examining the new shell holes with curiosity and wonder. Otherwise they went on with the routine of their lives, as if they had been interrupted by a heavy rainstorm but nothing more .[4]

The civil war in Spain was Gellhorn's induction into the role of war correspondent and marked the beginning of a canon of journalistic work that would encompass the major military conflicts of the twentieth century. According to media historian and theorist Fred Inglis (2002: 14): 'Martha Gellhorn bore witness to the endurance and heroism of ordinary men-and-women-become-soldiers, and to the conduct, mostly admirable, of those they had come to save from the most abominable and evil enemy history had ever seen.'

'Fiction is far more interesting'

Gellhorn often acknowledged the reliance she placed as an author upon her journalism. She constantly made notes of what she observed, characters she saw and dialogue she overheard, to compensate for what she perceived to be her defective memory. She would use these observations, kept in her diaries and notebooks,[5] to flesh the bones of her narrative. Gellhorn often spoke of her need to see for herself, witness first-hand, what she wanted to write about, both journalistically and as a writer of fiction. In a letter to Ernest Hemingway in 1943 she said: '... everything I have ever written has come through journalism first, every book I mean; since I am not Jane Austen nor the Brontë sisters and I have to see before I can imagine, and this is the only way I have of seeing' (Moorehead 2006: 158).

She also, more pragmatically, used journalism to fund her novel writing, as she told Nigel Forde in an interview for BBC Radio 4's *Bookshelf*: 'I earned enough money from journalism to buy me time to write ... I couldn't write one without the other' (Gellhorn 1990). This emphasis on the need for her 'writing' to be supported by her journalistic work is interesting and the same notion appears in her letters. Her assumption that journalism was not 'writing' is indicative of the greater significance she attached to her fiction and could perhaps have contributed to the greater challenge she found when composing novels and short stories. In evaluating her own career, Gellhorn asserted she found fiction 'infinitely more interesting than reporting' (ibid.). She attempted to make her narrative convincing through careful characterization, based on people she had known or seen, believing that by doing this she would be able to show rather than tell, making larger issues more personalized and thereby more comprehensible.

Whilst recognizing that her journalism informed her fiction writing, Gellhorn also acknowledged that she used literary devices to write her journalism and endeavoured to employ the same techniques 'to make the sounds, the smell, the look, the feel come through – although based on fact' (ibid.). Rollyson notes that from her earliest war correspondence, one of Gellhorn's first reports from Madrid, 'High Explosive for Everyone' (July 1937), her journalism was 'constructed like a story' (Rollyson 2002: 75). He continues:

> Using understatement ... Gellhorn alludes to her own hysteria by changing to the first person, describing her descent to the hotel lobby, concentrating on her breathing because the air sticks in her throat. The strict controls she puts on her language are themselves indicators of the discipline she had to maintain during the constant shelling. War is given a face, an intimacy and immediacy ... There is a delicacy, a light touch in the prose, that makes the ugliness of death and destruction all the more appalling.
>
> (Ibid.)

His observations are well illustrated in 'The Besieged City' (November 1937):

> There were ten little houses, huddled together, with cloth tacked over the windows and newspapers stuck in the walls to keep the wind out. Women with quiet, pale faces and quiet children stood by the trough and looked at one house, or what was left of it. The men stood a little nearer. A shell had landed directly on one flimsy shack, where five people were keeping warm, talking with one another for comfort and for gaiety, and now there was only a mound of clay and kindling wood, and they had dug out the five dead bodies as soon as it was light. The people standing there knew the dead. A woman reached down suddenly for her child and took it in her arms, and held close to her.[6]

Gellhorn understood the need to relate what was happening in Spain to her remote readership in the US.

> It seemed a little crazy to be living in a hotel, like a hotel in Des Moines or New Orleans, with a lobby and wicker chairs in the lounge, and signs on the door of your room telling you that they would press your clothes immediately and that meals served privately cost ten per cent more, and meantime it was like a trench when they lay down an artillery barrage. The whole place trembled to the explosion of the shells.[7]

In Gellhorn's journalism, first-person narrative and acute observations of people, their lives and situations, were dominant. She eschewed objective intellectual analysis; featuring an authority figure as the subject of her stories was of little interest to her. As Gellhorn told Nigel Forde on BBC Radio 4's *Bookshelf* programme in 1990: 'I don't like the people who sit at the top and decide for all the rest of us' (Gellhorn 1990). Gellhorn's greater emphasis throughout her work was on giving a voice to those who would not otherwise be heard, as with this piece she wrote after talking to three Polish men in London in 1944:

> It did not seem amazing to him that 85–100,000 children in the Warsaw district alone were going to secret schools. The Polish underground State paid the teachers and printed the text books, and carried education through from primary training to the final examinations and awarding of high school diplomas. If the Germans caught them, the teachers were shot; the parents of the students were sent to concentration camps, and the children who studied were deported for forced labor. But naturally the schools continued.[8]

In November 1943, Gellhorn travelled to Woodhall Spa, in rural Lincolnshire, to one of the RAF airfields used as a base for the Lancaster bombers. There she mixed with British, US and Polish airmen.'The land where they live is as flat as Kansas and cold now and dun-colored. The land seems unused and almost not lived in, but the air is always busy.'[9] A few years later, a short story, 'Week-end at Grimsby' (1951), was published in *The Atlantic*; it vividly describes the desolate Lincolnshire countryside in November.

> This was the shapeless weather all travellers dread. A smeared grey sky closed down over the smeared brown land. Cold leaked around the window-frames and the door of the railway carriage. England looked larger, flatter, and more desolate than was either possible or fair.
>
> (Gellhorn 1954: 41)

Yet Gellhorn seemed most at ease as a writer when she was most enraged or faced with extraordinary circumstances. She would never appear at these times to struggle with writer's block which could plague her in peacetime, most markedly when writing fiction. It seemed she needed drama and the necessity to rail against inequity and suffering to produce her best work. Without the adrenalin and the passionate indignation, Gellhorn could feel herself floundering and stagnating. In a letter to friends from Curacao in 1952: 'Am resting my soul … in this complete solitude and trying to write. I do write, hours every day, and I loathe increasingly each sentence as I make it … I wish I were an easy, happy writer; but there it is'. Moorehead 2006: 227).

Gellhorn and Hemingway: 'flint and steel'

Gellhorn's constant doubts about her own ability to write good fiction were hampered further by constant, and often critical, comparisons of her work with that of her husband of five years, Ernest Hemingway. They had first met socially whilst Gellhorn was on holiday with her mother and brother, Alfred, in Key West,

Florida, in 1936. It had been their first Christmas since the sudden death of her father George, an eminent gynaecologist. *The Trouble I've Seen* (1936), based on reports made by Gellhorn for a US government agency on the effects of the Depression on the United States, had been well received by the critics, giving her some status as a newly published author. After the New Year, Martha stayed a couple of weeks to continue with her writing and take advice and encouragement from Hemingway. Later they worked alongside each other in the Spanish Civil War – and so began their affair.

The tendency for the male author and journalist to dominate at that time made the long shadow cast by 'Papa', as Hemingway was affectionately known to his family and friends, inevitable. Gellhorn accepted these comparisons and frequently analysed their differences herself, their relationship an uncomfortable mix of jealousy and mutual admiration. It is clear from Gellhorn's letters that she felt she needed to strike a balance between learning from Hemingway and developing her own voice through her writing: 'I do not want to take his style, no matter how fine it may be … my own is my literary motto.'[10] During the early and best years of their relationship there is evidence in Gellhorn's letters that Hemingway supported and encouraged her writing and she admired his. He deplored her lack of discipline, in that she would only write when she felt inspired whereas he believed in regular writing whether the resulting material was acceptable or not.

Inglis believes that at times their styles are indistinguishable and he gives as examples sections of their reports from Madrid (2002: 7–9). While in London *The Times* was calling for appeasement with Hitler and newspapers in New York and Washington were downplaying the rise of the Nazis, Gellhorn reported for *Collier's*:

> An old woman, with a shawl over her shoulders, holding a terrified thin little boy by the hand, runs out into the square. You know what she is thinking: she is thinking she must get the child home, you are always safer in your own place, with the things you know. Somehow you do not believe you can get killed when you are sitting in your own parlor, you never think that. She is in the middle of the square when the next one comes.
>
> A small piece of twisted steel, hot and very sharp, sprays off from the shell; it takes the little boy in the throat. The old woman stands there, holding the hand of the dead child, looking at him stupidly, not saying anything, and men run out toward her to carry the child. At their left, at the side of the square, is a huge brilliant sign which says GET OUT OF MADRID.
>
> (Ibid.: 7)

As Inglis comments:

> The bite and dryness of the prose were already part of the almost-finished style of the twenty-nine year old; the solidarity with avoidable suffering, stiffened by her researches for the Relief agency, had struck deep roots in her character; the laconic diction, the American understatement, the domestic sympathy

('you are always safer in your own place') … and the admiration for everyday bravery are all distinctively hers.

(Ibid.: 7–8)

In focusing on 'everyday bravery', her subjects are, indeed, very often women. For instance, she continues her report on the Madrid bombings of 1937 with these sharp observations:

> Inside a shoe shop, five women are trying on shoes. Two girls are buying summery sandals, sitting by the front window of the shop. After the third explosion, the salesman says politely: 'I think we had better move farther back into the shop. The window might break and cut you.' Women are standing in line, as they do all over Madrid, quiet women, dressed usually in black, with market baskets on their arms, waiting to buy food. A shell falls across the square. They turn their heads to look, and move a little closer to the house, but no one leaves her place in line. After all, they have been waiting there for three hours and the children expect food at home.[11]

Rollyson also judges Hemingway a lesser journalist than Gellhorn: 'His work in Spain lacks Gellhorn's intensity, focus and unity – in part because he was expected to supply newsworthy articles, whereas she wrote for a weekly magazine that wanted human interest stories. She did not have to key herself around major battles or significant events.' He continues: 'Her range was narrower but more profound. She never approached her material with the great novelist's glibness, conscious of saving his best words for *For Whom the Bell Tolls*, which he hoped would be regarded as the definitive work of fiction on Spain. She put everything she had into her miniatures of war' (2002: 77).

By the start of World War Two, Gellhorn had matured and developed her voice as a journalist. This was not as a result of a calculated construction, rather that her journalism found its own distinctive timbre as a natural consequence of her temperament and need to 'bear witness'. There were times when the subject matter of Gellhorn's reportage was determined by circumstance; where, for example, she found herself denied access to the frontline, she would uncover alternative but equally valid subjects on which to report until she found a way to reach where she felt she needed to be.

During World War Two, for example, she reported from Finland and China with relative ease before the US entered the war, but after Japan bombed Pearl Harbor (on 7 December 1941) frontline reporting became more difficult, with the US military objecting to the presence of women correspondents in conflict zones. As Chambers, Steiner and Fleming report in their historical overview of women war reporters (2004: 202): 'US officials were averse to offering women credentials and mounted many barriers against them. In addition to the harassment they faced – in the form of sexist innuendoes and jokes – the lack of toilet facilities for women was used as an ongoing excuse by successive governments and the military to systematically bar women correspondents from the key events that needed to be reported on.'

Gellhorn commented:

> The US Army public relations officers, the bosses of the American press, were a doctrinaire bunch who objected to a woman being a correspondent with combat troops. I felt like a veteran of the Crimean War by then, and I had been sent to Europe to do my job, which was not to report the rear areas or the woman's angle.[12]

And in a letter to the then editor of *Collier's*, she wrote:

> it is really too late to do anything about my sex. That is a handicap I have been struggling under since I was five years old, and I shall just forge ahead, bravely, despite the army … This is going to be a nice long war, and sooner or later they are going to want to make it popular, and then folks like us can work.
>
> (Moorehead 2006: 123)

Significantly, comments on Gellhorn by men have tended to be highly sexualized. Inglis is typical when he says (2002: 8): 'Martha was an adventuress, she loved sex and good wine and, though with one caustic eye, men.' And his adulation of her culminates in this sentence: 'So it is worth making a statue of her, tall, beautiful, with brilliant blue, very slightly glaucous eyes and the proud curved beak of her nose lifted in scorn or in watchfulness' (ibid.: 15). Moreover, Chambers, Steiner and Fleming (2004: 202) highlight the sexism faced by women war reporters generally: 'The stories of several women who reported during the two world wars, and especially during the Second World War, underscore similar degrees of courage and determination, but also point to the heightened sexualization of women reporters, arguable to a far greater degree than women reporting in other arenas.'

But Gellhorn grew up in an environment that nurtured the intellectual and encouraged independence of thought: her mother was at the forefront of the suffrage movement in the US. So it never occurred to her that she could not function on a comparable level with men. 'It's assumed that men do whatever they want – I just assumed that I did whatever I wanted' (Gellhorn 1993). As Chambers, Steiner and Fleming (2004: 202) add: 'Some women seem not to have been particularly bothered by the attention to their bodies. Perhaps this is because they had no choice or perhaps it related to their willingness to acquire reporting assignments by claiming they would provide a different angle from that of male reporters.'

So, given the restrictions imposed by the US military on women gaining access to the frontline, Gellhorn went to where the war was accessible to her. In England she reported from Lancaster bomber bases in Lincolnshire and on the effects of the war on London; in Italy she travelled with European troops, who were more accommodating than the US forces. She was able to file a story on the D-Day landings by joining a hospital ship, and when the Allies felt the war was progressing in their favour and could perhaps be coming to an end, there was a greater relaxation on the control of journalists and Gellhorn was able to join the troops in mainland Europe, including Holland, Belgium and with fighter aircraft over Germany.

D-Day landings coverage: a study in contrasts

Hemingway, by contrast, had the name and the accreditation: moreover, he was male so could 'access all areas' with ease. For the D-Day landings, he crossed the Channel with a landing vessel but remained at sea off the coast of Normandy. His account of the D-Day landings, *Voyage to Victory*,[13] is as a participant and no doubt his status as America's best-known living writer at that time added to the seemingly heroic, iconoclastic theme running through the account. Gladstein notes that Hemingway would place himself in the foreground and emphasize his own role in the midst of the scene he was describing:

> Hemingway is definitely the protagonist of his reporting. He highlights his participation in the invasion both in his articles for *Collier's* and in his written recollections after the war. In *Voyage to Victory* he asserts his expertise ... As they roar in to the beach, he explains, 'I sat high on the stern to see what we were up against.'[14] He scouts the shore, spotting two machine-gun nests and warns the lieutenant. Writing later of his role as a correspondent, Hemingway saw himself as a key part of the war effort.
>
> (Gladstein 2003: 263)

Meanwhile, Gellhorn had surreptitiously joined up with an American medical team as their hospital ship was sent across the Channel in the wake of the flotilla to bring back injured servicemen. It is as a participant also that Gellhorn reports, but in her case from the D-Day beaches themselves rather than at a distance.

> Everyone was violently busy on that crowded dangerous shore. The pebbles were the size of melons and we stumbled up a road that a huge road shovel was scooping out. We walked with the utmost care between the narrowly placed white tape lines that marked the mine-cleared path, and headed for a tent marked with a Red Cross just behind the beach ... The dust that rose in the gray night light seemed like the fog of war itself. Then we got off on the grass and it was perhaps the most surprising of all the day's surprises to smell the sweet smell of summer grass, a smell of cattle and peace and sun that had warmed the earth some other time when summer was real.[15]

By this time Hemingway, who had needed much persuasion from Gellhorn to cover the war in Europe at all, had effectively usurped her position at *Collier's*, much to her chagrin, by offering to write articles for them. But he was scooped by his wife who, through her ingenuity and perhaps reckless bravado, managed to land on the beach, whereas Hemingway had, while writing himself into the landings, been careful to omit the fact that he did not actually touch sand. As a fully accredited journalist, but also a civilian, he was kept a little distance from the shore until the main part of the action had passed.

Objectivity and Gellhorn's 'journalism of attachment'

Gellhorn, as a war correspondent, employed a distinctive, contained, empathetic reporting style. For instance, during the Vietnam War she reported from Qui Nhon provincial hospital where civilians were treated 'under conditions suitable for the Crimean War'. She wrote:

> We, unintentionally, are killing and wounding three or four times more people than the Vietcong do, so we are told, on purpose. We are not maniacs and monsters, but our planes range the sky all day and all night, and our artillery is lavish and we have much more deadly stuff to kill with. The people are there on the ground, sometimes destroyed by accident, sometimes destroyed because Vietcong are reported to be among them. This is indeed a new kind of war.
>
> (Pilger 1986: 264)

Later she reported: 'We are uprooting the people from the lovely land where they have lived for generations. Is this an honourable way for a great nation to fight a war more than 10,000 miles from its safe homeland?'[16] Her articles were published in the London *Guardian* in 1966 but in the United States only the *St Louis Post-Dispatch* bought the series, yet it failed to publish the most polemical piece which raised forbidden questions over US involvement in Vietnam. 'All I did,' she later commented, 'was report from the ground up, not the other way round' (see Pilger 2004: 1).

As a result she was refused a visa by the Saigon regime and unable to return. Indeed, her disdain for objective reporting in conflict zones enabled her to produce the emotive journalistic prose for which she was known and which informed later work in the personalization of news and what has latterly been termed the 'journalism of attachment'.

This form of journalism has been defined by former BBC war correspondent (and later Independent MP) Martin Bell as 'a journalism that cares as well as knows ... that will not stand neutrally between good and evil, right and wrong, the victim and the oppressor' (Bell 1998: 16). The BBC's guidelines required reporters to be objective and dispassionate.

> I am no longer sure what 'objective' means: I see nothing object-like in the relationship between the reporter and the event, but rather a human and dynamic interaction between them. As for 'dispassionate', it is not only impossible but inappropriate to be thus neutralized – I would say even *neutered* – at the scene of an atrocity or massacre, or most man-made calamities.
>
> (Ibid.: 18)

The journalism of attachment has its critics, not only those who aspire to objectivity, impartiality and balance, but also those who feel that it polarizes and oversimplifies complex issues. According to Mick Hume, *Times* columnist and former editor of *Living Marxism*, the journalist following Bell's principles is in danger of 'playing the role of crusader' (Hume 1997: 4). Tessa Mayes, writing in the *British Journalism Review*, says that the journalism of attachment, in its anti-objectivity stance may engender a greater emotive response from the news consumer, but encourages speculative reporting.

> What appears to be a harmless new style to 'engage' people has altered journalistic standards – and not for the better. Worse, perhaps, is the possibility that this variation in news values may have contributed to the erosion of trust between the news media and the public. After all why should the public rely on news reporters if they're seen only to be offering yet another opinion?
>
> (Mayes 2004: 59)

And Greg McLaughlin (2002) suggests that the journalism of attachment leads to unacceptable moralizing and self-righteousness.[17]

Would Gellhorn have regarded herself as an early proponent of the journalism of attachment? Certainly one main element of this form of journalism, that a reporter can be nothing but subjective in a war zone, is something in which she believed. She was vehemently opposed to objectivity in her reporting, as she told Jenni Murray in an interview for BBC Radio 4's *Woman's Hour.*

> This objective stuff seems to me both rubbish and boring … if you are seeing something happening, the idea that you are so brain dead and stony hearted that you have no reaction to it strike me as absolute nonsense. You see appalling things happening to people … you are describing what you see, and what you see is awful.
>
> (Gellhorn 1993)

Yet commitment to a cause did not mean to Gellhorn that all critical attitudes had to be suspended. In an interview with the war correspondent and documentary filmmaker Max Ophuls she raised queries about any reporter who became so caught up in a cause that they lost all their critical faculties.[18] Moreover, the veteran investigative reporter John Pilger, whom she referred to as 'my spiritual heir' (Moorehead 2003: 478), says that Gellhorn would have had a problem with the label 'journalism of attachment'. He believes she would have dismissed it and argued instead: 'Before we label those who believe journalism is about humanity not power, let's deconstruct some of the distractions, such as the insidious institutional bias by the likes of the BBC behind its façade of "impartiality". Martha Gellhorn was a fine journalist because she gave priority not to a fake "balance" but to finding out the truth.'[19]

Pilger advises against framing the argument in traditional presumptions of 'objectivity' and 'subjectivity'. He agrees that Martin Bell was 'right about the "illusion of objectivity" which belonged to "bystander journalism"', but while rejecting objectivity as 'often merely a mask for an established consensus and bias',[20] he is wary of the term. Matthew Kieran agrees that the objectivity/subjectivity debate, when considering the journalism of attachment, is oversimplistic and that perhaps a redefinition of the key terms is needed:

> Objectivity is a matter of arriving at the appropriate report, interpretation *and* evaluation of a state of affairs. Impartiality, unlike neutrality does not preclude evaluative judgement. For good journalism should not just describe how and why an event happened but seek to show its true nature; and often what is most important is to highlight, in the case of a war massacre for example, the truly evil and horrific nature of what has been perpetrated.
>
> (Kieran 1998: xi)

Critics of the journalism of attachment, such as Hume, claim that it exaggerates the power of reporting as a potential force for good. But Gellhorn doubted that she could use her position as a journalist to directly influence the outcome of the events she was reporting. 'I do not believe in journalism; I think it changes nothing' (Moorehead 2006: 126). But she was driven to bear witness to what she considered man's inhumanity to man. In a letter to her mother written just before leaving to report from Vietnam in August 1966, Gellhorn said: 'All I know how to do is write: the only way I can write with any authority, in the hope of influencing even a very few people, is to write from first-hand knowledge' (ibid.: 329).

Conclusion: Gellhorn's legacy to journalism

A reader of Gellhorn's work, then, would have little doubt over her political leanings: it was clear she was anti-Reagan, pro-Clinton, anti-Thatcher, anti-war, anti-fascist, pro-Israeli. If there were contradictions in any of these stances, they did not concern her. According to Fred Inglis (2002: 16): 'She spoke some truths which cannot nowadays be spoken, about the mad rage and crazy credulity taught by some versions of Islam …'. In 1961 she was not afraid to compare militant Arabs to the Nazis. She wrote:

> In a new setting, Palestinian refugees assume the role of the *Sudetendeutsch*. Israel becomes Czechoslovakia. Propaganda prepares the war for liberation of 'our brothers'. Victory over – a minor near enemy is planned as the essential first step on a long triumphant road of conquest. A thousand-year Muslim Reich, the African continent ruled by Egypt, may be a mad dream, but we have experience of mad dreams and mad dreamers. We cannot be too careful. The echo of Hitler's voice is heard again in the land, now speaking Arabic.

Martha Gellhorn broke new ground for journalists and her legacy to journalism was to develop a different perspective for war correspondents; to show there were more dimensions to the reporting of military conflict. Her particular significance for her gender was the trail she marked for women reporters to follow and her determination that being a woman need not limit your ability to tell a story in places where women were traditionally denied access. Moreover. Gellhorn demonstrated, through the symbiotic relationship she had, initially unwittingly, forged between her reporting and her fiction writing, how combining journalistic and literary techniques can serve to tell a story with conviction and humanity.

Notes

1 See the full report in John Pilger (ed.) (2004) *Tell Me No Lies: Investigative Journalism and its Triumphs* (London: Jonathan Cape), pp. 1–9. Pilger says of it: 'Few pieces of journalism are finer' (p. 3).
2 From 'The War in Spain', November 1959, reprinted in *The Face of War*, Gellhorn 1998, p.14.
3 Ibid., p.15.
4 From 'High Explosive for Everyone', July 1937, reprinted in *The Face of War*, Gellhorn 1998, p. 21.
5 A number are kept in the Howard Gotlieb Archival Research Center at Boston University in the US.
6 From 'The Besieged City', November 1937, reprinted in *The Face of War*, Gellhorn 1998, p. 30.
7 From 'High Explosive for Everyone', July 1937, reprinted in *The Face of War*, Gellhorn 1998, pp. 18–19.
8 From 'Three Poles', March 1944, reprinted in *The Face of War*, Gellhorn 1998, p. 106.
9 From 'The Bomber Boys', November 1943, reprinted in *The Face of War*, Gellhorn 1998, p. 99.
10 'Letter to Pauline Hemingway', 14 January 1937, from St Louis. In Moorehead (2006).
11 See www.pbs.org/weta/reportingamericaatwar/reporters/gellhorn/madrid.html, accessed on 13 December 2006.
12 From 'The Second World War', London, 1959, reprinted in *The Face of War*, Gellhorn 1998, p. 96.
13 Published in *Collier's*, 22 July 1944.
14 From William White (ed.) (1967) *By-Line: Ernest Hemingway* (New York: Scribner's), p. 349.
15 From 'The First Hospital Ship', June 1944, reprinted in *The Face of War*, Gellhorn 1998, p. 126.
16 See www.iml.jou.ufl.edu/projects/Fall98/Bleichwehl/war.htm, accessed on 13 December 2006.
17 A useful, brief overview of the debate over the journalism of attachment appears in B. Franklin et al. (eds) (2005) *Key Concepts in Journalism Studies* (London: Sage), pp. 125–6.
18 See www.books.guardian.co.uk/news/articles/0,,1432426,00.html, accessed on 13 December 2006.
19 John Pilger in email to author, 16 December 2006.
20 Ibid.

References

Bell, M. (1997) 'TV news: how far should we go?', *British Journalism Review*, 8/1: 7–16.

—— (1998) 'The journalism of attachment', in Kieran, M. (ed.), *Media ethics* (London: Routledge), pp. 15–22.

Chambers, D., Steiner, L. and Fleming, C. (eds) (2004) *Women and Journalism* (London: Routledge).

Dimbleby, R. (1945) *Report from Belsen*, BBC Radio. Available online at www.bbc.co.uk/heritage/story/ww2/censor_prop.shtml, accessed on 6 December 2006.

Gellhorn, M. (1954) *The Honeyed Peace: A Collection of Stories* (London: André Deutsch).

—— (1961) 'The Arabs of Palestine', *The Atlantic Monthly*, October 1961. Available online at www.theatlantic.com/doc/196110/gellhorn/9, accessed on 23 December 2006.

—— (1978) *Travels with Myself and Another* (London: Allen Lane).

—— (1989) *The View from the Ground* (London: Granta Books).

—— (1990) Interviewed on *Bookshelf* by Nigel Forde, BBC Radio 4.

—— (1992) 'Ohne Mich: why I shall never return to Germany', *Granta* (December. Available online at www.granta.com/extracts/971, accessed on 13 December 2006.

—— (1993) Interviewed on *Woman's Hour* by Jenni Murray, BBC Radio 4.

—— (1998) *The Face of War* (London: Granta).

Gladstein, M. R. (2003) 'Mr. Novelist goes to war: Hemingway and Steinbeck as frontline correspondents', *War, Literature and the Arts: An International Journal of the Humanities*, 15/1,2: 258–66. Available online at www.wlajournal.com/15_1–2/gladstein%20258–266.pdf, accessed on 23 December 2006.

Hume, M. (1997) *Whose War is it Anyway? The Dangers of the Journalism of Attachment* (London: B. M. Inform Inc.).

Inglis, F. (2002) *People's Witness: The Journalist in Modern Politics* (New Haven and London: Yale University Press).

Kert, B. (1983) *The Hemingway Women* (New York: W. W. Norton & Company).

Kieran, M. (1998) *Media Ethics* (London: Routledge).

McLaughlin, G. (2002) *The War Correspondent* (London: Pluto Press)

Mayes, T. (2004) 'Here is the views-as-news', *British Journalism Review*, 15/2: 55–9.

Moorehead, C. (2003) *Martha Gellhorn: A Life* (London: Chatto & Windus).

—— (2006) *Selected Letters of Martha Gellhorn* (New York: Henry Holt & Company).

Murrow, E. R. (1945) *Report From Buchenwald*, CBS Radio. Available online at www.lib.berkeley.edu/MRC/murrow.html, accessed on 6 December 2006.

Pilger, J. (1986) *Heroes* (London: Jonathan Cape).

—— (2004) *Tell Me No Lies: Investigative Journalism and its Triumphs* (London: Jonathan Cape).

Rollyson, C. (1990) *Nothing Ever Happens to the Brave: The Story of Martha Gellhorn* (New York: St Martin's Press).

—— (2002) *Beautiful Exile: The Life of Martha Gellhorn* (London: Aurum Press).

Websites

www.bbc.co.uk/bbcfour/audiointerviews/profilepages/gellhornm1.shtml

www.granta.com/authors/95 (a collection of Gellhorn's reports for *Granta*).

www.nwi.net/~dorman/angie/gell2.htm (includes essay 'Reflections on the Human Legacy of War: Martha Gellhorn in Europe 1943–45' by Angelia Hardy Dorman).

Chapter 9

Cold-blooded journalism
Truman Capote and the non-fiction novel

Nick Nuttall

Truman Streckfus Persons was born on 30 September 1924 in New Orleans. His parents, Lillie Mae and Archulus 'Arch' Persons, divorced when he was six and his mother sent him to Monroeville, Alabama, where he was raised by her relatives. Eventually, in 1933, he moved to New York to live with his mother and her new husband Joseph Capote. In 1935 his stepfather renamed him Truman García Capote. An undistinguished student despite a supposed IQ of 215, Capote left school aged 17 and began working as a copyboy for the *New Yorker* magazine. He left the magazine under a cloud in 1944 and devoted the rest of his life to writing. Capote's first published work was a short story entitled 'Miriam' for *Mademoiselle* fashion magazine in 1942. It won an O'Henry Award for Best First-Published Story. His first novel, *Other Voices, Other Rooms*, was published in 1948 to great acclaim – staying on the *New York Times*'s bestseller list for nine weeks. *The Grass Harp* (1951) and *Breakfast at Tiffany's* (1958) were followed by his most famous book, *In Cold Blood*. This 'non-fiction' novel was serialized in the *New Yorker* in 1965 and became the publishing sensation of 1966. Capote also produced two collections of short stories, some travel writing and a collection of reportage, *Music for Chameleons* (1980), which included 'Handcarved Coffins: A Nonfiction Account of an American Crime', first published in Andy Warhol's *Interview* magazine. Apart from the unfinished *Answered Prayers*, however, he wrote no more fiction. He died in Los Angeles of liver disease and 'drug intoxication' in August 1984, one month short of his sixtieth birthday. Hollywood's treatment of *In Cold Blood*, the movie *Capote*, starring Philip Seymour Hoffman, appeared in 2005 to critical acclaim.

Blowin' in the wind

In Cold Blood has assumed iconic status not only in the world of literature, where it has always been marketed as the work of a novelist, but also in the world of journalism where it has been hailed, by Tom Wolfe among others, as the harbinger of the New Journalism of the 1960s and '70s (Wolfe 1990: 41). Wolfe's account of the New Journalism in Part One of his eponymous volume implied with little sense of irony that the post-World War Two American novel, far from heralding a new 'golden age', was caught between the twin poles of neo-fabulism and pulp fiction.

Neo-fabulism was Wolfe's term for 'a puzzling sort of fiction' in which 'characters have no background, no personal history, are identified with no social class, ethnic group or even nationality, and ... often speak, if they speak at all, in short and rather mechanical sentences that, again, betray no specific background' (ibid.: 56).

Pulp fiction was the equivalent of 'finding gold or striking oil, through which an American could, overnight, in a flash, utterly transform his destiny' (ibid.: 20). In 1966, the year *In Cold Blood* was published, these twin poles might best be exemplified by, on the one hand, Thomas Pynchon's reality-disconnection tour de force *The Crying of Lot 49*, and on the other hand Jacqueline Susann's raunchy extravaganza *Valley of the Dolls*, a tale with little literary or other merit that ended up as the second biggest-selling novel of all time. This 'retrograde state of contemporary fiction' convinced Wolfe that 'the most important literature being written in America today is in nonfiction, in the form that has been tagged, however ungracefully, the New Journalism' (ibid.: Preface).

However, Wolfe's Genesis moment, together with his suggestion of a new form of journalism, raises as many questions as it answers. Even the most enlightened reader is still entitled to ask, what exactly is the New Journalism? If it is a new genre of writing, what are its characteristics? The vexed question of genre, therefore, cannot be evaded or sidestepped if New Journalism is to claim its place in the 'Pantheon' as surely as Wolfe believed it should. Genres provide significant reference points in a culture that enable readers to identify, choose and interpret a text. Non-fictional forms, however, often resist the tight embrace of genre and to that extent *In Cold Blood* conforms to the stereotype. Its subject matter is typical crime story genre and Capote produces the suspense required of the genre by delaying the account of the main event (the actual murders) until the third part of the book. Capote himself invariably referred to it as reportage, as he noted in his Preface to *Music for Chameleons* (1981: xvi): 'Actually, in all my reportage, I had tried to keep myself as invisible as possible.' Yet its structure or form also suggests biography or even the nineteenth-century episodic novel. Such genre confusions are also apparent in the sheer number of terms used to describe what for simplicity's sake is here called the New Journalism.

But what on earth is New Journalism?

Capote himself said in an interview with the *New York Times* (Plimpton 1998: 197): 'It seemed to me that journalism, reportage, could be forced to yield a serious new art form: the "non-fiction novel," as I thought of it.' John Hellmann, in *Fables of Fact*, called literary journalism a genre of fiction (1981: 21). Buzz Pounds (2006), along with other current scholars, termed it literary non-fiction. In short, this taxonomical uncertainty offers few clues to identifying New Journalism in genre terms. And the ever-present 'empiricist dilemma', as proposed by Andrew Tudor (cited in Gledhill and Williams 2000: 223) has to be confronted. In other words, if we want to understand what a piece of New Journalism writing is, we must look at certain kinds of journalism. But how do we know which kinds of journalism to look at until we know what a piece of New Journalism writing is? To disentangle this conundrum and understand the complexity of New Journalism in genre terms we need first to examine what is sometimes described as the cultural consensus – those texts loosely agreed upon as examples of a journalism distinct from and atypical of the mainstream. It should then be possible to create a set of criteria from first principles or identify pre-existing criteria that can plausibly define this loosely-agreed-upon canon, being careful to reject the inappropriate or incongruous.

Man of constant sorrow

Perhaps the most readily understood genre distinction is that between fiction and non-fiction. The first is clearly novel territory whilst journalism is one of the most significant examples of the second. When Truman Capote first considered eliding these genres by writing a non-fiction novel, there was no 'cultural consensus' he could call on and, therefore, no pre-existing criteria to guide him in relation to form, style or subject matter. To that extent, as noted by Tom Wolfe (1990: 52), Capote was a pioneer. And he was never under any illusion about the difficulty of his task. Interviewed by George Plimpton for the *New York Times Book Review* in January 1966, he said:

> When I first formed my theories concerning the non-fiction novel, many people with whom I discussed the matter were unsympathetic. They felt that what I proposed, a narrative form that employed all the techniques of fictional art, but was nevertheless immaculately factual, was little more than a literary solution for fatigued novelists suffering from 'failure of the imagination'.
>
> (Plimpton 1998: 198)

This lack of sympathy was further aggravated by Capote's perennial problem of finding a suitable topic. As he explained in the same interview: 'The difficulty was to choose a promising subject … you want to be reasonably certain that the material will not soon "date". The content of much journalism so swiftly does, which is another of the medium's deterrents' (ibid.).

Capote goes on to relate how he found the story: 'One morning in November 1959, while flicking through the *New York Times*, I encountered on a deep inside page, this headline: "Wealthy Farmer, 3 of Family Slain"' (ibid.). Curiously, for a writer who boasted of his ability to remember without using notes or tape recorder, he had offered a different explanation a fortnight earlier in an interview with Harry Gilroy, of the *New York Times* (1965): 'Then one day I read in the *New York Times* a two-paragraph story under the headline "Eisenhower Appointee Slain".' Either way, Capote realized that a crime might provide the scale and scope he was looking for and that 'moreover, the human heart being what it is, murder was a theme not likely to darken and yellow with time' (ibid.: 199).

Simple twist of fate

In Cold Blood tells the story of the murder of a wealthy wheat farmer, Herbert Clutter, his wife Bonnie and the two youngest of their four children, Kenyon, 15, and Nancy, 16. They were found at their farmhouse in the village of Holcomb, Kansas. All four had been bound and gagged and then shot at close range. Herbert Clutter's throat had been cut. There were no signs of a struggle. Nothing had been stolen. According to the Sheriff, Earl Robinson, it appeared to be the work of a psychopathic killer. When Capote read about the murders the culprit was still at large. However, he wasn't interested in the murders as such. At one point he even told Alvin Dewey, supervising investigator for the Kansas Bureau of Investigation: 'It really doesn't make any difference to me if the case is ever solved or not' (Clarke 1988: 321). What Capote wanted to discover was the effect of the killings on such an isolated community, its inhabitants and the family itself. The *New Yorker* commissioned a shortish piece from him on this basis. But within a couple of weeks of Capote's arrival in Kansas, two suspects had been arrested in Las Vegas. The two men, Dick Hickock and Perry Smith, subsequently confessed to the murders.

The arrests and confessions significantly altered the angle and theme of Capote's projected story. Neither the two killers nor the reasons for their crime could now be ignored. Capote soon realized that the article he originally envisaged would be inadequate. But he also worried 'that he might be writing too much for the *New Yorker* to digest' (ibid.: 332). He had no idea that the finished 'novel' would be his longest, running to almost 350 pages. Through extensive interviews with both Hickock and Smith he explored their childhoods and their lives up to the moment of the killings. These stories provided a powerful counterpoint to the lives of the Clutter family and their friends. He discovered that the motive for the crime was robbery and that the Clutters' fate had turned on a single piece of flawed information given to Dick Hickock by a fellow inmate in Lansing jail.

Floyd Wells was a drifter and odd-job man who had once worked on the Clutters' farm for about a year. Wells met Hickock when they were both in Lansing, Wells for robbery and Hickock for passing dud cheques. Wells talked about the wealthy farmer he had once worked for and how Clutter had told him it sometimes cost him $10,000 a week to run the farm. Hickock asked Wells where the farm was, how to get there, how old the children were, did Mr Clutter keep a safe? Wells wasn't sure on the last point but told Hickock he believed there was a safe on the premises. The Clutter family's fate was sealed. When Hickock was released he teamed up with another old cellmate, Perry Smith, bought a twelve-gauge pump-action shotgun, and in Hickock's 1949 black Chevrolet sedan they drove the 400 miles to Holcomb.

Capote structured the story into four parts:

1   The Last to See Them Alive
2   Persons Unknown
3   Answer
4   The Corner

Part One offers the reader a counterpoint between the lives of the Clutters and those of Dick Hickock and Perry Smith in the days leading up to the murders. Largely descriptive, it ends with the killings themselves but gives no details apart from the immediate reaction of the Clutters' friends and neighbours.

Part Two continues this format, following by turns the developing police investigation and its effects on the people of Holcomb, and then Dick and Perry driving to Mexico after Dick passes a series of bad cheques to obtain funds. Capote here plants the first seeds of doubt about whether they left any clues. Perry is reading a story in the Kansas City *Star* headlined: 'Clues are few in Slaying of 4'. Perry doubts the truth of the story: 'Anyway, I don't believe it. Neither do you. Own up, Dick. Be honest. You don't believe this no-clue stuff?' (Capote 1966: 97). This section contains Perry Smith's biography and concludes with the two killers returning to California hoping to hitch a ride to Las Vegas.

Part Three introduces Floyd Wells in his role as *deus ex machina*. He hears the story of the Clutter murders on the radio while still in prison and eventually tells the warden all about Hickock. This section also contains Dick Hickock's biography. The two killers meanwhile drive a stolen car to Las Vegas and Perry visits the post office to pick up a large cardboard box he had posted from Mexico. Capote lists the contents: 'suntans, denim pants, worn shirts, underwear, and two pairs of steel-buckled boots' (ibid.: 217). This list, in the best traditions of crime fiction, gives the reader the other important clue to Dick and Perry's eventual downfall.

The stolen car leads to their arrest and after two days of interrogation in separate rooms Dick is shown their boots and pictures of the matching footprints taken in the Clutters' basement. Dick confesses: 'It was Perry. I couldn't stop him. He killed them all' (ibid.: 232). This section concludes with Perry telling the police what happened on the night of 15 November 1959. This is the first time the reader is confronted with the bald facts of the killings. Both men are driven in convoy to Garden City and the county jail.

Part Four covers the trial, their conviction on four counts of first-degree murder, the pronouncement of the death penalty and their execution. This section spans a period of five years and during that time Capote carried out extensive interviews with both men, especially Perry Smith. Three appeals were lodged with the Supreme Court. The third was denied in January 1965. The hangings were slated for 18 February but at the last minute were postponed until 14 April. Capote spoke to both men and accompanied them to 'the corner', the shed where the gallows was situated. Dick Hickock was hanged first. Capote later wrote (Clarke 1988: 355): 'I was there. I stayed with Perry to the end. He was calm and very brave. It was a terrible experience and I will never get over it.'

All I really want to do

Capote honed his non-fiction teeth on an earlier piece of reportage for the *New Yorker*. Published as 'The Muses are Heard' (1956), it chronicled a trip to the

Soviet Union by the Everyman Opera. They toured with Gershwin's *Porgy and Bess* and Capote went along to record the whole thing. He was aware, therefore, of the journalistic conventions he would have to acknowledge when beginning his *magnum opus* and he set out his journalistic credentials in the Acknowledgements at the beginning of *In Cold Blood*: 'All the material in this book not derived from my own observation is either taken from official records or is the result of interviews with the persons directly concerned.' One significant difference between the two texts, however, is that Capote is ever-present in 'Muses'. It is an 'I' story. He soon realized that this approach would not work with *In Cold Blood*:

> From a technical point, the greatest difficulty I'd had in writing *In Cold Blood* was leaving myself completely out of it. Ordinarily, the reporter has to use himself as a character, an eye-witness observer, in order to retain credibility. But I felt that it was essential to the seemingly detached tone of that book that the author should be absent.
>
> (Capote 1981: xv–xvi)

In some respects, as we shall see, he was moving in the opposite direction to the general thrust of the New Journalism that came later. As Buzz Pounds notes (2006: 2): 'The transition from object to subject in literary non-fiction has been a development of the "New Journalism" of the 1960s which has put less emphasis on the object of study, the thing or event, and has focused on the "subject" who is presenting.'

Although there was nothing intrinsic to the form or subject matter that demanded such a transition, journalists began to grasp that as soon as they intruded into an event to the extent that the New Journalism demanded they inevitably became a part of the action. It would be less than truthful, therefore, to ignore that participation. In Joe Eszterhas's 1972 piece for *Rolling Stone* magazine, 'Charlie Simpson's Apocalypse', he told the story of Charles Simpson who ran amok in Harrisonville, Missouri, killing three people and then blowing his own head off. Eszterhas wrote in the third person until the last few pages where he changed standpoint to the first person. The clue here is in the first sentence of the 'I' narrative (Wolfe 1990: 180): 'I got into Harrisonville about two weeks after the shooting.' If New Journalism claimed to be an encounter with the truth then Eszterhas had a duty to make it clear he was not a witness to the events he had described so vividly. Here the first-person narrative is a temporal device that maintains his journalistic integrity.

I don't believe you

Joan Didion's seminal collection of twenty essays, *Slouching Towards Bethlehem* (1968), consists mostly of first-person viewpoint stories. Indeed, one of the three sections is headed 'Personals'. The few third-person narratives deal with what might be termed more traditional journalism subjects – crime and celebrity interviews. Although she writes extensively about people like Howard Hughes, John

Wayne and Joan Baez, it is invariably from a Didion-centred perspective. As she confirmed in a *Paris Review* interview (Gourevitch 2006: 497): 'I can't ask anything. Once in a while if I'm forced into it I will conduct an interview …'. There is an engaging diffidence to her prose which at times has the reader wondering if, indeed, she did interview her subjects. And then slowly it dawns that the person she is always interviewing is herself.

Compare this with Capote's almost obsessive interest in the interview as a means of revealing character. For example, he spent three years on and off talking to Perry Smith and Dick Hickock. And as he noted in his *New York Times* interview (Plimpton 1998: 200): 'I suppose if I used just 20 per cent of the material I put together over those years of interviewing, I'd still have a book two thousand pages long.' Didion's subjective focus is at once softer and at times less forgiving than that of Capote and many of her other contemporaries: 'My only advantage as a reporter is that I am so physically small, so temperamentally unobtrusive, and so neurotically inarticulate that people tend to forget that my presence runs counter to their best interests' (Didion 2001: xiii).

Didion's shy defiance is at the opposite end of the spectrum to the journalism of Hunter S. Thompson. 'Gonzo' journalism was his take on the New Journalism and he made the 'I' story his territory. His first book, *Hell's Angels: A Strange and Terrible Saga* (1966), was pretty much standard journalism. Apart from one important factor: Thompson became part of the action. For a year he rode with the Angels, went home with the Angels, chronicled the sex lives of the Angels. There was no pretence here at traditional journalism's objectivity. His fiercely subjective style reached parts of society no other journalist reached. This was the era of flower power and the 'Summer of Love'. The establishment press had no clue how to report Black Panther rallies, Grateful Dead concerts, Beat writers' happenings or Hell's Angels' burn-ups. The first printing of *Hell's Angels* sold out within days of publication, the book going on to make the best-seller list of 1967.

Three years later Thompson penned 'The Kentucky Derby is Decadent and Depraved' for *Scanlan's Monthly* (June 1970). This story was by-lined: 'Written under duress by Hunter S. Thompson' and 'Sketched with eyebrow pencil and lipstick by Ralph Steadman' (Thompson 2000: 295). Thompson made it clear that he needed more time to hone the piece and complained about his treatment by *Scanlan's* editor in a letter to his agent Lynn Nesbit (ibid.: 300):

> I was locked in that stinking hotel room with a head full of pills & no sleep for 6 days, working at top speed & messengers grabbing each page out of the type-writer just as soon as I finished it. No carbon, no rewrite, no time to even look back on what I'd written earlier.

But the tight deadline was the catalyst he needed to produce what many believe to be the first piece of true gonzo journalism. In its book incarnation it is fifteen pages long. Only on page nine is there any mention of the Kentucky Derby itself. Thompson spends seven lines on the race. The remaining pages are a disjointed and querulous account of the types of people who frequented the Derby, mixed with descriptions of drinking, fighting, chaos and hangover. Ultimately, Thompson trying to get the story *is* the story. Capote's fabled pinpoint accuracy is ditched in favour of a kind of atmospheric authenticity which does not rely on the accumulation of facts so much as the accumulation of feelings, emotions, sensations. Who is to say that one is more 'truthful' than the other?

Yet friends and enemies alike have consistently questioned Capote's own adherence to the truth in his non-fiction writing. One friend, John Richardson, noted: 'Truman had absolutely no respect for the truth' (Plimpton 1998: 308). Another, Joanne Carson, ex-wife of legendary presenter of the *Tonight Show* Johnny Carson, explained: 'In Truman's mind, he doesn't lie, he makes things the way they *should* have been' (ibid.: 304). (Much the same could be said of Thompson's own journalism.) The ending of *In Cold Blood* was perhaps the most blatant piece of Capote fabrication. He agonized over whether to conclude with the executions or provide a more upbeat ending. He chose the latter. The chance encounter between 'Alvin Dewey and Susan Kidwell, Nancy Clutter's best friend, in the tree-shaded Garden City cemetery' (Clarke 1988: 359) is pure invention. It clearly suits the demands of a fictional narrative, providing a sense of life carrying on, bringing us full circle, back to the place where the story began, rather than the requirements of a piece of journalism that it stick to the facts.

This mischievous exploitation of 'truth' and the apotheosis of the 'I' story – the inconsequential nature of its subject matter, the focus on the journalist and his exploits at the expense of everything else, the mindscape so unfamiliar as to make questions of fact or fable not only unnecessary but irrelevant – is Thompson's *Fear and Loathing in Las Vegas*, published in 1971. From its famous opening riff – 'We were somewhere around Barstow on the edge of the desert when the drugs began to take hold' – to its Jack Kerouac-inspired tape transcript towards the end, Thompson here grabbed the New Journalism torch lit by Capote with *In Cold Blood*, blew the neat petrol of gonzo over it and produced yet another new form – subjective, hot, lethal, subversive.

It was this muscular style, Thompson believed, which set him apart from the 'prissiness' of rivals like Tom Wolfe. Weingarten records Thompson saying in a 1971 essay (2005: 117): 'Wolfe's problem ... is that he's too crusty to participate in his stories.' Thompson was always adamant, however, as Capote was of *In Cold Blood*, that *Fear and Loathing in Las Vegas* was more than anything a non-fiction novel (Thompson 2003: 188). Yet in *The Great Shark Hunt* he also described gonzo as 'a style of "reporting" based on William Faulkner's idea that the best fiction is far more *true* than any kind of journalism – and the best journalists have always known this' (Thompson 1980: 114).

I shall be released

Norman Mailer staked his claim to be among the 'best' journalists with his 1968 'hommage' to *In Cold Blood*, *The Armies of the Night*. It would probably not have been written, and certainly not in the way it was, without Capote's pioneering work. From that moment Mailer's name became inextricably linked with that of Capote, whom he memorably described as 'a ballsy little guy, and ... the most perfect writer of my generation, he writes the best sentences word for word, rhythm upon rhythm' (Clarke 1988: 314–15). Mailer's own view of journalism was somewhat ambivalent however. In an *Esquire* interview (June 1960) he said: 'Once a newspaper touches a story, the facts are lost forever, even to the protagonists.'

Mailer preferred his journalism long. *Armies* is the story of the 'citizen-army' protest march on the Pentagon in October 1967 against the Vietnam war. Mailer took part and was arrested. Although Capote worried about leaving himself completely out of *In Cold Blood*, he quickly understood that a first-person viewpoint would strike a false note in a story where he could not have been present during most of the action. Mailer, on the other hand, had no such problem. But even so, perhaps unconsciously acknowledging the primacy of Capote's text, he shied away from a straightforward 'I' narrative. Instead, he used the unusual device of becoming a character in the story but not the 'I' character. Mailer is the protagonist produced by Mailer the omniscient narrator. It is a subtle way of disguising the subjective reality of autobiography as the objective truth of biography. He could study his own reactions free from egotism and self-censorship. The following exchange, for example, takes place after he is arrested (Mailer 1968: 140):

> When Mailer gave his name, the man with the clipboard acted as if he had never heard of him, or at least pretended never to have heard of him. 'How do you spell it?'
> 'M.A.I.L.E.R.'
> 'Why were you arrested Mr. Miller?'
> 'For transgressing a police line as a protest against the war in Vietnam.'

This is a sort of halfway house along the object-to-subject transition noted earlier. For Mailer, like Capote, understood the seductive embrace of the 'I' story; the ease with which information could be manipulated, suppressed or exaggerated; the ways a writer could, if he wished, disguise his lack of candour. But Mailer was unable to expiate himself completely from his text, for as Joyce Carol Oates noted in her 1973 *Critic* essay on 'The Art of Norman Mailer', he was 'a "self" in search of an author' (Oates 1973: 1).

The tradition of journalistic objectivity was imbued in Capote through his writing for the *New Yorker* and he was aware of the subtle difference between telling a story as best remembered and one that was made up. Mailer, too, acknowledged the significance of objectivity. In his afterword to *The Executioner's Song*, the story of Gary Gilmore, a career criminal who killed a motel manager and a petrol station employee in Utah in 1976, and was executed by firing squad (1979: 1051), he wrote: 'This book does its best to be a factual account of the activities of Gary Gilmore ... and the story is as accurate as one can make it.' Here too, though,

Mailer seemed obstinately shy of using the first-person 'I' and sheltered behind the vaguely anonymous 'one'.

So far as Capote was concerned, objectivity was part of accuracy and accuracy was so important to him that he asked Sandy Campbell, a fact-checker at the *New Yorker*, to go with him to Kansas to check the correctness of all his information. Campbell 'verified such things as dates and distances. Sandy said that he had worked with many *New Yorker* writers ... but Truman was the most accurate' (Clarke 1988: 351). Yet Capote never took notes or used a tape recorder. He believed they inhibited candour and he trained his memory so he did not need them:

> Twelve years ago I began to train myself for the purpose of this sort of book, to transcribe conversation without using a tape recorder. I did it by having a friend read passages from a book, and then later I'd write them down to see how close I could come to the original ... I could get within 95 per cent of absolute accuracy, which is as close as you need.
>
> (Plimpton 1998: 202)

You go your way and I'll go mine

Part One of Wolfe's *The New Journalism* is an extended essay that attempts to place the New Journalism in a historical context but more importantly acknowledges the fictive qualities of the writing by suggesting that it shares four distinct characteristics or techniques with fiction writing, or at least the 'realistic novel' kind of fiction writing espoused by Wolfe himself (1990: 46–50). These four characteristics are scene-by-scene construction, realistic dialogue, third-person point of view, and the recording of people's 'status life'. They provide a useful marker for gauging how well Capote fulfilled his aim of producing what was essentially an oxymoron, the non-fiction novel. And by extension their role as identifiers of the New Journalism as a genre can also be evaluated.

Scene-by-scene construction

Wolfe contrasted scene-by-scene construction with 'sheer historical narrative' (see ibid.: 46). This first stylistic device takes the story forward moment by moment, gives it immediacy and, therefore, maximizes reader involvement. The other delays forward momentum by introducing background detail – the contextualization of character and place that provides the rich cultural and social mix of a novel. *In Cold Blood* quite clearly uses scene-by-scene development, but Capote was suddenly confronted with the problem, once the killers had been caught, of how to incorporate their stories into what until then had been a straightforward linear narrative. He solved this not by giving the reader 'historical narrative' but by using flashback to fill in the detail of the killers' lives – not as genealogy (third-person narrative) but as lived experience (first-person recollection). Thus he juxtaposes scenes involving Dick and Perry with those of the police, the Clutters, and the community of Holcomb. We experience the killers' road journey to Mexico and then to Florida as well as their 'life' journey. These scenes are not strictly chronological. They are often contemporaneous or use flashback for dramatic impact. One scene comments on another and this cause-and-effect see-saw maintains the forward thrust of the narrative.

Realistic dialogue

In Cold Blood uses dialogue lightly. As Capote was not present during many of the scenes he chronicles, he is clearly reticent about quoting those who were and he never intrudes himself as a character. However, much of the most riveting dialogue takes place when Capote obviously was not present, for example when Dick and Perry are on the road. They hitch a lift from a Mr Bell with the aim of killing him and stealing his car. Dick tells a joke for Bell's benefit (Capote 1966: 177):

> 'Here's a riddle. The riddle is: What's the similarity between a trip to the bathroom and a trip to the cemetery?' He grinned. 'Give up?'
> 'Give up.'
> 'When you gotta go, you gotta go!'
> Mr Bell barked.
> 'Hey, Perry, pass me a match.'

Unknown to Bell, Dick's match command was the cue for Perry, sitting in the back, to hit Bell over the head with a 'handkerchief-wrapped rock'. Even so, many critics questioned the authenticity of Capote's use of dialogue. In his *New York Times Book Review* interview, George Plimpton attempted to clarify the issue. Capote's response was typical:

> They ask, 'How can you reconstruct the conversation of a dead girl, Nancy Clutter, without fictionalizing?' If they read the book carefully, they can see readily enough how it's done. It's a silly question. Each time Nancy appears in the narrative, there are witnesses to what she is saying and doing – phone calls, conversations, being overheard.
>
> (Plimpton 1998: 207–8)

Clearly, the journalistic convention of corroboration was important to him and he was assiduous with regard to both the numbers of people he interviewed and the time he spent with each, often speaking to someone on two or three occasions in a single day (Capote 1966: Acknowledgements; Clarke 1988: 322).

Third-person point of view

Wolfe makes the point that a first-person viewpoint is limiting for a journalist 'since he can bring the reader inside the mind of only one character – himself – a point of view that often proves irrelevant to the story and irritating to the reader' (1990: 47). Capote had already decided that a third-person narrative was essential to maintain the detachment he felt essential for his story's integrity. And he also discovered that a longer, more complex piece of writing than his 'Muses' would soon begin to disintegrate under the subjective weight of an omnipresent 'I' character.

The recording of people's 'status life'

This involves noting such things as people's habits, gestures, manners; styles of clothing, furniture, travel, eating; ways of relating to children, workmates, bosses, inferiors; and other clues to a person's 'status'. Wolfe believed these 'status' clues provided the pure authenticity that brought characters to life. Capote used this element most tellingly to point up the differences in social status between Dick and Perry and the Clutters. Early on in the story Capote invites us to observe the Clutters' relative wealth: 'One of these barns was a mammoth Quonset hut; it brimmed with grain – Westland sorghum – and one of them housed a dark, pungent hill of milo grain worth considerable money – a hundred thousand dollars' (Capote 1966: 22). Contrast this with the list of Perry's possessions as discovered by Agent Nye in a Las Vegas boarding house: 'One dirty pillow, "souvenir of Honolulu"; one pink baby blanket; one pair khaki trousers; one aluminium pan with pancake turner' (ibid.: 181). Or the meal Perry and Dick contemplate on their way to Holcomb: 'The travellers stopped for dinner at a restaurant in Great Bend. Perry, down to his last fifteen dollars, was ready to settle for root beer and a sandwich' (ibid.: 63). Arguably these status details give the reader a greater insight into character, and at the same time attest to the veracity of that insight, than any amount of generic description.

Restless farewell: populating the domestic, domesticating the popular

These four devices clearly characterize New Journalism writing as defined by Tom Wolfe. Yet it is more difficult to ascertain their validity as a set of criteria by which all New Journalism can be identified. It would, indeed, be crass to expect or demand their inclusion as a requirement of the genre or their absence as confirmation of exclusion. For example, Robert Boynton in *The New New Journalism*, whilst acknowledging Wolfe's contribution, offers a more fluid and process-driven analysis of the way in which the genre has developed (2005: xiii):

> What Wolfe didn't anticipate was that a new generation of journalists would build upon (and ultimately surpass) his reporting methods, lengthening and deepening their involvement with characters to the point at which the public/private divide essentially disappeared. Wolfe went inside his characters' heads; the New New Journalists become part of their lives.

This becoming 'part of their lives' is one of the reasons for probably the most significant departure from Wolfe's four devices – the transition from his third-person to a first-person point of view. This is especially true of shorter New Journalism writing. Of the twenty-three stories in Wolfe's *The New Journalism* anthology, two-thirds are third-person point of view. In Sims and Kramer's *Literary Journalism* collection, published twenty-two years later in 1995, only two of the fifteen stories are third-person accounts, Calvin Trillin's 'First Family of Astoria' and Tracy Kidder's 'Memory'. Whilst this is obviously a crude statistical analysis, it is perhaps indicative of the trend towards first-person narrative in later New Journalism. And to that extent Hunter S. Thompson might be seen as its true progenitor rather than Truman Capote and Norman Mailer.

Yet Capote's assertion in the Preface to *Music for Chameleons* (1980) that when writing reportage he tried to keep himself as invisible as possible might seem at odds with the most celebrated piece in that collection, 'Handcarved Coffins: A Nonfiction Account of an American Crime'. This was written from a first-person viewpoint and he alternated between straight first-person narrative and dialogue presented in simple film script format, identifying himself as TC. The story is about a series of seemingly unconnected murders in an unnamed town in the American mid-West. It was, perhaps, a belated attempt by Capote to revive his fortunes by revisiting the formula of the non-fiction novel. Yet the story suffers from the inherent tension caused by Capote's desire to be 'in' the story on the one hand (the first-person viewpoint) and his equal desire for concealment (the film script format) on the other.

Despite this, much of the best book-length New Journalism, with the notable exception of Michael Herr's 1977 account of his experiences as a Vietnam war correspondent in *Despatches* and the work of Hunter S. Thompson, followed Capote's lead and used the third-person viewpoint, from Gay Talese's *Honor Thy Father* (1972) and Jane Kramer's *The Last Cowboy* (1977) to Mailer's 1980 Pulitzer Prize-winning *The Executioner's Song*.

Equally important as form is subject matter. Here Wolfe acknowledged the deficiencies of his four devices with reference to the '*higher* accomplishments of the great fiction writers' (1990: 49): character creation, psychological depth, a sense of history, the great themes of literature, etc. He placed responsibility for these squarely at the door of each writer: 'It depends upon the writer's experience and intellect, his insights, the quality of his emotions, his ability to see into others, his "genius"' (ibid.). And an important part of this 'genius' was the favouring of the quotidian as subject matter – New Journalists determinedly becoming part of their subjects' lives. Gruesome murders and murderers, large-scale protests, high-profile sports events, political scandals, famous people – these became the exception rather than the rule. The grand political gesture of the protest march is replaced by a story of the urban poor. The unique persona of the mass murderer is traded for the journalism of everyday misdemeanour. The walk towards destiny is exchanged for a stroll in the park. New Journalism has populated the domestic and domesticated the popular.

This concern with routine events at times belies the quality of the writing and the attention to detail of the typical New Journalist. But at the same time it has vastly expanded the range of topics considered worthy of journalistic attention. Perhaps the last word should go to Michael Lewis, one of the New New Journalists identified by Robert Boynton as having 'revived the tradition of American literary journalism' (2005: xxx). Lewis is the author of a number of books, including *Liar's Poker* (1989), an exposé of his time on Wall Street in the 1980s, and writes for *The New Republic* and the online magazine *Slate*. Interviewed by Boynton for *The New New Journalism*, Lewis said: 'Whereas journalists once felt humbled by the novel, we now live in an age in which the *novelist* lives in a state of anxiety about nonfiction' (Boynton 2005: xii). No doubt Truman Capote would have approved.

References

Boynton, R. S. (2005) *The New New Journalism: Conversations with America's Best Non-fiction Writers on Their Craft* (New York: Vintage).

Capote, T. (1966) *In Cold Blood* (New York: Random House).

—— (1981) *Music for Chameleons* (London: Sphere).

—— (2002) *A Capote Reader* (London: Penguin).

—— (2005) *The Complete Stories* (London: Penguin).

Clarke, G. (1988) *Capote: A Biography* (New York: Simon & Schuster).

—— (ed.) (2005) *Too Brief a Treat: The Letters of Truman Capote* (New York: Vintage International).

Didion, J. (2001) *Slouching Towards Bethlehem* (London: Flamingo) [originally published in 1968, New York: Farrar, Straus & Giroux]

Dunphy, J. (1987) *Dear Genius: A Memoir of My Life with Truman Capote* (London: McGraw-Hill Education).

Gilroy, H. (1965) 'A book in a new form earns $2-million for Truman Capote', *New York Times*, 31 December. Available online at www.nytimes.com/ads/capote/capote_12.html, accessed on 24 September 2006.

Gledhill, C. and Williams, L. (eds) (2000) *Reinventing Film Studies* (London: Arnold).

Gourevitch, P. (ed.) (2006) *The Paris Review Interviews*, vol. 1 (New York: Picador).

Hellmann, J. (1981) *Fables of Fact: The New Journalism as New Fiction* (Urbana: University of Illinois Press).

Hollowell, J. (1977) *Fact and Fiction: The New Journalism and the Non-fiction Novel* (Chapel Hill: University of North Carolina Press).

Kramer, J. (1998) *The Last Cowboy* (London: Pimlico) [originally published in 1977, New York: Harper & Row].

Lewis, M. (1999) *Liar's Poker: Playing the Money Markets* (London: Coronet) [originally published in 1989, New York: W. W. Norton & Company; London, Hodder & Stoughton].

Mailer, N. (1968) *The Armies of the Night* (London: Weidenfeld & Nicolson).

—— (1980) *The Executioner's Song* (London: Arrow Books).

Moates, M. M. (1996) *Truman Capote's Southern Years* (University of Alabama Press).

Oates, J. C. (1973) 'The teleology of the unconscious: the art of Norman Mailer', *Critic*, November/December. Available online at www.jco.usfca.edu/mailer01.html, accessed on 29 September 2006.

Plimpton, G. (1998) *Truman Capote* (London: Picador).

Pounds, B. R. (2006) 'Postmodernism – epistemological persona'. Available online at www.louisville.edu/a-s/english/subcultures/ideas/buzzpounds/pountheory.html, accessed on 22 September 2006.

Rudisill, M. with Simmons, J. C. (2001) *The Southern Haunting of Truman Capote* (New York: Cumberland House).

Sims, N. (ed.) (1990) *Literary Journalism in the Twentieth Century* (New York: Oxford University Press).

—— and Kramer, M. (eds) (1995) *Literary Journalism: A New Collection of the Best American Non-fiction* (New York: Ballantine).

Staff reporter (1959) 'Wealthy Farmer, 3 of Family Slain', *New York Times*, 16 November. Available online at www.nytimes.com/ads/capote/capote_13.html, accessed on 24 September 2006.

Talese, G. (1972) *Honor Thy Father* (London: Sphere Books).

Thompson, H. S. (1980) *The Great Shark Hunt* (London: Picador).

—— (1993) *Fear and Loathing in Las Vegas* (London: Flamingo).

—— (2000) *Fear and Loathing in America*, Brinkley, D. (ed.) (London: Bloomsbury).

—— (2003) *Kingdom of Fear* (London: Allen Lane).

Weingarten, M. (2005) *Who's Afraid of Tom Wolfe? How New Journalism Rewrote the World* (London: Aurum Press).

Wolfe, T. (1990) *The New Journalism* (London: Pan Books).

A special issue of the French literary magazine, *le magazine littéraire* (www.magazine-litteraire.com), of January 2007 was devoted to Capote (under the title An American Idol). It included articles by J.M.G. le Clezio, Philippe Besson, Geneviève Brisac and Michel Schneider.

Chapter 10

The journalist as philosopher and cultural critic

The case of Angela Carter

Linden Peach

Angela Carter (1940–92) is widely acknowledged as one of the leading British women writers of the twentieth century. She is best known for her novels and short stories, but she was also the author of numerous cultural commentaries in the form of essays and reviews which gave rise to two collections of journalism, *Nothing Sacred* (1982) and *Expletives Deleted* (1992). These were collected posthumously in *Shaking a Leg: Collected Journalism and Writing* (1997). Born Angela Olive Stalker, Carter was raised in Yorkshire during the war by her maternal grandmother and, although she spent most of her life in England, she also lived for short periods in Japan, the United States and Australia. Her father was a Scottish journalist and she herself began work in 1959 as a junior reporter on the *Croydon Advertiser* before reading English at Bristol University, 1962–5, specializing in the medieval period. Although she earned her living primarily as a writer, she also held a number of visiting and part-time positions in higher education, including Arts Council of Great Britain Fellow in Creative Writing at Sheffield University (1976–8), Visiting Professor at Brown University, USA (1980–1) and part-time teacher in Creative Writing at the University of East Anglia (1984–7), as well as appointments as writer-in-residence in Australia and the USA. In addition to the works of journalism referred to earlier, she published nine novels, four collections of short stories and *The Sadeian Woman: An Exercise in Cultural History* (1979). Other works include a volume of radio plays, a translation of the fairy stories of Charles Perrault, and edited collections of fairy and folk tales. She also edited *Wayward Girls and Wicked Women: An Anthology of Subversive Stories* (1986) and, in 1984, she wrote the screenplay for *Company of Wolves* based on *The Bloody Chamber*.

Resisting traditions and conventions

Angela Carter's journalism, like her fiction, spans almost thirty years. However, while her fiction after 1980 becomes larger, more carnivalesque and theatrical with *Nights at the Circus* (1984) and *Wise Children* (1991), her journalism, although still striving to be intellectually radical, becomes structurally and linguistically more constrained. One of the reasons for this was that much of her journalism during the 1980s took the form of reviews in the *Guardian*. However, over three decades her essays and reviews, published in that paper and in the *London Magazine* and *New Society*, cover a wide variety of literary and cultural topics and often display the linguistic and narrative experimentation that characterizes her fiction.

Carter's journalism has not received the critical and scholarly attention of her fiction, and usually it is seen as complementing her novels and short stories rather than as writing worthy of serious consideration in its own right. Since her essays and reviews cover, or allude to, subjects to which she returned frequently in her fiction, such as war, sexuality, feminism, pornography, sadomasochism, food, protest, fantasy, clothes and fashion, they provide valuable insights into the novels and stories. However, it would be wrong to suggest that Carter was a novelist who merely dabbled in journalism.

The daughter of a Scottish provincial newspaper journalist, Carter embraced journalism as part of a larger intellectual project that includes her novels and short stories, almost in equal measure. Indeed, they all share a daring conceptual reach, extravagant wit and cultural criticism. But they also all have an overarching concern to scrutinize and resist dominant, culturally determined and socially accepted ways of thinking that prevent or distort intellectual, emotional, sexual and aesthetic development. As cultural and political commentary, her journalism is as original, tough-minded, intelligent and astute as her other writings.

Carter would have greeted an attempt to place her journalism in any kind of tradition with derision. At a time when many critics were constructing continuities in women's writing, she distrusted them. A valuable insight into her thinking in this respect is provided by one of her early novels, *Several Perceptions* (1968), in which a key protagonist, opening a window, displaces his psychiatrist's papers which he then watches him trying, somewhat desperately, to gather together again. Carter's journalism shares with her fiction a desire to open windows and disrupt what she saw as our obsession with neat configurations and tidy classifications.

One of the key literary influences upon Carter's writing, as Lorna Sage points out (1994: 12), was the late eighteenth-century radical poet and thinker William Blake, particularly his protest against what he called, in one of his poems from *Songs of Innocence and Experience*, 'mind-forged manacles'. In Carter's view, there were no more inhibiting intellectual 'manacles' than custom and tradition. Her journalism, like her fiction, seems intent on demonstrating how different 'realities' appear when we step out of our usual ways of thinking and entertain new philosophical and sociocultural perspectives.

Carter's impatience with conventional thinking was matched, as is evident from her journalism in the late 1960s and '70s, by an obsession with exposing how the present is often 'pre-sent'. By this, I mean the way in which she believed that we never experience the 'pure' present but the present as it is mediated by preconceived perspectives. Thus, in her journalism, even more obviously than in her fiction, she is repeatedly concerned with exchanging one way of thinking for another. In her discussion of the male and female nude in *Playgirl* and *Viva*, 'A Well-Hung Hang-Up' (1975), published in *New Society*, Carter argues (1998: 62) that 'the picture of a naked man belongs to a different aesthetic convention than that of a naked woman'. The naked woman, she maintains (ibid.: 64), 'as the source of nourishment and sexuality is balanced by the icon of the naked man in physical torment'. The essay traces and contrasts the traditions in which the representation of the 'naked man' and the 'naked woman' are situated:

> And it isn't simply two thousand years of crucifixion and pietas working against the male body as an image of joy; it is two millennia of St Sebastian transfixed by arrows, St Lawrence with his gridiron, St Bartholomew being flayed, decapitated Holofernes, Prometheus with the birds gnawing at his liver, martyrdoms, executions, dissections. Marat stabbed in his bath. Against this rage can beauty hold a plea? Not, certainly, in the timorous hands of the male pin-ups.
>
> (Ibid.)

Carter and the construction of alternative traditions

Carter's version of the history of this particular sadomasochistic, aesthetic convention is driven by her critique of it, designed to persuade us to see it differently from the way in which we might have done previously. Despite her scepticism about 'received' traditions, Carter often constructs alternatives of her own. But this does not mean that she is simply exchanging one set of manacles for another. She avoids what she sees as the real manacle, the uncritical construction of continuities, and in writing from one aesthetic critique she is always aware of alternatives.

The boundary between the body and culture is a recurring motif in Carter's journalism. 'Lovely Linda' (1974), her essay on the pornographic model Linda Lovelace, demonstrates how her conviction that conventional wisdom inhibited original thought took her journalism into a new sophistry. Her argument is that Lovelace exemplifies a shift in the sex industry that occurred with its movement into the mainstream. With devastating wit, she maintains (1998: 55) that Lovelace has 'taken the repertoire and sexual display from the commerce and intimacy of the brothel and allowed her performance to be frozen upon celluloid, condemned to a sequence of endless repetitions'. Her mercilessly mocking critique of Lovelace is less about her than the different traditions in which commercial sexuality may be placed and the interlinking of the pre-modern and the modern. The ultimate issue with which this essay is concerned is the role of the spectator in the modern.

The pariah in Carter's journalism is the modern figure who is trapped like the spectator of Lovelace's films in one narrow perspective. Carter's enthusiasm for moving between different cultural traditions and perspectives is evident, as her journalism exemplifies, not only from the way she wrote but also from the interest with which she received particular works. One of her most positive reviews is of Jessica Kuper's *The Anthropologist's Cookbook*. She enthuses about this work (ibid.: 88) because of the way in which it 'zips about in space and time from the medieval English kitchen to the mountains of Laos'. Her journalism might be read as a record of the learning process by which she, as a writer, discovered how to handle such 'zipping' herself. This is all too apparent if we compare 'Lovely Linda' and 'A Well-Hung Hang-Up' with 'Bob Dylan on Tour' (1966). In her 1970s journalism the focus upon alternative traditions is more sustained and selective than in her 1960s work. At one level, the range of historical and literary references in her review of Dylan's Cardiff concert (1998: 323–5) – The Scarlet Hex Witch, Huck Finn-capped youth – is wittily illuminating. However, it is also bewildering because Dylan's literary heritage shifts in the essay as rapidly as his song list; he is linked to Twain, Kafka, Kierkegaard, Dostoevsky, Swift, Pope and Burroughs.

The Japan journalism

Whilst confirming some of the preoccupations of her 1960s fiction, Carter's time in Japan (1969–72) proved a watershed in her thinking about culture and this is reflected in her journalism about Japanese life and society published in *New Society* between 1970 and 1974. It is as if *New Society* provided Carter with a vehicle in which to reflect upon and develop different perspectives on Japan. The development of her thinking in this area informs the transition in her Japanese journalism from documentary, in the vein of travel writing, to cultural analysis and from empirical observation to scrutiny of language and image as 'sign'. 'Tokyo Pastoral' (1970) is a piece of travel documentary that discovers in the city's suburbs, where it always seems to be Sunday afternoon, a peace which in Western culture is normally associated with the rural. Although the focus in the description of the city environments is on the East, the reference point is frequently the West. Indeed, Carter's point that the heart of Tokyo 'ought not to be a happy city' is made with European cities in mind.

Her essay 'People as Pictures' (1970), on the Japanese art of tattooing, *irezumi*, is conceptually more ambitious than 'Tokyo Pastoral' and is concerned to place *irezumi* within wider cultural interpretations of Japanese culture. Thus, it is identified as an occupational badge worn by builders, other such manual workers and gangsters. However, it also sees *irezumi* as reflecting the wider sadomasochism of Japanese culture, an argument that is developed in subsequent essays such as 'Once More into the Mangle' (1971). The dense, vivid nature of *irezumi* is linked to the highly visual strip cartoon, which in turn is seen as promoting and legitimizing female masochism, and to Japanese hostess bars.

Thus, Carter's Japanese experiences proved important to her intellectual and aesthetic development and to her journalism. As I have argued elsewhere (1998: 20), Carter believed that in Japan she 'learned what it was to be a woman, and became radicalized'. However, the experience also extended her interest in sadomasochism, which eventually led to her cultural essay on Sade, *The Sadeian Woman* (1979). Writing about the comic strips, hostess bars and adult toyshops in her journalism made Carter aware of an apparent paradox in the West which she went on to explore further in her post-Japan novel, *The Passion of New Eve* (1977). Whilst women there were acquiring greater freedom from oppression, they were also becoming more interested in, and more likely to be voluntary participants in, sadomasochism, domination and bondage.

Japan also proved significant, as 'Tokyo Pastoral' (1970) makes clear, to Carter's approach to culture generally. In 'Tokyo Pastoral', Carter experiences what it is to be a minority and to be an object of interest in an alien culture. But what also fascinates her is the way in which she is regarded as 'white' in a way in which she might have seen other cultures as 'non-white', an experience that makes her realize that as a white person she is also 'coloured'. As her Japanese journalism demonstrates and explores, Japan defamiliarized culture for Carter and encouraged her to see not only Western culture but also culture generally from fresh perspectives. This is a key feature of her post-Japan fiction of the 1970s which is set in geographical and temporal locations increasingly removed from her early novels located in 1960s Bristol. In 'Ian Burum: A Japanese Mirror' (1986), Carter, in effect, revisits her 1970s journalism on Japan. Although she applauds the detail in which Burum writes of Japanese culture, the way in which he places modern Japan in a fresh cultural tradition is particularly welcomed. Carter highlights how in modern Japan (1998: 265) he sees evidence of pre-Buddhism and pre-Confucianism, especially the violence, sex and grotesque mythologies from that earlier period.

Japan and the links between sexuality and carnivalesque

Japan also encouraged Carter's interest in the links between sexuality and carnivalesque which are most fully developed in *Nights at the Circus* and *Wise Children*. In 'A Fertility Festival' (1974), she describes:

> The grannies thrust forward their empty prams and scream shrilly. The old men wave their female favours ecstatically. Here comes a jolly old dancing man bearing yet another phallus in his arms and, after him, a line of dancing men carrying a pole with, hanging from it, a six-foot phallus of unvarnished wood. Phalluses, phalluses everywhere.
>
> (1998: 261)

Here we can see the elements of carnival that Sarah Sceats says (1997: 111) Carter developed in *Nights at the Circus* even before she read Mikhail Bakhtin's work on carnivalesque, including 'association with popular culture, the subversion or reversal of the expected, overblown bodily function'. Ostensibly a description of the festival, this passage derives meaning from the way in which the words seem to acquire meanings by playing off each other, independent of their external referents. This reflects the way in which the festival itself is an enclosed event. The consonance and alliteration – 'scream shrilly', 'female favours', 'jolly old dancing man', 'phalluses, phalluses' – reinforce the linguistic interplay within the passage while absorbing the reader, like the later novels, into the theatrical and the bizarre.

Carter's long, densely packed, eclectic and highly allusive novels referred to above – *Nights at the Circus* and *Wise Children* – were written at a time when her journalism displays a new-found enthusiasm for 'zipping' between traditions, cultures and subjects matched with a more objective, critical perspective on this type of work. In 'William Burroughs: The Western Lands' (1988), she reflects (1998: 464) on Burroughs's 'densely impacted mass of cultural references' in a way she had not done previously and certainly not in her earlier essay 'William Burroughs: Ah Pook is Here' (1979). Valuing what she sees (1998: 465) as the 'shock of terror and pleasure' in Burroughs's work, Carter analyses (ibid.: 464) it in a way that suggests she is aware of the careful handling of the different literary techniques involved: 'The most urgent personal reflections are juxtaposed with jokes, satires, quotations, essays in fake anthropology, parody, pastiche …. piss, shit, offal, disembowellings. This is slapstick reinterpreted by Sade.' Here the focus upon literary features demonstrates how for Carter, as well as for Burroughs, disrupting the reader's conventional understanding of culture is a project that must inform not only content, offering the reader alternative traditions and perspectives, but also structure and style.

Radical structures

In 'A Busker (Retired)' (1967), Carter reveals one source for the way in which she wrote in the 1960s and 1970s. The quality that she most admires (1998: 325) in Charlie the Busker is that 'at the first signs of boredom, he nudges you into fresh attention'. In 'A Well-Hung Hang-Up', Carter, almost like a dispensing optician, places different lenses before the reader's eyes which embolden, distort or even blur what they see. Thus, 'A Well-Hung Hang-Up' moves through a series of paragraphs that, like different lenses, take the reader from pin-ups perceived as satisfying adolescent curiosity, through the nature of femininity in advertisements for sexual products, the butch imagery of the 'prick-and-bum mags', to sadomasochistic aesthetic conventions. Each paragraph appears designed to unsettle the reader who does not sufficiently question how received traditions can close off avenues of thought.

The constantly shifting viewpoint or lens in Carter's early journalism does not mean, however, that it has no centre. The second quality that Carter admired in her old busker friend (ibid.) was the way in which his walking stick symbolized a 'centre of gravity outside his body' and a 'silhouette'. Indeed, the technique of 'zipping' about between lenses, traditions and cultures is most fully exploited in Carter's most grounded journalism on topics about which she was particularly passionate, such as nuclear warfare. At the heart of 'Anger in a Black Landscape' (1983), this time literally and metaphorically, is her conviction that

> somehow the hideous poetry of the *terminal* nature of nuclear warfare can exist almost in a dimension of its own, that deforms thought. As if we still saw war itself as a metaphysical scourge, one of the four horse-men of the Apocalypse, arriving from nowhere and dominating the world, our real masters. Not as war really is, the product of interlocked tissue of political and economic causes,

of human actions and decisions. But as if nuclear weapons themselves – symbolized by the Bomb – were the very transcendental essence of war, and, more than that, an externalization of all our notions of the ultimate evil. The Bomb has become a very potent, perhaps *the* most potent, symbol of Original Sin.

(1998: 45)

Here Carter attacks what she sees as a conventional line of thought that can be traced to the vision of the Apocalypse in Revelations and to the first book of the Bible, Genesis, which introduces the notion of Original Sin. Countering this mythic way of thinking, which in theological terms links the beginning and the end, Carter suggests an alternative that places war in a complex web of sociopolitical and economic 'realities' which are constantly changing and unpredictable. Thus, although 'Anger in a Black Landscape' is primarily concerned with the 'evil' of nuclear warfare, it is also an argument against the solipsistic thought that makes the proliferation of nuclear weapons possible. It rejects the idea of arguing against such technology, as Carter says (ibid.: 44) at the outset: 'I've grown tired of rational, objective arguments against nuclear weapons.' Instead, it exemplifies the need for a different intellectual approach to the subject all together because, as Carter says (ibid.: 51): 'We have, indeed, learned to live with the unthinkable and to think it.'

Halfway through 'Anger in a Black Landscape' Carter declares (ibid.: 46): 'So. Let's start again from another angle.' Here, she refers to the essay's argument that we need an alternative to rational argument that seems to have proved ineffective in getting rid of nuclear weapons, but also to the way in which paragraphs in the essay tend to take up a different approach from the previous ones. Frequently, paragraphs have opening sentences that disrupt the line of thought before recovering the principal subject: 'Have you seen Goya's "black" pictures in the Prado, in Madrid?' (ibid.: 44); 'We think people who sell heroin are very evil and, if we catch them at it, send them to prison for a very long time' (ibid.: 45); or 'Surely you must have noticed what an exceedingly law-abiding race the British are?' (ibid.: 46). In the second half of the essay, which insists upon the importance of rage, the paragraph sequence becomes more fragmented not only in content but in form. It does so in order to insist upon the importance of not being hoodwinked by what might appear to be logical discourse:

But this is no argument at all against women taking their fair share of policy- and decision-making, and, since it hasn't been tried before, it might well make a difference, in the long term. If there is a long term.

It is certainly no argument against asking all women, all normal, everyday women who tend and nurture children, make them clean their teeth and eat up their greens so they'll grow up big and strong, to appreciate that such an activity might well be futile. If.

That such an activity probably *is* futile. Because …

(Ibid.: 50)

In this section of the essay, there is an ostensible tension between this kind of structure that insists upon more thought – 'If there is a long term', 'If' and 'Because' – and an increasing rhetoric:

> We must plead, harangue, protest, demand – all kinds of things! A lot more democracy, a lot less secrecy; make (oh, horrors! oh, embarrassment!) a fuss, then a bigger fuss, then a bigger fuss again. The peace movement in the USA didn't rationally argue troops out of Vietnam. It harangued. It shouted. It screamed. It took to the streets.
>
> (Ibid.: 52)

However, the rhetoric here is paradoxically a kind of 'anti-rhetoric'. It balances the conventions of rhetoric – repetition, balance, assonance, connotation – with a vagueness in the writing that exposes the imprecision which rhetorical devices often obscure: 'all kinds of things!', 'A lot more …' and 'a lot less …'. At the same time, it employs the kind of asides that traditionally would have no place in rhetoric: '(oh, horrors! oh, embarrassment!)'.

The structural techniques which make reading Carter's journalism like looking successively through different lenses are particularly suited to her essay on her father, 'Sugar Daddy' (1983). The essay reads as if the author is turning over pages in a photograph album of him. The different 'snapshots' which the reader has of Carter's father are not simply a literary technique to hold the reader's attention. As each lens presents him somewhat differently in a different context, the reader is made aware of how it is difficult even for a daughter to know her father fully and how each of us presents a different face in different situations. Thus, the structure of the essay is appropriate not only because it mirrors the process of looking through a photographic album, but because it also reflects the difficulty of completely knowing another person.

An ambition reflected even in Carter's early journalism is to write in a style that is integrated with its subject matter. Although the apparent spontaneity of 'Bob Dylan on Tour' (1966) now has a dated, American Beat feel to it, it provides a good early example of how Carter, like the American Beat writers William Burroughs, Jack Kerouac and Allen Ginsberg, sought to break conventional syntax, so that her writing has an energy and breath commensurate with its subject matter, in this case the Dylan performance (1998: 323): 'Bang, bang, drums, organ, amplified guitar.' Sentences are broken irreverently in mid-structure and clauses employed to start a new paragraph in a way she can get away with in the *London Magazine* in the 1960s more than in *New Society* in the 1970s:

> … But what matters most is the songs.
>   Which now have a tough urgency, a strained sense of critical involvement with twentieth-century America and a kind of moral satire …
>
> (Ibid.: 324)

The radical nature of this writing, when compared with the more constrained style and more muted visual imagery of 'A Busker (Retired)' (1967), published in *New Society*, reveals the influence upon Carter's journalism of the different publications for which she wrote simultaneously: 'He reeled off a bunch of music-hall tunes, using much double and treble stopping and a very flamboyant bow technique, he grunted alarmingly as he played' (1998: 323). There is no attempt to encapsulate in the writing itself the 'double and treble stopping' or the 'flamboyant bow' which Carter may have attempted if she were writing for the *London Magazine*.

Moving through and between different lenses is not simply a device in Carter's journalism. As the epigraph to her novel *Several Perceptions* (1968) demonstrates, it is fundamental to her aesthetic: 'The mind is a kind of theatre, where several perceptions successively make their appearance, pass, re-pass, glide away, and mingle in an infinite variety of postures and situations.' It might appear to be responsible for an anarchic quality in her fiction. Sage maintains (1994: 11) that Carter's 1960s fiction has a 'cabinet-of-curiosities or mausoleum shape'. However, her journalism clearly demonstrates the extent to which the eclectic nature of her fiction, its speculation and its constant disruption of the linear by the radically episodic were the products of careful thought.

Words, images and 'theatre'

Carter's critique of William Burroughs's *Western Lands*, referred to earlier, suggests that we should pay attention not only to the content and structure of her journalism but the sentences in which she wrote. Her journalism shares with her fiction a fondness for following, as Lorna Sage argues (ibid.: 19), the way in which William Blake took the 'formal shape of the balanced, aphoristic sentence and use[d] it to advance the most heterodox suggestions'. The strategic employment of such a sentence is used to close the discussion of sadomasochism in 'A Well-Hung Hang-Up' cited above: 'Against this rage can beauty hold a plea? Not, certainly, in the timorous hands of the male pin-ups' (1998: 64).

The technique is used extensively in 'Anger in a Black Landscape' in lines such as: 'Women have always had a tendency to despise men for their emotional impoverishment. Men feel superior to women for the same reason. Impasse' (ibid.: 50). However, the literary influence in this essay comes not only from William Blake but also from Dylan Thomas. This is especially evident in the last sentence: 'War is no longer the province of men and, as its most vulnerable potential victims, we *must* arm ourselves – not with weapons, but with rage, rage as if against the dying of the light' (ibid.: 52). Clearly, Carter has in mind here the last line from Thomas's poem (Davies and Maud 1988: 148) addressed to his father: 'Do not go gentle into that good night': 'Rage, rage against the dying of the light.'

At times, the way in which aphoristic sentences are employed in the 1960s and 1970s to advance heterodox ideas seems too obviously a contrived journalistic technique. This is the case in 'Theatre of the Absurd' (1978) which opens: 'I suppose that, of any form, the television commercial has most in common with the limerick' (1998: 401); and in 'Much, Much Stranger than Fiction' (1979) which announces that 'Autobiography is closer to fiction than biography' (ibid.: 358). In fact, Carter is much more effective in using literary devices which have an element of theatricality. Thus, the opening of 'In Pantoland' (1991) reflects the expertise she had acquired in writing *Nights at the Circus* and *Wise Children*: '"I'm bored with television," announced Widow Twankey from her easy chair in the Empyrian, switching off "The Late Show" and adjusting his/her falsies inside her outrageous red bustier, "I will descend again to Pantoland!"' (ibid.: 393). And she is effective when her visual and literary imaginations come together, as in the opening of 'Robert Coover: A Night at the Movies' (1987): 'The American cinema was born, toddled, talked, provided the furniture for all the living-rooms, and the bedrooms, too, of the imagination of the entire world, gave way to television and declined from the most potent of mass media into a minority art form within the space of a human lifetime' (ibid.: 382). What is especially potent here is the way in which Carter juxtaposes two powerful images, of American cinema shaping the entire world's perspectives and then of its sudden decline.

Apart from the sometimes giddying range of incongruent literary and historical allusions, referred to earlier, Carter's 1960s journalism is marked by its imagery. Unlike in the 1970s writing, the highly entertaining imagery sometimes seems to strain for effect. Bob Dylan in 'Bob Dylan on Tour' (1966) is captured with merciless sharpness (ibid.: 323) as 'a Beardsley hobgoblin'. Demonstrating her flair for this kind of theatrical mockery, she refuses to let him off the hook, highlighting how 'the little pointy face, so white it is almost blue in the spotlight, is shadowed by a baroque mound of curls'.

The epigraph to *Several Perceptions*, referred to earlier, highlights the way in which Carter herself linked her work with 'theatre'. The implications of this for her journalism are suggested by Sue Roe who, in a discussion of the novel *Love* (1971), points out (1994: 65) that Annabel's favourite painter is Max Ernst, known for his collage novels which 'consisted of a series of cut-up and reassembled nineteenth-century book illustrations' in which 'words interact with images and function as images'. Carter appears to capture the surreal energy of Ernst's imagery. In 'A Well-Hung Hang-Up' she describes (1998: 62) how 'Almost all the young men exhibit pale bikini marks on their deeply tanned, terribly hairy frames. They are joy through strength. The beaux of Muscle Beach engaged in as narcissistic a cult of the body as Hitler Youth.'

This sentence demonstrates the way in which Carter generally employed one image in close proximity to another that contradicted, challenged or undermined it. Here the young strong men in their 'terribly hairy frames' are feminized by their 'pale bikini marks' and the 'beaux of Muscle Beach' is rendered sinister by the allusion to the homoerotic muscularity and fitness of Hitler Youth. The points are made not simply through words but through the jostling of incongruous imagery and allusion in a single sentence. In other essays Carter uses this technique to summarize her authorial position, as in the essay on Linda Lovelace referred to above: 'She is a shaven prisoner in a cage whose bars are composed of cocks' (ibid.: 56).

Even her more restrained journalism for the *Guardian* in the 1980s occasionally betrays her enthusiasm for surreal, theatrical imagery. In 'Vladimir Nabokov: *The Enchanter*' (1987), Carter (ibid.: 581) says of the novel's plot how 'the effect is that of raw liver exquisitely arranged in a pink frilly box'.

On the whole, though, Carter's review of *The Enchanter* exemplifies how her journalism, published in the *Guardian* in the 1980s and shortly before her death in the early 1990s, is different from her work of the 1960s and 1970s in its more mature critical reflection. This is encapsulated not only in the content but also in the more conservative style and structure of her review essays. The short opening sentence, designed to nudge if not shock the reader into attention, is replaced by a more academic style of writing, evident from the opening of 'The German Legends of the Brothers Grimm' (1981): 'Unlike the Grimms' collection of fairy tales, without which no home is complete, their collection of German legends has never been translated into English before' (ibid.: 465).

The structure of the essay is more linear and the paragraphing is more conventionally sequential than in the journalism of the 1960s and 1970s. The rhetorical techniques that so boldly characterized her earlier work are more carefully integrated in this case with the discursive tone of the piece as a whole. In her essay 'Christina Stead' (1982), published in the *London Review of Books*, Carter (ibid.: 572) observes: 'Fine writing must have come easily to her; roughness, ungainliness, ferocity were qualities to which she had to strive.' The reverse appears to be the case for Carter. In her introduction to her collection of journalism, *Expletives Deleted* (1992), she admits (ibid.: 604) that 'I am known in my circle as notoriously foulmouthed'. Certainly, she feels at home with importing into her writing what she describes (ibid.: 574) as 'the real structures on which our lives are based'.

Carter's interest in what she calls 'real structures' is evident in her lecture 'Love in a Cold Climate', delivered to a Conference on the Language of Passion, University of Pisa, Italy, in 1990, which invokes the British tabloid press, the *News of the World*, and the *Sport*. Here she contrasts the British, Protestant cleansing of the language of passion with D. H. Lawrence's attempts to reclaim the profane language of proletarian sexuality (ibid.: 592). She places the dichotomy of 'fine' and 'naturalistic' writing, which she discusses in 'Christina Stead', in a different context by tracing two traditions in the language of English sexuality which have been previously ignored. It also places her admission in *Expletives Deleted* that she is generally regarded as 'foul-mouthed' in a new perspective by arguing that 'we are essentially a Northern peasant culture, of the earth, earthy' (ibid.). This remark alerts us to a creative tension that runs throughout her writing between the 'naturalistic' – sexual, profane, subversive, rebellious, carnivalesque, theatrical – and the 'fine' – the intellectual, analytical, sceptical, philosophical and literary.

Journalism and fiction as a single, ongoing project

Thus, journalism offered Carter a mode of writing overtly linked to worldliness. However, it alerts us to the fact that for all its flights of fancy, Carter's fiction is also grounded in cultural and political 'realities'. Together her fiction and non-fiction engage the reader in a critique of the ways in which our identities and thoughts are mediated and defined by language and culture. Through socio-cultural critique and philosophical/historical speculation Carter's work decentres and offers alternatives to dominant, defining discourses. Her fiction and journalism are a part of what for her was a single ongoing project.

In her fiction and her journalism, Carter's 'ongoing project' frequently returns the reader to subjects, such as war, sexuality, gender identity, pornography, violence, fantasy and fashion, that preoccupied cultural criticism and commentary in the late twentieth century. Her non-fiction, her novels and her stories share a conceptual reach that is daring in two respects. Through their extravagant wit and devastating cultural critique they undermine traditional classifications and configurations but they also embrace new, disturbing perspectives. This does not mean that one set of viewpoints is simply exchanged for another. At the heart of both Carter's journalism and her fiction is recognition of the importance of what might be described as creative, critical thought.

The fusion of creativity and cultural criticism in Carter's various modes of writing is partly a product of her experiences in Japan which defamiliarized for her the whole concept of culture. Although Carter's early writing and her pre-Japan journalism demonstrate an eclectic interest in different cultures, the Japan and post-Japan writings are characterized by a deeper understanding of the significance of being able to think and work across and outside different cultures. At one level, this realization affected her fiction and non-fiction in different ways. Whilst her fiction became larger, more carnivalesque and more bizarre, her journalism, partly due to the papers and magazines in which it was published, became ostensibly more disciplined, even restrained, in its scope, structure and style. However, the difference between the fiction and the non-fiction in the 1980s is not as wide as might appear.

Carter's abiding interest in theatricality and incongruity, which came to a head in *Nights at the Circus* and *Wise Children*, did not desert her journalism, even in the *Guardian* writing of the 1980s, where ostensibly incongruous images are frequently juxtaposed to undercut conventional lines of thought and to suggest alternative, radical perspectives. Moreover, the later fiction, once one looks beneath the entertainment, and the journalism demonstrate Carter's developing awareness of the careful, highly disciplined deployment of linguistic and rhetorical techniques underpinning the literary representation of the incongruous, the theatrical and the bizarre.

In conclusion, it is worth remembering that the tutor who taught the craft of writing to such luminaries as Kazuo Ishiguro, Pat Barker and Glenn Patterson was the daughter of a journalist and began her own professional life on a newspaper. It is not difficult to imagine that from these beginnings, Carter inherited the capacity to work across different modes of writing, including short stories, novels, essays, introductions, translations, reviews and cultural commentary, with respect for each as a vehicle to further her philosophical thinking, develop her cultural criticism and dismantle the barriers to creative, critical thinking.

References

Carter, A. (1968; 1995) *Several Perceptions* (London: Virago).

—— (1971; 1988) *Love* (London: Picador).

—— (1977; 1982) *The Passion of New Eve* (London: Virago).

—— (1979) *The Sadeian Woman* (London: Virago).

—— (1982; 2000) *Nothing Sacred: Selected Writings* (London: Virago).

—— (1984; 1994) *Nights at the Circus* (London: Vintage).

—— (1991; 1992) *Wise Children* (London: Vintage).

—— (1992) *Expletives Deleted* (London: Chatto & Windus).

—— (1997; 1998) *Shaking a Leg: Collected Writings*, Uglow, J. (ed.) (Harmondsworth: Penguin).

Davies, W. and Maud, R. (eds) (1988) *Dylan Thomas Collected Poems 1934–53* (London: Dent).

Peach, L. (1998) *Angela Carter* (Basingstoke: Macmillan).

Roe, S. (1994) 'The disorder of love: Angela Carter's surrealist collage', in Sage, L. (ed.), *Flesh and the Mirror: Essays on the Art of Angela Carter* (London: Virago), pp. 60–97.

Sage, L. (ed.) (1994) *Flesh and the Mirror: Essays on the Art of Angela Carter* (London: Virago).

Sceats, S. (1997) 'The infernal appetites of Angela Carter', in Bristow, J. and Broughton, T. L. (eds), *The Infernal Desires of Angela Carter: Fiction, Femininity, Feminism* (London and New York: Longman), pp. 100–15.

Index

Related titles from Routledge

English for Journalists

Third Edition

Wynford Hicks

Praise for previous editions:

'For those uncertain of their word power and those who know in their bones that they are struggling along on waffle, a couple of hours with this admirably written manual would be time well spent.' – Keith Waterhouse, *British Journalism Review*

'*English for Journalists* is a jolly useful book. It's short. It's accessible. It's cheap. And it tells you what you want to know.' – Humphrey Evans, *Journalist*

'It makes a simple-to-use guide that you could skim read on a train journey or use as a basic textbook that you can dip into to solve specific problems.' – *Short Words*

English for Journalists is an invaluable guide not only to the basics of English, but to those aspects of writing, such as reporting speech, house style and jargon, which are specific to the language of journalism. Written in an accessible style, *English for Journalists* covers the fundamentals of grammar, the use of spelling, punctuation and journalistic writing; with each point illustrated by concise examples. This fully revised and updated new edition features a brand new introductory chapter which includes:

- a discussion as to why 'good English' is now such a hotly debated subject
- an introduction to the anti-correctness arguments of academics
- a look at the increasing informality of journalistic writing in general, and in particular, the growth of personal columns and other fun features written in a colloquial – therefore sometimes ungrammatical – style
- the role of house style
- fully up to date examples of mistakes published by magazines and newspapers.

Other chapters include examples of common grammatical errors and how to avoid them; lists of problem words and a discussion of spelling rules; notes on style; and information on reporting speech.

ISBN 13: 978-0-415-40419-8 (hbk)
ISBN 13: 978-0-415-40420-4 (pbk)
ISBN 13: 978-0-203-96766-9 (ebk)

Available at all good bookshops
For ordering and further information please visit:
www.routledge.com

Related titles from Routledge

Ethics for Journalists

Richard Keeble

'Richard Keeble's book asks questions which dominate our working lives and it is invaluable not just to working journalists and students, but to the reading and listening public on whom our work depends. There isn't a journalist who would not benefit from reading this book especially if he or she attempts to answer some of the questions in it.' – *Paul Foot*

Ethics for Journalists tackles many of the issues which journalists face in their everyday lives – from the media's supposed obsession with sex, sleaze and sensationalism, to issues of regulation and censorship. Its accessible style and question and answer approach highlights the relevance of ethical issues for everyone involved in journalism, both trainees and professionals, whether working in print, broadcast or new media.

Ethics for Journalists provides a comprehensive overview of ethical dilemmas and features interviews with a number of journalists, including the celebrated correspondent Phillip Knightley. Presenting a range of imaginative strategies for improving media standards and supported by a thorough bibliography and a wide ranging list of websites, *Ethics for Journalists* considers many problematic subjects including:

- The representation of women, blacks, gays and lesbians, and the mentally ill
- Controversial calls for a privacy law to restrain the power of the press
- Journalistic techniques such as sourcing the news, doorstepping, deathknocks and the use of subterfuge
- The impact of competition, ownership and advertising on media standards
- The handling of confidential sources and the dilemmas of war reporting

ISBN 13: 978-0-415-24296-7 (hbk)
ISBN 13: 978-0-415-24297-4 (pbk)
ISBN 13: 978-0-203-18197-3 (ebk)

Available at all good bookshops
For ordering and further information please visit:
www.routledge.com

The Routledge Dictionary of Literary Terms

Peter Childs and Roger Fowler *The Routledge Dictionary of Literary Terms* is a twenty-first century update of Roger Fowler's seminal *Dictionary of Modern Critical Terms*. Bringing together original entries written by such celebrated theorists as Terry Eagleton and Malcolm Bradbury with new definitions of current terms and controversies, this is the essential reference book for students of literature at all levels. This book includes:

- New definitions of contemporary critical issues such as 'Cybercriticism' and 'Globalization'.
- An exhaustive range of entries, covering numerous aspects to such topics as genre, form, cultural theory and literary technique.
- Complete coverage of traditional and radical approaches to the study and production of literature.
- Thorough account of critical terminology and analyses of key academic debates.
- Full cross-referencing throughout and suggestions for further reading.

ISBN 13: 978-0-415-34017-5

Available at all good bookshops
For ordering and further information please visit:
www.routledge.com